Show-Me Sportscasters

Joe Moore, Ph.D.

*For my dad, Leon Moore, who taught me
to love the games.*

Acknowledgments

As a professor, I'm not sure what is cooler, that I had the opportunity to interview the likes of Nate Bukaty, Ryan Lefebvre and Mitch Holthus, or that it was two of my former students who are now living the dream and working in sports talk radio who helped me secure those interviews. Thanks, Derek Haglund and Dusty Likins. You make the old man proud! I also have to thank BJ Kissel and Kelly McCabe for helping me track down Mitch Holthus; that was no easy task in the middle of one of his busiest seasons!

Having never written a book before, it was critical I find some advice from those who have been down that road. Thank you to John Wilson, Matt Fulks, and Rob Rains for all your advice and guidance at the genesis of this project. Then, near the end, three wonderful people helped me bring this project to the finish line. A very special thank you to my editors, Debbie Cunconan and Bill Turnage, and to my cover designer, Amy Kenney. You cannot begin to realize how much I appreciate your yeoman's work.

Naturally I have to thank the gentlemen who allowed me their time for the interviews. What a thrill it was to travel across our great state to visit with you, pick your brains, and hear your stories. I hope I have translated them in a way that makes you proud.

To my mother, Judi Moore, thank you so much for your enthusiasm, support, and publicity efforts right from the beginning of this project. You've always had my back.

Gaby, Gavin and Grant, you all gave up a lot of dad time while I was on the road conducting interviews, at the office transcribing and writing, and begging for quiet so I could complete this project. You are my heroes.

To my wife, Heidi, where do I begin. You are the reason I get up in the morning, you are my best friend, you are the great love of my life. Thank you for never giving up on me and for believing in this project as much as I do.

Most of all, I must thank God and my Lord and Savior, Jesus Christ. Colossians 3:23 tells us, "Work willingly at whatever you do, as though you were working for the Lord rather than for people." I pray I have always had that in mind and that You have been glorified through this work.

Table of Contents

Introduction. 6

Brad Boyer
   KRES 104.7 FM - Truman State University 9

Nate Bukaty
   Sports Radio 810 WHB - Sporting KC 19

John Coffey
   KXCV 90.5 FM - Northwest Missouri State University 31

Art Hains
   KTXR 101.3 FM - Missouri State University 39

Greg Hassler
   KOKO 1450 AM / KWKJ 98.5 FM - University of Central Missouri 51

Mitch Holthus
   KCFX 101.1 FM - Kansas City Chiefs 61

John Kelly
   Fox Sports Midwest - St. Louis Blues 73

Kevin Kelly
   KWOS 950 AM and 101.1 FM - Jefferson City, Helias, & Blair Oaks high schools . .83

Mike Kelly
   KMOX 1120 AM - University of Missouri 95

Ryan Lefebvre
   Fox Sports Kansas City and Royals Radio Network - Kansas City Royals 105

Mike McClure
   McClure Broadcasting, ESPN+, ESPN3 - Missouri Southern & Missouri State 115

Dan McLaughlin
   Fox Sports Midwest - St. Louis Cardinals. 127

Greg Schmidt
   KMMO 1300 AM and 102.9 FM - High School Game of the Week. 135

Erik Sean
   River Radio - Southeast Missouri State University. 143

Adam Winkler
   KNEO 91.7 FM - Webb City High School 155

Tips and Strategies from the Pros 167

Introduction

Two calls defined my love of sports when I was a boy. One was Al Michaels' "Do you believe in miracles?" call as the U.S. hockey team defeated Russia in the 1980 Winter Olympics. The other was Marv Albert's call as Arkansas' U.S. Reed hit a half-court shot to beat Louisville in the 1981 NCAA Tournament: "It's in! It's in!" The fact that his voice cracked on the second "it's in" only made the call more dramatic. I can still picture my father and I leaping into a mid-air embrace as Marv described our beloved Razorbacks' improbable victory. After we moved to Missouri and joined Chiefs Kingdom, Kevin Harlan's "Oh, baby, what a play!" became synonymous with Sunday afternoon.

Of course, as a sports fan, the men and women who called the events I loved to watch were a huge part of the experience. But it was not until I began a career in college athletics that I realized what went into play-by-play. I, like many other fans, assumed these professionals just had great heads for sports trivia and superior voices for sharing those nuggets of information while watching the game. Boy was I wrong. For 15 years I worked in sports information, 12 years as a director. I developed media guides, wrote news releases and feature stories, produced game notes, provided statistics at sporting events and served as host to countless media. The one group that always amazed me during sporting events: the play-by-play announcers. I was always astonished at how they could remember the names that matched the numbers and how they could recall this information in real time (actually in really fast time). Until then, I never realized how much homework they did before the event—checking stats, scouring game notes and media guides for any useful bit of knowledge, interviewing coaches and players, watching game film, examining trends and so forth. The fact that they could so poignantly articulate what was happening and draw on their preparation just fascinated me.

When I decided to begin this project, telling the back stories of some of my favorite sportscasters from across my home state just seemed to make sense. I have also always been a fan of the back story. "Batman Begins" and "Captain America: The First Avenger" are two of my all-time favorite movies. While I am not a fan of the Star Wars prequels, I watch "Rogue One: A Star Wars Story" at least once a month. I find it intriguing and even inspiring, to see how our heroes became who they are today. As a sports fan, this is the type of book I would like to read because it is through the eyes of these gentlemen that I often get to "see" the game (if I'm listening to the radio) and that I get to really know the players and coaches who make it happen (if I'm watching on television). As an educator who teaches sports broadcasting, this is the kind of book I would want to recommend for my students who are interested in being on-air talent.

Missouri is where some of the greatest sportscasters of all time have hung their hats: Jack Buck and his son Joe, Harry Caray (even if he did cross over to the Cubs), Kevin Harlan, Bob Costas. It is home to KMOX, the legendary CBS Radio affiliate in St. Louis. The goal of this project was to feature some of the men who are keeping the legacy of sports broadcasting alive in the Show-Me State. The tradition continues with men like Greg Schmidt, who is on the cusp of calling 5,000 games; Kevin Kelly, who calls some of the toughest action in the Capital City; and Adam Winkler, the voice of eight state football titles for Webb City High School. It continues with Dan McLaughlin, whose St. Louis Cardinals are one of the most storied professional franchises in American sports history, and with Ryan Lefebvre, who survived three straight 100-loss seasons with the Kansas City Royals before they won the 2015 World Series. The list includes Missouri Sports Hall of Famers Art Hains from Missouri State and Mike Kelly from Mizzou. It includes John Kelly, the son of St. Louis Blues icon Dan Kelly, who is quickly becoming a legend in his own right, and Erik Sean at Southeast Missouri State, who cut his teeth in small towns before becoming the Voice of the Redhawks. It also features Mitch Holthus, he of the great "Touchdown—Kan-SAS City!" call that sends chills down Chiefs' fans' spines. Also included are gentlemen who have been in the game for decades (Brad Boyer at Truman State University and John Coffey at Northwest Missouri State) and professionals who are early in their play-by-play careers (Nate Bukaty of Sporting KC and Greg Hassler at the University of Central Missouri). And it includes an innovator in Mike McClure, who started his own internet broadcasting service.

They are journalists, entertainers and storytellers. They've adapted to technology, learned to roll with the punches and never forgotten the listener or viewer. To a man, they demonstrated great humility during the interviews for this project and seemed eager to share what they have learned with the next generation of play-by-play announcers. Two lessons that jumped out to this college professor: You better continue to develop your writing skills and there is no substitute for experience.

I hope you enjoy hearing from the pros as much as I enjoyed talking to them. In the following pages, you'll get to hear their stories in their words. They'll share their experiences, their joys and frustrations and some of their greatest challenges. They will also wax poetic about their heroes. Finally, they all share some of the tips and strategies they have learned along the way. So, settle in, grab a snack and enjoy the call.

Photo courtesy of Brad Boyer

BRAD BOYER
KRES - 104.7FM
TRUMAN STATE UNIVERSITY

I first met Brad Boyer when I became the sports information director at Missouri Southern. When I got to Joplin in 1996, Brad had been broadcasting Truman State University football and basketball games for about a year. And while I have been through three career changes in that time, he has been a staple at KRES (104.7 FM) for more than three decades. KRES is a 100,000-watt station located in Moberly, Missouri that along with sister stations KWIX, KIRK and KTCM is owned by Alpha Media. KRES airs classic country music with spot news and agriculture reports and is the Moberly affiliate for St. Louis Cardinals baseball. Brad began his career with the superstation while a prepster at Scotland County High School.

Brad is now the operations manager at KRES, covering Truman, with the occasional Moberly High School game mixed in. A native of Arbela, Missouri, where he grew up on the family farm, Brad graduated from Scotland County High in 1986 and then earned an associate's degree from Moberly Area Community College.

He and his wife, Kristi, have three grown children: Brett, Lindsey and Brandon, and one granddaughter, Braelynn by Brett and his wife, Brittany.

As the Voice of the Bulldogs, Brad has seen a little bit of everything. He has watched as Truman transitioned from a charter member of the Mid-America Intercollegiate Athletics Association to one of the newest members of the Great Lakes Valley Conference. He has witnessed a football program that during his tenure has lost 12 more games than it has won, but that produced the 1996 Harlon Hill winner, Division II's answer to the Heisman. Bulldog men's basketball has a winning percentage of .452 since 1995 but made a D-II Final Four run in 1999. And the Truman women's basketball team has been to the national tournament twice in Brad's time on the mic while producing a record of 329-329.

In 2015 Brad was inducted into the Missouri Basketball Coaches Hall of Fame, and in 2016 he and his broadcast partner, Hank Janssen, were inducted into the Truman State Athletic Hall of Fame. Now in his 32nd year as a broadcaster, Brad is also a Missouri State High School Activities Association Distinguished Service Award recipient (2008) and a Moberly Area Community College Distinguished Alum (2016). He also served 20-plus years as president of the Northeast Missouri Sportswriters and Sportscasters Association.

THE SECRET TO LONGEVITY

Thirty-plus years is a long time to spend in one place, especially when the national average is 12 job changes in an adult's lifetime (according to the U.S. Bureau of Labor Statistics). So for Brad to have been in the same position since the mid '90s, clearly he has found something that works.

"I like what I do. I enjoy it. I hope it's because my superiors like what I do, too. I'm hanging around, so I guess the listeners like what I do. I get an adrenaline rush just calling a game. I love just calling the game.

"I like the fact that I have families come up to me, and they can only make it to one or two games in a season, and I'm their picture. I'm their voice for their kid or their cousin or their nephew. That's very satisfying.

"I've thought about a lot of different things I could possibly do. We've gone from a family-owned group of stations to a corporately owned station. There's many a day where I think maybe this is it. Maybe it's passed me by, it's time to look for something different. But there's just something, you know ... It's just like today. We're getting ready for our all-star banquet tomorrow. We let the coaches vote on an all-star team and then we bring them in, and we honor them with a dinner in the program. A few years ago I started this legends program where I bring back a former coach, present him with an award just to kind of highlight his career for this new generation. Duane Schnelle (Milan High School football coach from 1970-2000), who I haven't seen for probably 20 years, he drops by the station because I'm presenting the award.

"It was just like old times. It's just the people that you get to meet, it's a real blessing. You can't meet as many people in any other job as you can in my occupation. You see different people all the time. It's just neat to learn about them. I guess that's part of it, too. It's the uniqueness every day you come in. You're not sure what you're going to find. Last week we covered a tornado that ran through Randolph County. December tornadoes? How many times does that happen? Well I found out today; I had a guy from The Weather Service on and the last time it happened was in the Pleasant Hill area, and that was 35 years ago. So you're never quite sure when you come to work what you're going to get here."

FROM THE DRIVEWAY TO THE HIGHWAYS

Like many in his field, Brad says he can trace the beginnings of his career to when he called his own games. That experience has since led him across the Midwest.

"It probably started in the driveway when I was calling my own games when I was playing. I'd go outside and shoot baskets and I would call my games. I watched a lot, as much as you could watch. There weren't nearly the games on TV as there are now. But I'd watch a game and then I'd go out and I'd play the game and I'd do the play-by-play.

"I've always had an interest in writing and telling stories. I think the two things—my interest in sports and my interest in writing—led me to sports broadcasting. I couldn't play anymore, so this is where I landed."

Brad Boyer is a member of the Missouri Basketball Coaches Hall of Fame and the Truman State University Athletic Hall of Fame.

IT'S NOT JUST THE PLAYERS WHO AIM FOR THE TITLE

Every boy or girl, man or woman who has stepped into the athletic arena has dreamed of hoisting a trophy. It is in that moment when the athlete feels he or she has reached the pinnacle. The same could be said for a broadcaster. That's when Brad says he knew he had arrived.

"It was a Final Four year; I'd have to go back and look at the exact year. I want to say 1990. We had three high school teams in our coverage area that were in the Final Four in Springfield for the Show-Me Showdown that year. We had a gentleman who was going to go down there, but his dad died, so I got called in kind of last second. At that time I was taking every game I could get, so yeah, my hand went up real quickly when they asked for someone to go. But anyway, they needed somebody to go. Our program director at that time was heavy with the junior college program, and so I got sent down there, and that was a lot to take on because three teams, two games, back-to-back days. I guess I did well enough that from there on I felt good about what I was able to pull off for the station. They were big sellers, and they were exciting games.

"I think I pretty well knew that this is something that I could handle and take on more responsibilities. I think I proved myself to the stations, too. And then, Ken Kujawa, who is somebody I give a lot of credit to, kept continually giving me opportunities to do more. Obviously, I consider him a mentor. (*Kujawa served as operations manager at KWIX/KRES/KIRK in Moberly, Missouri for nearly three decades. He also was the voice of the Moberly Area Community College basketball team for 28 years and the Truman State University football team for 15 years. Ken is now the director of the Viking Sports Network at Missouri Valley College in Marshall.*)

"I got the opportunity to do the junior college women here when they got to a national tournament. He was occupied with the men, so he would send me to the women's national tournament. And then it got to the point, even when the women went by themselves, he just told me to go. It kind of built from there."

11

PARTY LIKE IT'S 1999

For someone like Brad Boyer, who has been in the broadcasting business for more than three decades, picking a single game that stands out can be a monumental task. While Brad ultimately was able to come up with one game, he can be forgiven if, when asked to recall a favorite game, he focused more on a full season.

"I would say the cool thing about sports is when you go to a game, you never know what story you're going to get to tell. Even this season I can think of two or three games where it's just something unique that happened that you're not expecting. I'm calling a Truman football game this year, and for the first time in my career, in the midst of a play in the third quarter, the lights go out, and I've never had that. We don't even know where the running back is.

"If I had to pick one, I would have to say the triple overtime Elite Eight game for Truman against Saint Rose New York in '99. Actually, the entire 1999 Truman basketball season I could put there. I mean, now that was a sportscaster's dream. You probably remember, the Bulldogs were picked seventh in the conference that year and they made the Final Four. (I didn't remember until Brad mentioned this fact and then it all came flooding back to me; that team had no truly exceptional players but was one of the best Division II basketball teams I've ever seen).

"We go to Missouri Western and get thumped by 20 points on a Saturday night then we got to go to Washburn on a Monday night and we're down 20 points there and it looks like the season's going to tank, and we come back and beat them and didn't lose again until the semifinals. But that Elite Eight game was a triple overtime game. That one has to be the at the top of the list. I won one of my awards on that one, but that was—just for the magnitude of the game …

> *"I like what I do. I get an adrenaline rush just calling a game."*
>
> *~ Brad Boyer*

"They had a 6-10 All-American center, and it was just a classic. Nearly won it in the first overtime. Jason Ramthun hit a circus shot off a rebound as the buzzer sounded. Just threw it up and it went in and they waved it off—that was before we had replay, even though CBS had already set up and people were testing the replay then and saw that the shot should have counted. Anyway, they won the game, but yeah, that one by far is probably the best."

A FATHER FIRST, SPORTSCASTER SECOND

The natural progression in my line of questioning, after asking for a favorite game, was to ask Brad to pinpoint a specific favorite call. Again, you're talking hundreds, even thousands, of games, to come up with one specific call. After a very long pause, he was able to come up with one. And it was every father/sportscaster's dream.

"I called a Moberly Spartan playoff game. It was my son. We played Lutheran North in the first round of the playoffs, and the Spartans were getting beaten pretty good, and he made a play where they were driving in. It was in essence going to put the game away. This kid goes sweeping around the end, and my son went over and just ripped the ball away, wrestled it away and went 80 yards for a touchdown. From a personal standpoint that's probably it. That put everything together—big game, great play, and my son making the play. Just to be able to do that was pretty special."

OF ALL THE SPORTS IN ALL THE ARENAS ...

When you have a career in athletics, people always want to know what your favorite sport is. In one sense, Brad is not unlike any other professional I've ever known. His immediate response was, "Whatever is in season." But he also can pinpoint one sport that rises above the others.

"They've all got different things about them. I guess basketball is probably the favorite. I love the speed of it. That was my favorite sport to play, so I probably gravitate to that.

"Football I enjoy because there's stoppages; it's not continuous action, so you can use some of the material that's on your board a little bit more. And then, you know, baseball is cool because it's basically telling the story. You've got so much downtime between pitches. But basketball is my favorite."

It therefore comes as no surprise which event Brad would like to call.

"I guess the NCAA Final Four. Did you know I called an NCAA regional prep game? (I did not). The organizing committee was needing a game at the Edward Jones Dome in St. Louis, I'd have to go back and look what year that was; I think early 2000s, but maybe earlier than that. Anyway, they had to have a game before they hosted the regional, sort of as a tune-up, and so Truman played Harris-Stowe at the Edward Jones Dome. I called that game in front of a couple hundred people.

"It's funny. They're trying to work out the kinks, and we had a jump ball situation. They're trying to find the possession arrow and they'd forgotten to account for that, so some guy had a wood block. I'm thinking, that's probably something you better get taken care of before March. There's your trivia—first NCAA tournament game at the Dome. Who was it on the call? Me! Wasn't really a tournament, game; it was a prep game but still, I got to call it."

JACK BUCK: A MODEL FOR SUCCESS

KRES and its sister stations have been a launching pad for many in sports broadcasting. So, it would stand to reason that for many young broadcasters Brad Boyer is a legend. To him, though, there is nobody like Jack Buck.

"Jack Buck was my favorite. I grew up on Jack. I listen to play-by-play on the radio and it's just a picture that you paint. That's what I strive to do every day. From colors to weather conditions to uniform, you know everything that you can to present a picture. That's what he did for me."

So, has Brad also followed Jack's model and tried to prepare for a call, as Buck did for Mark McGwire's record-setting home run?

"I'm sure Jack Buck thought about some things, but when you say, 'Go crazy folks! Go crazy!' that to me is not a scripted thing. That's a totally out of the blue description of what happened when Ozzie Smith hit that home run (in game 5 of the 1985 NLCS). I don't know that I would have come up with something like go 'Go crazy folks! Go crazy!' and yet when you listen to it, it's perfect, it's ideal and it'll stand the test of time. But if you sat down and tried to write out, 'What if Ozzie Smith hits a home run, how am I going to do this?' How are you going to do that? And I think he had so many other calls that were just like that from, you know, 'We'll see you tomorrow night' (when Kirby Puckett hit a walk-off home run in Game 6 of the 1991 World Series) or whatever. I don't know how you can script something like that. He was the greatest in my mind.

"When I do listen, I listen to a lot of people. I think you're foolish if you don't listen to people to at least get ideas. There are certain phrases that I'll use that I've picked up along the way. I listen to a lot of guys. You know broadcasters have a certain catchphrase they use all the time, but I'm not one of those. I like variety, so I will describe in a variety of different ways."

A NEW GAME IN BROADCASTING

In 30 years in broadcasting, Brad has seen lots of changes. He can point to one thing, though, that has made the biggest difference in the game.

"Technology. From a radio standpoint, from actual printed copy to computers and from carts to computer. That's obviously the biggest thing. Social media is the other huge change.

"You know, I jokingly say I never had to worry about my face being seen in pictures and I never had to spell right, and now those things have changed because we obviously put our stories up on the website, and social media has become huge, like it or not. It's a huge part of what we do, trying to reach the ever-changing audience and so Twitter and Facebook, and there's other social media we haven't totally gotten into yet. But that's the big change."

Asked if technology and social media have made broadcasting better or worse, Brad says it's just different.

"I'm old school and, you know, I like the written story. I will say websites have made preparation time so much easier. In the old days, you had to do everything by phone. That has been a big positive in preparing for games. But I'm just huge storyteller. I love to write the story and incorporate sound with it, so I don't know if that detracts. You can still get those stories out.

"I don't want to be a curmudgeon and say 'the good old days', but I think that the frustrating part for me is you write this detailed story and from management it's like, 'Okay, now what have we done from the social media aspect? I'm like 'You don't care about my stuff! Look at my story! I spent a lot of time putting this together and all we're worried about is the presentation and how it's put together on social media.' That can be frustrating."

HOME SWEET HOME

Sports fans have varying opinions on the subject of "homers," those announcers who work for one specific team or whose station is a program's flagship and broadcast as though they are on the sidelines with the participants. Is it appropriate to say "we" when referring to the team one covers? Should equal excitement be provided to calls for either squad? Is it okay to praise the opponent or criticize the home team? I was eager to hear the answers to this question. Brad did not disappoint.

"My first response is no, but I do think that you can't change nor would I want to change, what my Truman audience thinks of me. I am their voice, so I guess from that

14

standpoint it's okay. But my goal is to never be viewed as a homer. I think part of that is the way we do things here in our operation. We have always taken the stance that we're regional radio, so we don't just do Moberly games, even though our station is in Moberly. We incorporate Shelby County, we want Macon County to think we're their radio station. So, we try to get out and do all of these high schools. Well when we do that just about every high school match up we do is two-sided, so you learn to present the game right down the middle. You're just calling the game. You're excited when they score, you're celebrating these kids. That's the way I have always called games when I was coming up in high school, and I hope it hasn't changed.

"I like to give credit to Central Missouri when they do something well, but I'm also going to celebrate Truman's plays a little bit more. You'll probably be able to tell a difference, but I'd like to think that if Central Missouri fans were listening to me they'd say that was a pretty enjoyable broadcast even though they would know that I was the Truman broadcaster.

"I just don't like that word. A homer to me is everything is about your team, and while I celebrate the Bulldogs, you know not every play goes right, and the other team has something to do with that too, so I think they deserve credit and that should be pointed out in the broadcast. And I would like to think that the Truman listener also wants to know who statistically is leading for the opposition, what background they may have. I want to know the whole game picture; I don't want to just know my Truman players so there's some context. When the running back for the Mules accomplishes something, you have some context to build on. 'You know, that kid was an all-state running back in the state of Texas'.

Photo courtesy of Brad Boyer

Brad has been calling games for KRES 104.7 FM since 1995. For all of the thrilling Truman State University action he has seen, it was a play in a football game that featured his son Brandon (left) that stands out as his favorite call.

15

"I think also with the officiating aspect, there's no doubt that there are calls that I can say, 'That certainly didn't go our way' or whatever. And I'm sure in the heat of battle there are times when I've gotten mad at an official, maybe questioned something. But I think it can get to be too much, and even if I'm listening with my Bulldog ears on or my Moberly Greyhound ears on, there comes a point where it's like, 'I don't want to hear anymore about the officiating'. It overshadows the actual game to focus too much on it. Then you lose the actual the picture that you're presenting of the game."

JUMPING CONFERENCES

Northeast Missouri State University was one of charter members of the Missouri Intercollegiate Athletics Association. Of course, Northeast became Truman State University and the conference changed its name to the Mid-America Intercollegiate Athletic Association when teams from Kansas (and later Oklahoma and Nebraska) joined the league. But the biggest change for Brad and Truman came in 2013 when the Bulldogs, witnessing the geographic shift in both leagues, took their teams to the Great Lakes Valley Conference.

"It was hard. You get used to guys like you and the other sports information people and the relationships that you made. You know where to go and you know where to plug in and you know where to park, and so you have to learn all the nuances of the GLVC.

"The two conferences are vastly different in the makeup of the schools, and that's really the big difference. I mean the urban areas, you've got schools in Chicago and Indianapolis and St. Louis and Kansas City. And so here you are traveling in these urban areas for a Division II Thursday night doubleheader. It's just totally different. Then a lot of the schools are private. It's just a different makeup.

"So yeah, it was a transition. Again, figuring out all the different, you know, where my equipment works to broadcast, what backup I need to have. But, you know, getting to meet new people is nice. Football is certainly not nearly at the same level as the MIAA; that's a whole different deal."

Besides the logistics, I was curious what Brad did in order to acclimate himself with the new professionals with whom he'd be working.

"Even in the MIAA, even though I was familiar, I was always in contact with sports information people and the coaches, and so I just keep that up. I call the coaches and I talk with them. I call sports information people, or email these days. Communication. Bottom line, calling a game is still calling a game.

"From what I do, it doesn't change how I call a game in any way. It's just the other factors, just getting on the air and whose phone line works with your equipment or whose wireless is working with your equipment to get the game on, meeting new sports information people, trying to figure out how to drive through Chicago and Indianapolis.

"The other part of it is, with the football side of things, there are a lot more open (non-conference) dates. There's some good to that. You get to see a variety of different places. But, ours is maybe a bit too much. We need a few more football schools. We end up on the road to Michigan (for games) quite a bit."

PERFECT CHEMISTRY

I had the great pleasure of working with two of the most brilliant NCAA Division II play-by-play announcers I know. At Missouri Southern, I spent a year working side-by-side with Kevin Greim to call Lions basketball. At the University of Central Missouri Shawn Jones and I teamed up for six seasons calling Mules football with the occasional basketball game mixed in.

Obviously Brad and his partner, Hank Janssen, know a thing or two about the chemistry needed to succeed in sports broadcasting. That tandem has been on the call since 1995.

"Hank knows when I leave off and he knows where he picks up. It's become seamless. Don't ask me how it happens other than reps. We really never knew each other before we kind of jumped into this thing together, but we went and now we have fun with it. I mean we try not to take ourselves too seriously and yet at the same time we don't want to get too goofy with the game either. But we have some fun with it.

"You know, just the other night we came out of a timeout. Hank mentions some concession stand offering, the cat dog at McKendree. So, he proceeds to describe what all is on the cat dog. Little things we can throw in.

"Then there is historical. You've got a new audience each year. They don't know the '99 team. They don't know the '79 NCAA team. They don't know some of these playoff teams, so there's an education. You can slip in some of these players of the past that have kind of built the foundation of Truman. We even do a football segment, what's called 'Hank's History Book', and we just kick around old games, old dates—On This Date type thing—and that kind of brings the past to the future a little bit."

RESTING IN HIS FATHER'S ARMS

One thing I know about Brad is that he is a man of great faith. As I did my research prior to writing this book, one of the things I continually saw was that you have to find a way to take a break from the game. I asked Brad if his faith served as an escape.

"I don't know if I've ever really thought about it that way, but I'm a man of faith, so you know my spirituality is probably the big thing. My church and Bible study, things like that. Through my church I have a life group that I participate in. It's totally different than sports, you know. We can get together, study the word and that type thing.

"The other part is just family. That's one thing that I really try to separate. It's really hard because a lot of times, I have to take my preparation home to get done what I need to do. But at the same time, when it's family time my wife does a great job reminding me. I focus on family. And that's good. It's good to get away. I like Christmas break. I'm going to enjoy that time. I'm not preparing, I'm not doing those things. Just flush my mind for a little bit. So, family and faith. That's my getaway.

"I hope that's apparent because my story is not traditional, and there's only one reason that I've had the honors and success and that's the good Lord has blessed me and that's it. There's no other way to explain how I've been able to achieve what I have, and that he would receive the glory for it.

"It's just not a traditional story. I'm not the traditional bachelor's degree, master's degree in journalism. That was my goal, and it just it took a different path. I would have never … I didn't know anything about Moberly, and it's where I've raised my family, my grandkids and everything. It's cool how things work. I was raised in Northeast Missouri. Now I end up that's where my career is. Good people and Truman and the great relationships I've had, you know, how does that story ever happen? But a university in Kirksville decides they want Moberly, Missouri to be their flagship station. That's a unique story in itself and how I ended up involved in that. So yeah, I certainly don't want to take too much credit. Pride can be a bad thing, man. I think you could be proud of your work, but you don't want that to get in the way. That is the root of a lot of problems in our world, so I try to be humble. There's no doubt you feel good when somebody comes up and tells you they really enjoy something. I could certainly do a lot better job in giving glory to God, but I try at least."

ADVICE FROM A MENTOR

As much as he loves being a play-by-play announcer, I got the sense in talking to Brad that he may enjoy being a mentor even more. So, when I asked him for his final thoughts, he jumped right into advice for aspiring young broadcasters.

"You have to love to do it. It's not a home run. That's what I love about the kids I got on my staff right now, you know? They get it. I mean they know they're not here to get rich, but they're here to get reps. I try to take care of them because I've been there. I still work a lot of hours, but they know they're going to put in the hours and to get to do what they want to do. They have to do the extra stuff and the less glamorous part of radio to get to do what they want to do. A lot of them have moved on from here and taken that next step, and that's what they all want to do. I have a guy from New York City on my staff. I got a guy from Chicago on my staff. They've come from all over.

Photo courtesy of Brad Boyer

Brad was joined by his children (l-r) Brett, Lindsey and Brandon as he received a Moberly Area Community College Distinguished Alumni Award.

"The other thing is just the relationships with coaches and people. That's a cool thing to get to know people, to meet people. SIDs, coaches … Fact is, I was just thinking about that this morning, how many different people that I get to meet during the season. It's just a neat thing to learn about people and their lives.

"I was raised on a farm. I have so much greater appreciation for the farm than I did when I was growing up. That was where I wanted to get away from. I could probably retire there. I don't think I'd be a very good farmer, but I love the farm now. That was not my gift. But it probably goes back to that driveway. Night light under a broken rim with an uneven gravel driveway, trying to shoot baskets. That was good, good life. Kept you out of trouble."

NATE BUKATY
SPORTS RADIO 810 WHB
SPORTING KC

Growing up an American football fan, I just never got soccer. How could anybody think this was an exciting sport? Why on Earth would people all around the world put themselves through this torture of watching men and women kick a ball around a field for 90 minutes only to see a 0-0 or 1-1 draw? I actually never even saw a full game until I was hired as sports information director at Missouri Southern. It was there that I started to appreciate the beauty of the sport. I now coach my son's team, and I truly love the game of soccer. But it still takes someone with a smooth baritone voice that can erupt into shouts of ecstasy in an instant to make the game come alive for television viewers, even more so for radio listeners.

Enter Nate Bukaty. We met at a Starbuck's in Overland Park. Even for 1:30 on a Monday afternoon it was bustling with activity—patron's chatting, business men and women preparing for the next meeting, baristas serving up espressos and lattes.

Incidentally, you never realize how loud an espresso machine is until you try to conduct an interview. Little did I know that the frantic pace of the world's most famous coffee shop was a metaphor for the dizzying routine Nate keeps on a daily basis.

Okay, so Nate Bukaty is not "technically" a Show-Me sportscaster since Children's Mercy Park is in Kansas, but Sporting KC does train at Swope Park on the Missouri side, and both sides of the state line claim SKC as their own. Now in his fourth year as the Voice of Sporting Kansas City, Nate has been with 810 WHB since 2003. Prior to that, he was with News Radio 980 KMBZ from 2000-2003, 1250 The Game in Kansas City from 1999-2000, and KRES in Moberly from 1998-99, where he covered high school and junior college sports, provided the farm report and was a country music deejay. He also worked with the KU Jayhawk Radio Network from 2000-2014. Today, in addition to his duties with Sporting KC, Nate is co-host of the Border Patrol at 810 and is a correspondent for MLB Network. He also does some freelance college basketball when he has time.

Nate graduated from Bishop Ward High School and went on to earn a degree in broadcast journalism from the University of Kansas in 1998. He and Kelly, his wife of 11 years, have two children, Ben and Ophelia.

A VOICE FOR THE PEOPLE

They say that a play-by-play announcer should be able to talk to "every man", meaning fans of all backgrounds should be able to relate with the announcer. Given his background, that task is pretty easy for Nate.

Photo courtesy of Nate Bukaty

Nate, here with Jake Yadrich and Andy Gruenebaum, has been the Voice of Sporting KC since 2014 and has been on the call for a pair of U.S. Open Cups.

"It's a whole confusing story. I went to kindergarten and public school in KCK; my parents moved me to Overland Park and I went to the suburban, white picket fence, soccer mom community from first grade through fourth grade. My parents got divorced, and my mom moved me to a small town in southern Kansas called Arkansas City, which is about an hour south of Wichita, where she married a farmer. So, I went from inner-city public school to suburban public school to rural farm. After two years there, I didn't like it, and so I moved back with my dad to Wyandotte County, which is where he was originally from. Then I went to Catholic school in inner city KCK from seventh grade through high school. I consider KCK to be my hometown. When people ask me, I tell them that's where I'm from."

FATHER KNOWS BEST

For some people, their career path takes a long and winding road. Through a series of events, they just seem to stumble into it. But Nate Bukaty can pinpoint when he knew his business card would read "Sportscaster".

"I could say the exact moment: It was while my parents were divorced and I was living in Arkansas City. I was in about fifth grade. At that time, every other weekend we would come up and visit my dad in Kansas City. One of the times I was driving with him on I-35 somewhere around Emporia, he asked me what I wanted to be when I grew up, and I said, 'I don't know. Maybe a point guard or a shortstop.' He was very ... my dad's a very brutally honest person, and he was like, 'the odds of that happening are slim to none.' So, he started going through the odds of even getting a Division I scholarship, a person my size and athleticism and all that, and so he says, 'You really need to think about some fallback plans.' This is in fifth grade, you know, and I was really kind of hurt by that at the time. But we were in the car and we were listening to a game on the radio, I said, 'All right, what about the guys that broadcast the games?' and he said, 'Well, there's a road map there. You go to journalism school' and all that stuff.

"That's when I decided that's what I wanted to be. So, it was about fifth grade, and I was really singularly focused. I mean that was what I told anybody who was going to listen—middle school, grade school, high school, college--that I wanted to be a sportscaster when I grew up."

SET YOUR GOALS

Hockey great Wayne Gretzky is famous for having said, "You miss 100% of the shots you never take." Nate was not about to let that happen to him. From the time he decided he wanted to be a play-by-play announcer he started making a plan, setting goals and then taking aim. Along the way, he says, he always reminded himself never to get comfortable.

"You know, I think if you ever feel like you've made it in this business you're about to be done. You can't ever relax because there's a hundred people that are willing to take your job tomorrow. You're always replaceable, so you can't ever feel like you've made it. But my dad always taught me that successful people have set incremental goals, so I feel like there were times when I realized I've checked some of the boxes on things that I wanted to be.

"One of the first things was I just wanted to get paid to cover a sporting event; that would make me an official sportscaster. My first gig I ever got paid to do was while I was in college at KU, I started working at a small town south of Lawrence called Ottawa,

Kansas, and I got to do the play-by-play for their high school American Legion baseball team. Got paid probably about 30 bucks, but I got paid to do a game. So that was the first incremental goal.

"My next goal was to get a full-time job that involved me broadcasting sports, and I got to do that in Moberly. But it wasn't a full-time sports job. My next goal was get a full-time sports job where I got paid to do nothing but broadcast sports, and I got that at 1250 The Game.

"I wanted the chance to do Division I athletics or professional athletics, and I got to do the Kansas women's games and work on the sidelines for the Jayhawk Radio Network. I was the sideline reporter and pregame show host for KU football for 10 years. I got to broadcast four or five KU men's basketball games over that time, a couple on the radio, a couple on TV. So those were all kind of little incremental goals.

"One of my goals was to be the play-by-play voice of a major league franchise, and when I got the Sporting Kansas City job, that was probably the biggest of my dreams to come true. That was a huge moment for me."

WINNING THE U.S. OPEN CUP

Any broadcaster who works for a specific squad is going to experience highs and lows with his or her team. Nate is no exception. So, when asked to pick a favorite game he ever called, it didn't take long to come up with a response.

"Well, the first two that come to mind are when Sporting Kansas City won the U.S. Open Cup. The one in 2015 was the first real championship I was ever lucky enough to broadcast. To me, that's what it's all about, right? Winning, being a part of something, seeing somebody win a trophy, being a part of an organization that wins a major trophy. And I was on the sidelines when KU won the Orange Bowl. That was pretty tremendous because it's the only Orange Bowl in the school's history. I wasn't doing the play-by-play at that time; I was a sideline reporter, so that's a little different.

"I've been fortunate enough in my first three years at Sporting to get to broadcast two U.S. Open Cup finals. That's something you just can't take for granted because there's all kinds of guys I'm friends with that broadcast sports. Look at Mitch Holthus. He's been broadcasting the Chiefs for, what? Two or three decades now, and he's still looking to go to his first Super Bowl. Ryan Lefebvre is one of my best friends in the broadcasting business and he'd been the play-by-play guy the Royals for 20 years before they won the World Series. You just never know. And some guys have never gotten to do it.

"Winning the Open Cup isn't the same thing as winning the Super Bowl or the World Series because it's a secondary competition, but still it's a major trophy, it's a major opportunity, it's a national championship. There's a champagne celebration in the locker room and all those things. It's all-night celebration afterwards. I feel like as a play-by-play guy, the legacy that you get to leave behind is when they play back the call of a moment like that in the stadium or on social media, videos, whatever. Your call is going to be heard every single time they play it. There's some pressure that goes into that--you want to deliver. But it's exciting. It's your chance to be a part of history."

SPEAKING OF CALLS ...

One of the questions I enjoyed most was asking about a favorite call. Was there one moment, one call that really stood out, where they said, "Yeah! That's poetry." Nate's response, for me, perfectly summed up why I love sports.

"Every moment in a sporting event is a unique moment in and of itself, and I believe it deserves a unique call, a call that describes that particular moment. For me, if I say the same thing every time someone scores a goal, that doesn't do that goal justice, particularly in a sport like soccer where the goal is so precious. I mean if there's 50 baskets in a basketball game you're going to call some of them the same. But for me, in a soccer game each goal is such a momentous occasion that I believe it deserves its own call that's worthy of that moment, so I've never scripted those things.

"Now, I've scripted two things that I can remember in my entire career, and those were what I was going to say when Sporting won the Open Cup because that goes back to what we talked about. That moment is unique, but I can script what I'm going to say in that moment because I know what the moment is. If a guy scores a bicycle kick from 20 yards out, I don't know that moment is coming and if I just say the exact same thing I said when a guy scored a little tap-in from two yards out, that doesn't do it justice. But winning the Open Cup, I know what this moment is. I know this moment is the team winning a cup, and it's my job to put in perspective in a short period of time what this means. So, I did script those two calls.

In addition to providing play-by-play for Sporting KC, Nate Bukaty is co-host of the Border Patrol on Sports Radio 810 WHB in Kansas City.

"I remember what I said when they won in 2015: 'For the glory of the city, and for the third time in four years, a major trophy is coming back to Sporting Park!' That's one of the things that the fans say. I feel like this year's was more special because one of the team owners and his wife, Neal Patterson and Gene Patterson, both died of cancer this year. Neal Patterson is one of the founders of Cerner, one of the biggest financial giants in the history of the city. His presence here literally transformed the economy of the city. Cerner employs thousands and thousands of people in this town, and they saved the team. He and Cliff (Illig) and the other owners, they bought this team when it was going to be sold to a team in Rochester, and so when he died it was a big deal. The team went out and won an overtime game in which they got a red card; they played down a man for 80 minutes. They just held strong, fought their butts off, and then one of Sporting's players got kicked in the head, and that leveled both sides because Dallas got a red card. Sporting scored three goals in extra time to win. It was like they played that game for Neal Patterson. They even had a logo painted on the field that said 'Neal'. Players all wore patches the rest of the season that said 'Neal', so when they won the Open Cup my call was, 'This one's for the Patterson family! The club that they saved has brought glory to the city once again.' That one was something personal."

SEVEN DAYS OF WORK FOR 90 MINUTES OF ACTION

Ninety minutes. That's the length of a typical professional soccer game. Ninety minutes of action, 90 minutes to dissect strategy, to tell the story of the game and the stories of the individual participants, to bring the fans closer to the action. To do justice to those 90 minutes, Nate Bukaty puts in seven days of study and research. And then, it's game time.

"In soccer, you have all week to prepare for the game. Gameday itself for a Sporting game begins at 7:30. I usually get to the stadium at around 3 o'clock, and the first thing that I and my broadcast partners do is go to the TV truck and we meet with our producer and director and replay coordinator and graphics coordinator and we go over what we call a script. It's really an outline of what we're going to be doing for the pregame show and during the game. You look at all the video clips, highlight packages, things like that they're going to show. We look at any graphics that they're going to have, and we discuss those things.

"Then I go upstairs and I kind of do some last-minute prep. I really just go back over all the preparation that I've done all week; hopefully all my preparation is done before I ever get to the stadium, so I kind of just read through all the notes. I have my spotting boards and all that, and then we're on the air at 7 o'clock.

"One thing that's really huge for me, for home games anyway, is my wife and kids come to all the games. If it's a 7:30 game, at 5 o'clock I go down and have dinner with my wife and kids for about a half an hour, which is really important to me. I was a season ticket holder for Sporting before I ever got the job, and I used to take my kids to all the games. It was a great thing for us to do as a family, and when I took the job I wanted to maintain a little bit of that. So, when they come to the games and they get to have dinner with me, it becomes a family outing instead of just another day where dad's off at work and they don't get to see me.

"Then it's back to work and we're on the air at 6:30. We go for a half an hour after the game's over and then that's it. I usually go down to the field club where the players and owners all kind of gather. Sometimes I'll have a postgame beer, just make sure to go down there and show my face. If people want to talk to me, I'm there to talk. If they don't, I leave them alone. It's always just good to show the team you support them and that you're there. It's always good to be seen."

PAVING THE WAY: ANOTHER LEGENDARY SHOW-ME SPORTSCASTER

Asked which broadcasters he most admires, Nate did not hesitate before describing one of the legends. He speaks with something akin to reverence about the broadcaster he holds in highest regard.

"I respect all of them because I know that it's all in the eye of the beholder. When I was a kid, Bob Costas ... I wanted to be like him. I went to a sportscaster camp in high school in St. Louis because he was going to be the keynote speaker. I saved up all my money for the summer and went to it. I got his autograph, and I was really excited.

"The thing I loved about Bob Costas back then was that he did everything. He did play-by-play and was really good at it. He did a talk radio show that was syndicated back before there was 24-hour talk radio. It was called 'Costas Coast-to-Coast' where he'd sit down and do an hour-long interview with some sports figure. I used to take a tape recorder, and I would record it and listen back to it. I was mowing the lawn and things like that. I went over it again just to get down the way he asked questions and how he got things out of people. He obviously could do the studio stuff like the Olympics. I was always fascinated by his ability. I think he's great.

"When it comes to soccer, I find soccer to be really fascinating because there's so many different cultures. I listen to a lot. I listen to Hispanic broadcasters from the Mexican League and places like that. The way they call the game is so different from the way the English guys in the English Premier League call the game. I'm a big fan of Arlo White; he does EPL games on NBC. John Strong is, to me, the best American soccer voice right now. He's the lead play-by-play guy for Fox on soccer. He's really good. I actually

Being a professional sportscaster provides Nate the opportunity to interview some high-profile professionals, including former U.S. Men's National Team coach Jürgen Klinsmann.

communicate with him a lot; pick his brain on how he's calling the game, his approach, and stuff like that."

CALLING THE BEAUTIFUL GAME

Soccer is arguably the most popular sport in the world. According to FIFA's most recent Big Count survey, there are about 265 million individuals playing soccer worldwide. In the United States, however, it is still about fourth or fifth on the list when fans talk about their favorite sports to watch, trailing football, basketball, baseball and, in some circles, hockey.

Nate Bukaty was no different growing up; he admits being a soccer announcer wasn't one of the goals he discussed. But he has definitely grown into the role, and he says he sees a bright future for the beautiful game.

"Obviously it was not a childhood dream of mine to be the play-by-play voice of a Major League Soccer team because Major League Soccer didn't exist until I was in college. And even at that point I don't feel like it really existed as a quote-unquote legit player on the scene until the last 10 years or so. There were worries that this league was going to fold and all that stuff. Now, all of a sudden, it's growing exponentially. Its teams have found ridiculous amounts of money for expansion teams, so it's grown a lot.

"I became a die-hard soccer fan over the past 11 years. Now, it was really the World Cup in Germany. I had some soccer experience; I played it in high school and I always liked it, but the World Cup in Germany ... I just caught the bug and I became a die-hard soccer fan. So, the opportunity to be the voice of the Major League Soccer team in Kansas City, which we've claimed ourselves the soccer capital of America, it's really exciting.

25

"I just finished my third year, and I hope to do it the rest of my career. I hope I'm lucky enough to get to do it for a few more decades. I know we (U.S. soccer) just suffered a huge setback with missing out on the World Cup, but I'm not any less convinced that the sport is going to continue to grow for the next 30 years in this country. I'm just convinced of it. I'll give you an anecdotal reason. When we get college interns now, almost every single one of them, if I ask them, 'Hey, who's your soccer team?' They'll have an answer, whether it's Bayern Munich or Barcelona or Chelsea or one of the European giants. Almost every one of them has an answer. Ten years ago—just 10 years ago—you ask that same question to every college intern we have, and they look at you like, 'What are you even talking about?' If you asked them who is Bayern Munich, they wouldn't even know. Even the kids who don't like soccer now know who these teams are and know about almost all of them because of growing up playing FIFA Soccer.

Nate is a bookworm who loves to read almost as much as he loves calling Sporting KC games and working The Border Patrol on 810 WHB.

"The world has changed. When you look at the demographics of the average age of the season ticket-holder for Sporting Kansas City versus the average season ticket-holder age for the Kansas City Chiefs or the Royals, you're talking about people in their upper 50s (for the Chiefs and Royals) versus people in their early 30s or late 20s (for Sporting), and I don't see any reason to believe that trend is going away. You look now and Sporting Kansas City gets 20,000 fans at their games. You're looking in markets like Atlanta, they launched the team this year, and they literally had over 70,000 fans for multiple games this year in their first year in MLS. There are 40,000 people going to the games in Seattle. Not every market is taking off like that, but if I told you just 10 years ago that was happening, you'd say they were crazy.

"Now, I still think the league has a long, long way to go. I mean, I'm under no illusions about that, but I just see the arc, and I see a sport that parents are more willing to let their kids play. I see a world that continues to shrink, and again it goes back to that anecdote I told you. While I was growing up and I liked soccer and I was looking for soccer heroes, I didn't know where to find them. We had the Kansas City Comets in town for a little while when I was a kid, and then there was pretty much nothing. That was a quick fad that didn't last. The best players in the world were playing in other parts of the world, and there was no way to watch them or learn anything about them. Now you turn on the TV on a Saturday morning, the German Bundesliga is on Fox Sports One, Premier League games are on NBC—these games are everywhere. Kids are playing these video games, too. Games are played around the world, and they are there for everyone to see. So, I just think soccer is going to continue to grow. It is the world's game, and the more that we as a country become a part of the world itself, the more embracing of soccer we become."

THE LIFE OF A PROFESSIONAL SPORTS FAN

Kansas City sports fans know that if they can't get enough of Nate Bukaty during Sporting KC games all they have to do is turn on Sports Radio 810 in the mornings to catch "The Border Patrol". While that's great for the fans (and Nate admits he loves the action and the pace), it can be quite a challenge to basically hold two full-time sports broadcasting jobs.

"Yeah, my wife doesn't get to see nearly as much of me during soccer season as she would like, or maybe it's good, maybe she enjoys the break. To me it's all about time management. You sit down every Sunday and you map your week out and you figure out how you're going to fit everything that needs to get done into the week ahead. To be honest with you, the more difficult challenge is with balancing the two jobs and balancing having two kids, still being a part of their lives and helping with soccer practice and all those things. Luckily for me I like to work. I love sports; I want to consume sports. My morning show allows me to pick my kids up from school, spend a couple of hours with them, eat dinner with them, and then once they go to bed I go back to the basement and I work for two or three hours getting ready for the next Sporting game and multitasking. I'll have the Royals game or whatever NFL game on; I've got a basement with the multiple TV setup, and I'll have all the games on while I'm sitting at my computer working on the game so I can kind of keep track of what's going on.

"I try to make sure that I get a couple of hours each day during the week in on preparing for the next game. I also spend a lot of time preparing for the games at the gym because I take my iPad, and I go and I'll walk or run on the treadmill or ride the bike and I'll watch games. I'll watch Sporting's opponents, their last few games or whatever and do those things. And I can get exercise while doing work all at the same time. That's one of the benefits of getting paid to watch sports for a living—part of work is watching sports!"

THE GREAT ESCAPE

Even for a die hard sports fan, sometimes it's important to take what elementary teachers call a "brain break". For Nate Bukaty that means reading and spending time with the family.

"I love to read non-sports, and I love to read fiction. I will read nonfiction as well. I'll alternate; I'll read one fiction book and then one non-fiction book. That's one of the main ways I love to get away from doing sports.

"My wife and I love to cook together. I feel like I spend a lot of time with my children. I will say, though, that a lot of that time is sports-related. I coach my son's soccer team. We play ball together a lot. But I love to watch movies. I don't really watch TV shows, but when I get a chance, especially on flights and things like that, I like to watch movies. I like to write. I try to write on a relatively consistent basis. I just think it's good for your brain; you can kind of exercise your mind.

"I love to exercise. A lot of times while I'm exercising I'm still consuming sports, but I will say this: I don't feel like I need to get away from sports much. I love it. If I wasn't getting paid to watch sports all the time I'd be finding another reason to watch sports all the time, so it's great for me because I get to have a reason, there's a purpose behind my love of sports that I've invented for myself, which makes it nice because then I get to feel like I'm not just wasting my time watching sports; I have to!"

When Nate mentioned coaching his son's soccer team, it reminded me of my own career in sports and as an educator who teaches sport communication. I have experienced some great victories and some painful defeats, but nothing I've ever done in sports has brought me as much satisfaction as seeing my children perform, be that on the soccer pitch, in a vocal competition, or in theatre. I thought I knew the answer, but I had to ask: Dad to dad, how does something like winning the Open Cup compare to watching his children compete?

Photo courtesy of Nate Bukaty

Nate, along with sideline reporter Carter Augustine and color analyst Matt Lawrence, provides Sporting KC fans with the insights that have helped make Kansas City the Soccer Capital of America.

"I remember when I was covering the Royals on a daily basis, John Wathan's son Dusty got a cup of coffee with the Royals. John Wathan was one of the all-time great Royals. I got to go out and sit with him in the stands on the day that his son had his first Major League game, and I asked him about that. I said, 'How does this stack up to the biggest moments in your career?' I mean, he won a World Series, and he said, 'This is the best! This is better than anything I ever did on a baseball field.' I mean, every dad can identify with that.

"My son, this year was his first year playing in the Heartland League, the club soccer league. My buddy and I have been coaching the last three years. My buddy played Division I soccer; he really knows what he's doing. I'm the assistant coach. We put them in a club league this year—it's eight-year-old and under—and they won their division. They went undefeated, and the last game of the season they happened to play against the only other undefeated team. I'm thinking, 'Oh gosh! This is going to be a big-time battle!' It's second-grade soccer, but both teams were undefeated. The other team had scored a ton of goals all year, and I had to miss the game because Sporting KC was playing against Real Salt Lake.

It was one of only two games I missed the whole season. I had my wife video the whole game. She was sending me text updates and everything.

"I got home that night from the Sporting game, and I knew my son's team won 2-0. They went undefeated for their first season, and I watched the whole game back with my son. I couldn't believe how into a second-grade soccer game I was. You just don't get it until you're there. I was always like, 'I'm not going to be one of those dads'. And I'm definitely not one of the ones that yells at the refs or anything like that, but I mean you want to see your kids succeed, and have fun and, yeah it's better!"

IF YOU HAD ONE PIECE OF ADVICE TO SHARE . . .

Nate advises those interested in a career in sportscasting to go in with eyes wide open and to understand what they are about to encounter.

"I remember a professor in college telling me you can't get into this business because of the money, you can't get into this business because of the potential for fame because those things are either entirely fleeting or non-existent altogether for sportscasters. There are better ways to make money and get famous. Fame is a fickle thing. Get into this business because you love it. The thing that will keep you in the business is the people, and I do like that. I meet so many great personalities and great people. I now have so many great relationships. If you're motivated by those types of things you'll find a lot of joy.

"The other thing is you need to go into it with your eyes open because my eyes weren't open to it until later on. Getting paid to talk about sports seems like a great deal, and it is, but it is still a job. And you're going to be working hours that your friends are not. You're going to sacrifice a lot of time—nights, weekends, holidays—because if you think about it, sports are played when everybody else is off work. So, when everybody else is playing, you're working. You just have to be open for that.

"You're not going to be broadcasting the Super Bowl when you get out of college. The odds are you could be calling a high school game that you don't think anybody is listening to on Super Bowl Sunday. I broadcast some women's basketball games on Super Bowl Sunday when all my friends are at their Super Bowl watch

> *"If you ever feel like you've made it in this business you're about to be done. You can't ever relax because there's a hundred people that are willing to take your job tomorrow."*
> ~ Nate Bukaty

parties, and I'm doing a game where my team I'm broadcasting for is getting beat by 40 points. You have to find a way to call that game just like you are calling the Super Bowl because all the parents on the team are listening to that game, and to them it's the most important game in the world.

"You have to have realistic expectations. I'm not going to be calling the World Cup, maybe ever, but definitely not in the first three years I've ever done soccer. You have to be willing to go where the games are and call what games are available to be called, even if they're not glamorous and sexy. If you just want to call the biggest games ever, you might work your whole career to get to call one U. S. Open Cup final, and you have to be able to find every single sporting event compelling and motivating and interesting in order to have a chance at it."

Photo courtesy of John Coffey

JOHN COFFEY
KXCV - 90.5 FM
NORTHWEST MISSOURI STATE UNIVERSITY

As you roll into Maryville, Missouri along I-29, there are two signs. One reads "Northwest MO State University, NCAA Division II National Football Champions 1998, 1999, 2009, 2013, 2015, 2016". The second reads "2017 Division II Men's Basketball National Champions".

Turn left off I-29 and head about 2.5 miles west on Business 71, and you'll come to your stereotypical small-town college hang out, Carson's Sports Grill (I recommend Heidi's Special and steak fries). Two pool tables sit prominently by the bar on one side. On the other side is a big screen TV where every fall Saturday, Maryville fans cheer on their beloved Northwest Missouri State University Bearcats. John Coffey has been calling the action for those games for the past 33 years. Even though our teams have been rivals, he at Northwest and I first at Missouri Southern and now at Central Missouri, I have been blessed to call John a friend for 23 of those years.

John is the news and sports director for Northwest Missouri State University's KXCV-90.5 FM, the flagship station of the Bearcat Radio Network. KXCV-KRNW provides in-depth news, information and entertainment to 32 counties in the "Midwest four-corners region" of Missouri, Iowa, Kansas and Nebraska. The station features programs and news from National Public Radio as well as Americana, jazz and classical music, along with a variety of entertainment and topical programs.

John was at KNIM in Maryville from 1983-1999 before joining the staff at KXCV. Now in his 36th year as a broadcaster, John used to do Maryville High School as well, but since joining the team at KXCV, he has focused on the Bearcats. The Albany, Missouri native graduated from Albany High School before earning his degree in broadcasting from Northwest in 1982 and has been recognized by the Missouri Broadcasters Association throughout his career for his news coverage and play-by-play prowess.

JACK, HARRY AND JOHN

For as long as he can remember, John says he had designs on the broadcast booth. It all stemmed, not just from his love of the St. Louis Cardinals, but from his fascination with the men who called the game.

"It probably started when I was eight or nine. I was as much a fan of Jack Buck and Harry Caray as I was the Cardinals themselves. I could look forward to turning on the radio and listening to the games, and that's something that I've had an interest in really ever since."

Photo courtesy of Brent Barnett

Fast forward about 17 years. Where Buck and Caray were how John connected with the Cardinals, in the mid-1980s many would begin to identify John with Northwest Missouri State University. It was then, he says, he started to think he could have a career in broadcasting.

"Just doing the Northwest games that first year. Doing that, I started to feel like I'd made it, that I could do this. That first year doing Northwest games in 1985."

Good thing it worked out because if it hadn't ...

"I don't know really (what else I would have done). Seriously I don't because this is what I wanted to do all my life. I guess probably something in

John and his broadcast partners, including Matt Tritten, have watched as Northwest Missouri State football has risen from afterthought to national power.

media or PR or something like that. I never wanted to do anything else. Sometimes I wonder about the sanity of that, but this is it."

RETURN OF THE BEARCATS

In 1989, the Northwest Missouri State football team finished 9-3 and advanced to the NCAA Division II playoffs. Over the next six years the Bearcats went 22-43-1. But then their fortunes changed. In 1996 Northwest went 11-2, finished as MIAA co-champions, and went back to the playoffs. Their first opponent: the University of Nebraska-Omaha. Not surprisingly that game stands out as John's favorite.

Six times Northwest Missouri State has won the NCAA Division II football title. And six times John Coffey has been on the call.

"That's one that came right down to the end of the ballgame, and a touchdown pass from Greg Teale to Jessie Haynes that we won it there. That was a great ending to the game. That was also when they made that first step up. We knew there's a future for this team. They went twice before that and then we'd take a step backwards, but it just felt like this was a stepping stone to something special."

JUST ANOTHER DAY AT THE OFFICE

When I worked in college athletics, game days meant I got to the office early and I was always the last one out of the stadium or arena. Second in and next to last out? Usually the broadcast crew. So, while I knew what I did on a gameday, I was curious to learn what all went into the play-by-play announcer's preparation.

"For football, I like to get to the stadium no later than an hour and a half before airtime. Right now we go on an hour before kickoff time, so it gets me there and I really—I'd like to be there a little earlier as far as that goes—but, if you're on the road traveling with people they don't want to be there quite that early. But I figure an hour-and-a-half before airtime gives you time if something goes wrong with the equipment, we've got time to troubleshoot it and get it fixed before you're on the air. Then it gives you time to talk to the other announcers, SIDs, different things, and see if we come up with a few nuggets that you didn't have in your notes as you prepare for a game. Then you can just sit back and relax a little bit. Nothing I hate worse than I have to rush into a broadcast. You're still in rush mode once you get on the air, and I just never feel like I've quite hit the stride even after you get into it a little bit. I like to be there and just have a chance to relax a little bit before we go on.

"For basketball, same way. Again, I like to get there about an hour and a half ahead of time and get set up and ready to go and make the rounds, talking to different people and just again maybe sit down for a little bit, take a deep breath before we go on and just enjoy the atmosphere a little bit."

WWW.BROADCAST-GAMECHANGER.COM

When John began broadcasting, if you didn't live in the immediate coverage area of the radio station or newspaper, you were going to have a hard time keeping up with your team. That all changed with a little invention called the World Wide Web.

"Oh, I think the internet has changed a lot of it. It's just from the standpoint of who your audience is because we will now get emails or texts during the game from people all around the world. We've gotten emails from people from Germany to, I think, one time somebody was on a ship just off the China coast. One game last year, we asked the audience to let us know where you're at, and we were getting messages from Australia, England, different places around the states. Alumni and friends. The audience has certainly grown because of that. They'll call the station and they'll relay it on to us and want a mention. Normally those come during games when we're up in the second half; we'll try to make it a little more fun."

JACK BUCK: BROADCASTER, ARTIST, IDOL

I knew from his opening response that John was an admirer of Jack Buck. But I wanted more detail. What was it about the legendary Voice of the Cardinals that made such an impact?

"One of the things about Jack, I always looked at him as more of a broadcaster than a sportscaster because he could do football, he could do basketball, he did Sports Open Line on KMOX and he was just very versatile. Growing up I loved to listen to Harry Caray, but I think of him as a baseball announcer, and Jack was more of a complete broadcaster. Jack probably was my hero growing up. I looked forward every night to turning on Cardinals baseball, and when he was doing Monday Night Football on CBS radio, things like that, I was tuned in. I would just try to, I don't want to say mimic him because obviously there was only one Jack Buck.

> *"What young people need to know is that initially they're not going to make a lot of money at this. (But) we can touch people in ways you don't know."*
>
> *~John Coffey*

"The thing I took from Jack is number one have fun at the game. It's not deadly serious. And number two is, if you tune into just the radio and listen to Jack, you know immediately where you're at in the ballgame, even without the scoreboard. Just by the inflection in his voice you knew this is an important part of the ballgame. And he's not screaming either, like something you'd see now. Hopefully I'm able to get some of that across because you don't want a touchdown in the first quarter to sound like a game winner. You want to kind of build to that level at the end of the ballgame. That's part of what I took from listening to Jack growing up."

FROM THE FIELD TO THE ARENA TO THE DIAMOND

One of the great things about working for a radio station that covers a university is the diversity. Football in the fall, basketball in the winter, baseball in the spring. Just as you are ready for a change, a new season arrives. Like his counterparts, John has a hard time pinning down the sport he likes to call most.

"Oh gosh that's tough because I enjoyed doing baseball. I've done it the least just because of the economics of broadcasting in the area I'm in. Football in the regular season from the beginning is fun. I think consistently from game one to the end of the season, football is exciting because each game means a little bit more.

34

Photo courtesy of Brent Barnett

John has not only covered one of the most successful NCAA Division II athletic programs in the nation, he has also helped jump start many young broadcast careers, including those of Matt Tritten and Ryan Elliott.

"Basketball, once you get past November and get into the conference games, to get in close games and then tournament time especially, that's a lot of fun. I mean the excitement level is there for both, but there's something about a tournament game of basketball that's going right down to the wire, and in a lot of places you're sitting right in the middle of fans, kind of getting into it. That's fun. But basketball games, where you're playing 30 games or so (if you're lucky), some of those early games against NAIA schools can kind of drag."

While picking a favorite sport to call may be a challenge, John has no problem identifying a dream event to cover.

"I'd say World Series. I think just growing up listening to baseball and the nightly aspect—every word—the announcers really become part of your family to a large degree. I would like to have been at that level, I think. I just love sitting back and watching a baseball game in the summertime."

THE VOICE OF CHAMPIONS

The first nine seasons of John's tenure as Voice of the Bearcats, Northwest went a combined 37-61-2 and had only two winning seasons. Then Mel Tjeerdsma came to town. His first team went 0-11, but over the next two-plus decades, Northwest Missouri State gave John a new brand of football to call. From 1994 through 2016, the Bearcats went 259-51 with 16 MIAA titles, six NCAA Division II crowns, and had four undefeated seasons. The Bearcats also won the men's basketball national title in 2017, though John did not get to call the championship game because he got sick.

Given Northwest's struggles the first part of his tenure and the unbelievable success over the next 20 years, I was curious if winning made calling the games easier or if it became so expected coming up with exciting calls actually made it more difficult.

"I don't know. Even when they were bad they weren't terrible. They didn't win a game Mel Tjeerdsma's first year, but you could see that they were building on something, and the nice thing is the community's always been pretty supportive, even during the years when they were down. You could see a good contingent of people from the community. There are several games that are built in that you're going to have a big crowd—homecoming, family day— and you could see there was still some excitement around the program, even when they weren't winning consistently.

Back to my original question, Does the performance of the team impact the call?

"There's some games, you know, that probably the game is going to go downhill from the kickoff. But I just kind of look at it as you owe it to your listeners and your underwriters or sponsors to do the best job you can do, whether the team's 11-0 or 0-11. You have to give them their money's worth and prepare for a game just like if they were going to play for a national title that day. So I enjoy both. I mean, obviously it's easy to say now after you've won some championships, but I just enjoy broadcasting sporting events. You know there's a chance you're going to see something that you've never seen before.

"Especially now, with the internet, you know people that can't travel to all the games are listening. You owe it to them not to get too negative on the team. They're 18- to 22-year-olds and their doing the best they can. Just describe what you're seeing out there. Even the pros, I don't think being negative really helps you that much. I hate to hear an announcer that starts bashing the officials or bashing the players, you know saying 'I can't believe you made that error' or anything because even at that level, those guys have some talent or they wouldn't be out there playing. But you just describe what you see and then go on to the next play. Even with officials, if he makes a bad call, and you know in your heart they made a bad call, most of the time the coach is going to be up arguing that call. I never say, 'Man I can't believe the official made that call' because normally you can get that across by just telling how the coaches or players reacting."

BEING THE VOICE

I've always wondered if a guy like John Coffey, who has been at a radio station calling the action for a small—albeit highly successful—NCAA Division II athletic program, has ever gotten the itch to try for a network job. Or is basically working for one team more gratifying.

"Well, you get to be known as the voice of the university to a large degree. I think, even though I had a good relationship with the coaches before I came over to the university, you're part of the same team to a certain degree, although again during the broadcast I'm playing it straight, trying to be objective throughout the entire broadcast. But you're essentially working for the same people here, and that's the constituency of the university and the fans, and so I think you get a little bit more access to the coaches now than what I did at the commercial station.

"Plus, I enjoy the aspect of working with the students as they come through, developing a good relationship with them. Like our sideline reporter every year is a student who is going through our program, and it's nice to help them out and then see how they blossom when they graduate, to know you had a little something to do with helping them succeed."

Just to clarify, I asked John if KXCV is a teaching station.

36

"Yeah because we train the students when they come through the program, whether it's in the newsroom, on air, sideline reporting. And then we also hire students to do the engineering behind the scenes to send it out to our affiliates and work with them, so there's a lot of different skills that they can get by coming through the program. It's just nice to be able to see most of the guys and gals that come through our program, whether as a sideline reporter or as an engineer behind the scenes. They normally do pretty well when they get out because that looks really good on the resume. Just to know you've helped them a little bit and given them a start. It's something that I get from being at the university that I didn't at the commercial station across town."

So, I asked, do you prefer working for the university or would you like to work for a network?

"Oh, I think it'd be fun to do it just to see what it's like and to do a Division I game. We got a few with basketball where we play Division I teams, so you kind of get a sense of that a little bit anyway. But it would be nice to see what it's like at that level. I would love to have that opportunity. But right now, as far as where I'm at, I think I've got the best job in Division II, just from the coaches I work with to how easy they are to get along with. The games are always competitive and the conference we are in …. it's a fun conference to be in from the standpoint of all the play-by-play guys get along, you make good friends with them, good friends with the sports information people and people around all the universities that we go into. I don't know if you can top that."

Photo courtesy of John Coffey

John Coffey has broadcast Northwest Missouri State football and basketball for more than three decades, and he says he has no plans to hang up the headset any time soon.

MAKING A DIFFERENCE

"When my run calling games comes to a close what I'll miss most is the people I've gotten to know around the conference. I think what young people need to know is that initially they're not going to make a lot of money at this, unless they hit it big. But I think in sports you can really be an important part of somebody's life. We can touch people in ways you don't know. I always go back at times when I think of, 'Oh man, I've got a game and I'd like to be home doing this or that'.

"There was a time when I was doing high school games as well as the college and the high school team was playing in a holiday tournament at William Jewell College between Christmas and New Year's. It's one of those nights I'd like to be doing anything other driving to Liberty, Missouri to do a high school game. But I got a letter in the mail the next week from a lady in town that listens to all the games and it said that she was going through chemotherapy at the time and said that the thing that helped her get through chemotherapy was knowing that she was going to be able to turn on the radio and listen to the games. She was always at all the high school and college games, and she looked at all those guys as her kids. To be able to follow them, she said, that's just one thing that helped her get through chemotherapy. That's how you can make a difference in this business."

38

Photo courtesy of Missouri State University Athletic Communications

ART HAINS
KTXR - 101.3 FM
MISSOURI STATE UNIVERSITY

The Meyer Alumni Center, home of the Missouri State University Office of Development and Alumni Relations, is located in an old bank in downtown Springfield. Travel to the third floor, and that is where you will find Art Hains, MSU marketing specialist, licensing director, and Voice of the Bears and Lady Bears. A 1976 graduate of Southern Methodist University with a broadcast journalism degree, Art got his start in college, working as a student assistant in the sports information department while also calling games for the Mustangs.

Art's professional career began in his hometown, as he spent one year at KMMO in Marshall, Missouri, living in his parent's basement and covering the Marshall Owls and the Missouri Valley Vikings and going "to everybody else's fraternity parties because all my friends were still in college".

From there he moved on to KGBX in Springfield, where he covered the Bears and the High School Game of the Week from 1977-1981. That is also where he got his first taste of sports talk radio, as he produced "This Week in High School Sports". He moved back to Dallas from 1981-1985, serving at KRLD, where according to his Missouri State bio, he hosted the Dallas Cowboys' pre- and post-game shows and served as studio host for the Southwest Conference Radio Network. He also was involved in coverage of SMU football and basketball, as well as PGA Tour events in the Dallas-Fort Worth area. Part of his duties with SMU football had him covering the famed "Pony Express" featuring Mustang running backs Eric Dickerson and Craig James.

In 1985, Art returned to the Ozarks, where he has been the Voice of the Bears ever since. For 10 years he was the director of marketing in the Missouri State Athletic Department before joining the KTXR team from 1995-2008. He has been back full-time in his present role at Missouri State since 2008. He has hosted the daily Sportstalk radio show since 1995, and since re-joining the staff at MSU, he has also anchored the pre- and post-game shows for the Kansas City Chiefs on the Chiefs Radio Network.

Art and his wife, Lisa, have two grown children: Chris and Kathleen, and one grandchild (from Chris and his wife). He is a member of both the Springfield Area Sports Hall of Fame (2003) and Missouri Sports Hall of Fame (2017). So trusted is he as a sports authority that Art was recognized as "the most knowledgeable sports fan in the Ozarks" during his Missouri Sports Hall of Fame induction.

Photo courtesy of Missouri State University Athletic Communications

For Art and his broadcast partner, Missouri State business professor Ben Goss, calling Bears baseball is a dream come true.

SMALL-TOWN BOY WITH BIG-TIME DREAMS

You might think someone who has been in broadcasting for 40 years would have forgotten why he got into the business. You would be wrong. Art says he first caught the sportscasting bug when he was growing up in Marshall, Missouri, population just over 13,000.

"Our house was a neighborhood Athletic Club. We had a regulation-size goal post in the front yard that my mother and grandfather constructed. It was either a landmark or a monstrosity, depending on your point of view. The area between the hash marks down the middle of our front yard was skinned up every fall from the football games we would have.

"I was a front yard neighborhood star but that really didn't translate on the real level, so where everybody else was studying players I was kind of studying broadcasters. I knew who did what in TV and radio, and I kind of made it my goal to get into that."

In Art's bio for the Missouri Sports Hall of Fame he described himself as "lucky to live in a town big enough to have a radio station but small enough to let a high school kid on the air." I wanted to know more about that.

"Our family had owned the newspaper in Marshall when I was growing up. My granddad owned it. The radio station was kind of a competitor, but we'd sold the newspaper—my dad still worked for them. But Marshall is a small town; everybody knows everybody. My mom ran into the radio station general manager in the grocery store and said, 'Well, you know, Arthur would like to get into radio sports' and he said, 'Well, have him come out and see me.' They started me out doing preseason reports on Marshall football—how the practices were going and things like that—and do like a one-minute report three mornings a week that August. And then the games started, so they let me tag along in the press box and keep stats, and after about three weeks they let me talk. Finally, the next the last game of the season the general manager went off to a Missouri broadcasters convention and left me there to do the play-by-play, so I made my play-by-play debut when I was 17. Just that one game, but then that next summer before I went away to college, I wanted to do some baseball, which has always been my favorite sport.

"They then—and still do—carry the Royals on KMMO, so I looked at the schedule and I looked at the Legion schedule and picked out about seven games that we could do that didn't conflict with the Royals. Mr. Douglas, the station manager, said, 'Well, okay we can do those, but we need some advertising, so you need to go out and get some support to make it worth our while.' That was an early lesson that radio is not all just a public service; it's a business. So, I went out and drummed up enough advertising to do those seven games and had that experience.

"Then I get to SMU, and nobody else has ever really been on the radio before, and I had, so I got kind of the better assignments on the student radio station. I was the play-by-play baseball announcer for three years, and that was a horrible baseball team. And that was good experience because it's a lot easier when your team is good than when your team is 2-36, like we were my senior year. That takes quite a bit to keep the broadcast going, and we were probably awful, and you know, irreverent and probably, you know, cruel to our classmates because they're just so bad. But we had four scholarships and everybody else had 12 or whatever the NCAA permitted then, and we're playing Texas and Texas A&M and Arkansas and just getting mauled. That was good experience, even though at the time it was kind of kind of rough to get beat that bad regularly."

41

MAKING IT IN THE BIG D

The small-town boy from Marshall had to grow up fast when he went off to college at Southern Methodist University in Dallas. He wasted little time in doing so, immediately beginning work in the university's athletic department so he could get the lay of the land in big-time college sports media.

"When I was in college, and this is hardly making it because these are just little assignments, but I worked in the sports information office at SMU. I would have never thought of that, but my dad had a friend in Marshall named John Waldorf, who was director of football officials for the Big Eight Conference. He told my dad, 'Well, if Art wants to get into media he needs to get into sports information at a Division I school.' I kind of learned the ins and outs, so I met all the media people—electronic and print—in Texas and Arkansas through that, and I also got involved with KRLD radio in Dallas, which was and still is the big station there for news and sports. They wanted SMU students to go out and report on high school games on Friday nights, so they had three of us and they'd send me to a game and I'd take notes on a notepad and then go to a pay phone and call in my report and they'd record it and play it back on the scoreboard show.

"My senior year I got to host the scoreboard show. This is a 50-thousand-watt station in Dallas. I got to do that. I got to do color on a couple of SMU basketball games."

Finally, after demonstrating his commitment and knowledge of the game, Art got his big break.

"This is January of my senior year. The Cowboys were going to the Super Bowl in Miami, and the people who did the Cowboys also did the SMU games. I got a call at my parents' home in Marshall; I'm home for Christmas. It's Al Wisk, who for one or two years was the Voice of the Chiefs in the late '70s, and he said, 'Got a situation here where Frank (Glieber) and I are going to be in Miami for the Super Bowl and SMU plays Baylor the night before in a basketball game. Have you ever done basketball?' Well I hadn't. I'd done baseball and football, but I said, 'Oh yeah, yeah! Basketball, sure!' and he says, 'Well, you're doing the SMU-Baylor game a week from Saturday.' I said okay, no problem. I hung up and thought, What have I done? I remember I went to Sweet Springs one night, you know, just wherever I could find a game and I'd sit there in the stands with a program and kind of think to myself what I would say and how I would describe it. And then I went back down there to Dallas, and they had a high school kid for a spotter for me, and I did that game by myself. I thought well, you know, I can do this.

"I went home for a year after graduation and did the Missouri Valley and high school games, kind of waited for something to come along, and in 1977 the Springfield newspapers sold to Gannett, and right next door to the newspaper was KGBX radio and they were co-owned. Well the FCC rules at that time required Gannett—the previous owners were grandfathered—but the newspaper had to divest of the radio station; Gannett could not acquire it. So, Stauffer Communications out of Topeka bought KGBX. That was who we'd sold the newspaper to in Marshall, so they had both radio stations and newspapers, so I kind of knew it was coming and bided my time there in Marshall and then that sale went through. Before I could get the job, I had to come down here and bring some tapes and do an interview, and I got the job. The guy that hired me 40 years ago is still around; we go to church together. I came down here in May of '77 and with the exception of those four years in Dallas have been here ever since."

BEATING THE HOGS

For all the SMU games he worked, calling games with Eric Dickerson and Craig James—the famed Pony Express—and countless action-packed games in the old Southwest Conference, Art says it was a recent game involving Missouri State that stands out as his favorite game.

"When we won the baseball regional (in 2017) at Arkansas, and not because it's recent.

"You know, I'm a huge Royals fan and brought my son up to be a Royals fan. Most people here are Cardinals fans. When you suffer, it means so much when you finally win. Other than the actual birth of my kids, those two World Series (in 1985 and 2015) mean more to me than anything ever because I got to be there with my son for those things.

"I say that to circle back to two years ago. We lose at Arkansas in baseball. First game we get blown out, and that night at the restaurant everybody's, 'Oh, you know, it was just a bad game. Y'all will do better tomorrow.' These are Arkansas fans. Second night after we beat them they weren't quite so friendly because now they're feeling that they may lose. And then they did beat us by one run in the deciding game.

"Well, now this year we go down there for the regional and play them on the third night, and we had a rain delay at 11:30 p.m. I thought surely they're going to just suspend this and we're going to come back tomorrow. Nope. We came back and resumed the game at 12:45 a.m. and played on. It got to 3 a.m., and it is pouring. I've never seen a game played in these conditions. The umpire was going to bring the tarp out, and clearly somebody at Arkansas had

Art Haines got his start at KMMO in Marshall, Mo. Know who else has ties to KMMO? Greg Schmidt (the subject of Chapter 13).

gotten to the grounds crew and said you do not bring the tarp out unless we say so, and they convinced the NCAA rep that no, we can play. It was a joke. We finished the game, and they won. So now we have to come back and play the once-and-for-all game the next day, and we beat them. And I think I said something like, 'There's a dog pile in the Boston Mountains and the Bears have beaten the Razorbacks.'"

SPOON-FEEDING A MISSOURI COACHING LEGEND

Not only do play-by-play announcers get to call some exciting action; they also get to interview some of the biggest names in sports. Former Bears head basketball coach Charlie Spoonhour was a personal favorite of Art's, as much for entertainment value as for his knowledge of the game.

"You know, people used to tell me when Spoon was here that for a home game, they'd race out to their car after the game because they wanted to hear what he had to say. It was like I was the foil. You know, I just served him up and he hit 'em out of the park, like Rowan and Martin or Abbott and Costello. He was a dandy.

"I remember one night when we had given out seat cushions for a promotion, and at the end of the game somebody sent one sailing down. Well that started just an avalanche of people throwing them down and the court was just pelted with maroon seat cushions. Charlie came out for the postgame, and he said, 'Well, thank God it wasn't cutlery night!'"

A CALL OF REDEMPTION

When I asked Art about Jack Buck, thinking about how he would call Mark McGwire's record-breaking home run, I was thinking he might have practiced a call for a big touchdown run, a three-pointer at the buzzer, or a called strike three for the final out of an important game. Instead, he shared a call that was all about propping up his Bears.

"There are only a few times, when it's a huge game. I keep going back to baseball, and this was in '03 when we went to the College World Series. The week before at the conference tournament we had lost at Wichita State, our archrival, and there was a question whether we'd even get in the NCAA tournament. We had brought back our first day starter in relief in the conference tournament championship game and he pitched about three innings of relief and they beat us in extra innings. It got back to me later that the Wichita State broadcaster, who's a friend but he's very, very partisan on-air, said, 'Why would any parent send their kid to Missouri State to have them abuse their son's arm like this?' He found fault with our pitching choice that we brought this kid back.

"The next week we're in the regional finals at Nebraska playing Nebraska, and it was a cakewalk. We win 7-0, so I could kind of see it coming about three innings early that we're going to win, and I'm thinking how am I going to call this last out? I just hope it works out, and it did. It's a pop up on the infield, and I said, 'The question was asked, Why would any parent send their son to Missouri State to play baseball? To go to the Super Regional, that's why! The Bears are going to Columbus.' So, I did have some time to think about that."

Art's second favorite call also involved the Bears and Shockers, this time on the hardwood.

"2011 was the last time we beat Wichita State in basketball. It was the last day of the season, on ESPN, the Conference championship on the line, at our place, packed. We win the game and confetti comes raining down. That's probably my very favorite moment ever at Missouri State, winning that game and having the confetti come down and beating Wichita and winning the conference, although we didn't end up going to the NCAA because we lost in the finals of the tournament the next week by four points. But I said, and we've got it on tape, 'For the first time ever we can say the Bears are Missouri Valley Conference champions'."

EXECUTING THE GAME PLAN

Reviewing statistics. Studying game notes. Watching game film. Reading press clippings. Those are just some of the sportscaster's activities while preparing to call a game. Take care of business and it should be smooth sailing once the game begins. Fail to do it ... When I asked Art what a typical game day looks like, he supported that notion.

"For the most part, the hay is in the barn. I've done the preparation. Now you just have to execute. I just get there in time to set up the equipment, connect to the station, and eat. Obviously home game days are very different from road.

"During the 10 years that I also did promotions and marketing, now that was different because I had to prepare the PA announcer script, and I was in charge of the timeline, the national anthem singer and when that's going to come. We had some interesting moments there. A couple times the national anthem singer didn't show. One time a guy forgot the words, and of course he was right in the middle of it, so what can you do? I kind of prided myself on scouting out good national anthem singers. This guy I'd taken sight-unseen on a recommendation from a fan who had seen him in Las Vegas and said he's great, and he was performing in Branson. We got him up here and he had this big leather jacket and his shirt unbuttoned, you know, like a lounge singer. He got out there and not only forgot the words, he forgot the tune, so he just kind of went off and 'doobie-doobie-doobie'. It was horrible, and I'm just sliding under the table because what can I do? But I jumped over that

table many a time to go run over and check on something and then run back and put the headset back on. That was a little more hectic back in the days when I was doing that.

"If we're on the road, I jump on the bus with the team to the game, hook up, eat, do the game. Pregame we've always done day of, about an hour and a half before the game, except our current football coach Dave Steckel wants to do it a day ahead. That's good and bad. It's good in that it's taken care of ahead of time so you don't have to worry about it on game day. But that obviously causes us to pick out a time the day before or two days before.

Art Hains is a renaissance man as a broadcaster. Not only is he the Voice of the Bears, but he also hosts Sportstalk on KTXR and anchors the Kansas City Chiefs pre- and post-game shows on the Chiefs Radio Network.

"But no, I don't get there overly early because, you know, as far as prep work, I've got all that done. I usually shoot for about an hour and a half before I go on the air."

TRIPLE THREAT

Most of the high school and college sportscasters I interviewed called football and basketball. The pros called football, baseball, soccer or hockey, with a few games from another sport mixed in. Art was one of the few who broadcasts football, basketball AND baseball. Naturally, I wanted to know which is his favorite.

"Baseball is my favorite sport. Football probably flows the best. Call a play, color man analyzes the play, time for the next play. That really goes well. The only thing with football is recognition because you're so far away. I always use binoculars. Always have. If it's a pass play, I have to pull them down to follow the ball. If it's a running play I stay with it. So identifying, you know, not getting faked out and things like that can be a challenge. But as far as the flow is concerned and the pageantry of it, I think football is maybe my favorite.

"It's also the sport in which we've had the least success. As I've told young broadcasters all the time, you do the same job whether your team is horrible or championship. People will say, 'Oh boy, you called a good game last night' and I'll say, 'Well it was a good game, and I called it.' They call themselves when it's such a good game. You know, down to the wire, that's not hard to do. It's hard to do when it's 50-7, but then we've had some of that too, going back to my SMU baseball days.

45

"Basketball, the trick is just not to say too much. You're going to get behind if you call every pass, every bounce, every nuance, they're going to be pulling it out of the basket and going the other way, so you have to develop a shorthand that the listener hopefully can follow. The color man really has to jump in and jump out because there is not much time unless the ball is dead and there's a timeout or whatever. Now, that's the sport for which we are best known, and probably by extension I'm best known because there's just so much interest and history in that."

"Baseball, the challenge there is all the dead time and filling that in some way. I haven't done much TV, but on the radio side—no dead air, no dead air! To a point, if there is a crowd, you can let the ambient crowd noise fill the time. But sometimes in baseball season in March, we're at Central Arkansas, there's a hundred people in the stands, so not much ambient sound there and you have to fill the time somehow. That's the trick. But I just love being in a baseball park and doing a game. I'm a nut for that. My kids went to Parkview High School, but I go to other high school games just to see them. Every time I go to a football game at Kickapoo, about once a year, their baseball field is right behind the football stadium, and they usually have it lit up on football game nights for some reason. I kind of pause on the stairs to the press box. You know it's just a field, but all baseball fields are beautiful."

Recognized as "the most knowledgeable sports fan in the Ozarks", Art Haines is a member of the Springfield Area Sports Hall of Fame and the Missouri Sports Hall of Fame.

A FAN OF THE POETS

While Art is a fan of many different sportscasters, two gentlemen stand out above all the others. Not surprisingly, as an avid baseball fan, they are two of the game's icons.

"I didn't hear Ernie Harwell that much, but Jack Buck and Vin Scully, I think, were the best ever at calling baseball. Growing up I had relatives in Texas and I followed the Kansas City A's when they were there when I was a little kid, but I also was an Astros fan from going down there and visiting my grandparents and aunt and uncle in Houston and Beaumont. I got to go to a game in the Astrodome the first year it opened and they were playing the Cubs. I would listen to Astros games on AM stations crackling in at night up in Marshall, Missouri Gene Elston was their broadcaster. He just passed away within the past few years, but he was very smooth and very understated—and I'm probably neither—but I really liked him at the time. I liked the way he called a game.

"You know the Chiefs have been blessed with such, oh my God … Wayne Larrivee, and Kevin Harlan, and now Mitch (Holthus). Just three outstanding broadcasters, all with great enthusiasm, so you know, those are some of them.

"(Royals announcer) Denny Matthews is as technically good a baseball broadcaster as there is in his description of the ball in play and his knowledge of the game."

Like many of the gentlemen I interviewed, Vin Scully and Jack Buck came up in my conversation with Art. So I asked him, What was it about these two icons that everyone finds so awe-inspiring?

46

"Well, I mean it's just poetry that comes out of Vin's mouth. It's often said when he is in the middle of telling a story, the baseball gods do not permit the inning to end until he finishes the story. So, if he's in the middle of a story, there's going to be a visit to the mound or there's going to be a couple of foul balls, but something's going to happen and when he gets to the end of his story the inning ends. I mean his timing, it's just lyrical, so I admire that from him.

"Jack just had such a command, such an authoritative demeanor, but I'd say at the same time a humility. Authoritative and humble don't always go together, but I think in his case they really did."

CALLING THE WORLD SERIES
So, a dream event to call would be ....

"I've already gotten to do one College World Series. That's the one sport that the mid-majors like us can compete in and beat Mizzou and Arkansas on a fairly regular basis. I really think now that Wichita State has gone into decline that we're kind of the 'it' school in the Midwest for baseball. We've got a great facility.

"Something I'd love to go back and do is another College World Series. If you're just saying any event, oh yeah, I'd love to do a World Series. But you know, and people ask me about that, you kind of cast your lot. If you're going to do baseball, you have to do baseball and pay your dues and do minor league games and ride a lot of buses and do all that. I chose to go more the college route, which is maybe more stable and long-lasting, but that kind of forecloses the possibility of, say, getting into professional baseball."

ART HAINS—SPORTSCASTER
Art Hains fans do not have to wait for a Missouri State game to hear their man on the air. "The most knowledgeable sports fan in the Ozarks", as he was called during his Missouri Sports Hall of Fame induction, has continued working with professional football teams throughout his career.

"Doing college play-by-play is my favorite but being involved with the Chiefs is a close second. And early in my career in Dallas I did the same work for the Cowboys for three years at KRLD. I kind of took it for granted back then. It was just part of the job. I worked Monday through Friday. Saturday there for two years I was the studio host on the Southwest Conference Radio Network, so all the Southwest Conference schools except Arkansas (they did their own), those broadcasts all came into one studio in a strip mall in Dallas. There might be six games going and they each have their own board operator in this room, and then I would do pregame, halftime, and postgame for all of them. So that was pretty hectic. You know, am I talking to the TCU-Texas audience? They don't need to hear their own highlights; they want to hear about Baylor-SMU. So I'd do that on Saturday and we'd do Cowboys on Sunday.

"It was very similar to what we do with the Chiefs now, except that after the game, about an hour after all the locker room interviews were over, then we would do a call-in show and we'd have a former Cowboys player in studio with me. One year was Charlie Waters, and one year it was Preston Pearson, and one year was Cliff Harris. I don't know why it kept changing, but those fans could be pretty irate after a Cowboys loss, so fortunately we had a former player there to kind of calm them down. So, you know, that's seven days a week, and it was kind of a toll.

Art and Missouri State football coach Dave Steckel chat during an MSU Bears basketball game. Art's job provides him a front-row seat to some of the best action in the Show-Me State.

"So all these years later now Mitch Holthus gets me involved with the Chiefs broadcasts, and that has really been a blessing. Dan Israel, the executive producer—I've gotten to be really close friends with all of them—his commitment to putting on a great broadcast ... I've not always been in those situations. A lot of time, you know, it was just get it on the air, get the commercials played, we really don't care. But Mitch and Dan really care about all aspects.

"We've had some bumps. This year we've had some new people on the broadcast, and we've had some technical faux pas, and that's been a little rough to work through. But just getting to be part of that, growing up a Chiefs fan and hearing that music, going to games at Arrowhead for years, and now I hear it and I'm on ... It's a lot of work but I look forward to it every week."

ART HAINS—TALK SHOW HOST

Art also hosts his own sports talk show. Compared to play-by-play and hosting an NFL pregame and halftime show, I wanted to know if sports talk presents its own challenges.

"When the phone doesn't ring, that can be a problem. My show is pretty caller-driven. I do about 20 minutes of top stories and opinion at the start, I'll have at least two guests usually along the way, and I don't keep guests more than 10 sometimes, 15 minutes unless it's something really special. And then I'm dependent on the phone calls. If the phone is not ringing then I just talk until it does. The current trend is good in that almost all sports talk shows have at least two hosts so they can bounce things off each other. It really makes for a better show. The other trend is that hosts will make outlandish statements or say something outrageous to get the phones to ring. Well, I work by myself, and I won't do that. Reluctantly, I've gotten into the National Anthem thing (the NFL players protesting by kneeling during the National Anthem) and that'll get the phone ringing. I really don't want to talk about players beating up their wives and the sordid stuff. I'd rather talk about who's going to play second base for the Royals next year or are the Cardinals going to re-sign Lance Lynn and things like that. But sometimes that doesn't get the phone to ring, so I have to talk till it does.

"Some people will do a topic show. They say, 'Well, what do you think the score of the Chiefs game is going to be this week?' I don't like doing shows like that, so I make it harder on myself because of these things that I mentioned. During the day I listen to talk shows and I build a pile of news releases and things that I'm going to use and that gets me up to a point, but it doesn't get me two hours. I'm always thinking about do I have enough to get through this show? Thank God for the internet because I can go to espn.com or go to Kansas City Star or St. Louis Post-Dispatch and there's usually something there that'll trigger something that I can talk about, and maybe that'll generate some phone calls."

ART HAINS—MENTOR

One thing Art mentioned is that it is tough on young broadcasters because play-by-play jobs don't open very often. I learned from a lot of my interviews that, to help young men and women break in, there seems to be a brotherhood, a mentorship that happens. I asked Art about his involvement in guiding young broadcasters.

"Because of all the digital opportunities now, there are more chances for young broadcasters to get some experience. I mean, every high school in the country just about streams their games, and if you can get involved with that then you don't necessarily have to get on with the hometown radio station and get out over the air. So there are more opportunities to get experience, which is huge. But there aren't any more actual jobs that pay a lot and that is a problem, and it is true that most of us stay forever in these positions. I am 38 years into football here, and the guy at Southern Illinois is 39 years in, and the basketball guy at Bradley is 39 years in, and Mike Kennedy at Wichita is about 40. So they don't turn over very often. For example, Kevin Greim is one of the guys that I mentored a little bit when he was in school here, and he just helped set up the equipment and would go run stats and things like that, but he was around it and he made a career out of it for a number of years."

Kevin is a mutual friend; he was the athletic marketing director at Missouri Southern when I served as sports information director there, and he often spoke fondly about the impact Art Hains had on his life. Others are obviously getting the same benefit.

"I've got a young man coming Thursday who was a neighbor in Marshall that lives here now and they had kids on the swim team, and this kid is on our swim team, and he wants to get into broadcasting. So I'm going to visit with him and maybe that'll result in him hanging around courtside with us like Kevin did all those years ago, kind of get him started. I haven't met him yet so I'm anxious to do so. But yeah, anybody that wants to get into this business, anything I can do to help, I'm glad to do."

CALLING IT OLD-SCHOOL

We had a Division II baseball championship tournament game with the Mules where Shawn Jones was our play-by-play announcer and Bob Jackson was providing color. Because of space and technology issues (the perfect storm for a broadcaster), they had to call the game on a cell phone, passing the phone back and forth between pitches. Surely, I asked, in 40 years did Art have a similar story to share. Boy, did he!

"Oh yeah. I've had to do that. One night during football we had a power outage. It was a night game, so everything went out—lights, power, phone line. So obviously the game is halted until they get the lights back up. But the university phone system was out—and this is before cell phones—so I mean we're screwed. Well there's a pay phone in the back of the press box, and it was not part of the university system, and it had a dial tone. So I went to the pay phone, and you know it had one of those little short hard chords that didn't go very far. But I got ahold of the radio station and said, 'Okay, put me on the air because now the lights are back on and the game was going to resume.'

"Ned Reynolds (former sports director at KYTV in Springfield) was doing color with me at the time. The cord did not reach far enough for me to see around the corner to see the field, but he gave me hand signals like 'He's back to pass' (Art pantomimes a passing motion) and, you know, 'He hands off' (Art acts out a football hand off) and then he would give me like one or two fingers for what player had the ball. We had to do about the last quarter of the game that way. It was almost like sign language what he was giving me. He'd give me hand signals and then I would call the game that I couldn't see from this pay phone. Now, by the time the game ended, the phone system came back up, and we were able to go back into the press box and do the postgame show normally. But that would be an outrageous example of what you have to do to try to stay on the air. And we did."

LIVING THE DREAM AND COUNTING HIS BLESSINGS

For more than four decades Art Hains has been able to call the broadcast booth his home. From the front lawn in Marshall, Missouri to the Big D and SMU to the Ozarks, he has been living his dream of calling the action and talking sports. And he's not about to take it for granted.

"I'm just very blessed to be in this circumstance. It's what I've always wanted to do and I've gotten to do it now for more than 40 years. We're probably going to wind down some of the activities, but yeah, I guess I'll know when it's time on the Bears, and the Chiefs will probably let me know when it's time. Those are the two things that I want to go on doing here for a while because I still get excited about, 'Oh, I'm going to get up this morning and go to Carbondale and do a game'.

"Curt Gowdy was in town some years ago for the Springfield Area Sports Hall of Fame speaking on behalf of Johnny Morris, the Bass Pro guy, who we inducted. He gets Curt Gowdy to come to town and speak for him, and he said for young broadcasters 'never get jaded'. When you lose the excitement, when it becomes, 'Oh, man, I've got a job to do' then it's time to get out. You can't get jaded about it, and I haven't. I still look forward to the broadcast."

Photo courtesy of Greg Hassler

GREG HASSLER
KOKO 1450 AM / KWKJ - 98.5 FM
UNIVERSITY OF CENTRAL MISSOURI

Greg Hassler did not take what many would consider the "traditional" route to the broadcast booth. But, then again, he hasn't been traditional in much of anything in his career. He started at Park University right after graduating from Washington High School in Kansas City, Kansas but left to be a golf professional before coming back to graduate with a degree in management in 2001.

He came to Warrensburg in the late '80s and served as a golf pro in Kansas City and then in Warrensburg from 1984-1997. Greg also worked in real estate before joining his friend Vance DeLozier to purchase D&H Media, home of 1450 KOKO/98.5KWKJ, on August 6, 2001. Since that time, he has provided play-by-play for Warrensburg High School, sideline reports for University of Central Missouri Mules football, color commentary for UCM basketball and finally play-by-play for the Mules and Jennies.

Broadcasting for one of NCAA Division II's top programs (five top three and seven top 10 finishes in the Learfield Director's Cup over the past 10 years), Greg has naturally had the opportunity to call the action for some stellar teams. Included in that list are three football playoff berths and three bowl games; eight women's basketball regional tournament berths and a regional title; and eight trips to the men's basketball regional, including three championships. He has also called the action for a pair of men's final fours. The highlights, though, came March 29, 2014 in Evansville, Indiana when Greg was on the call for the Mules' 84-77 win over West Liberty to claim the NCAA Division II National

Championship and on March 23, 2018 when the Jennies ended Ashland's 73-game win streak with a 66-52 win for the National Title.

Greg and his daughter, Ally, live in Warrensburg. He is vice president, co-owner, and sports director for D&H Media, where he wears many hats, including accounting, programming and scheduling. He took second once in a Missouri Broadcasters Association but says he doesn't regularly submit for competitions. He is currently back in school, pursuing a master's degree in communication at the University of Central Missouri in hopes of landing an opportunity to teach one day.

Greg and I sat down to visit at his office in Warrensburg. While he is one of my closest friends in the media (we have been broadcast partners for seven years as I provide color analysis for Mules football), I learned a lot I never knew about Greg and his approach.

OTHER DUTIES AS ASSIGNED

From a golf pro to a real estate agent to a radio station owner. As I said, Greg did not take the traditional path to the broadcast booth. So how did he get into radio and from there into sportscasting?

"Vance (DeLozier) and I had an opportunity to bring an FM station to town because KOKO was just AM and it was owned by somebody else. But we had an opportunity, and word got out that we were going to bring an FM in. The company that owned KOKO wasn't from here and realized that's probably a very good deal for them because we are local guys, we know everybody, so they said let's just sell. So, we bought KOKO and now we had both of them. We have a plaque on the wall that shows we played our first record in 2001.

Before partnering with Vance DeLozier to create D&H Media, Greg Hassler served as a golf pro in Kansas City and Warrensburg, Mo.

"Sports broadcasting was just a by-product of being an owner. Somebody had to do it, I had an experience in it, and so I started out at the lowest level. I put a lot time in as a football sideline guy for Mules football. That's all I was did. And then I started doing color for UCM Mules and Jennies basketball, and then it progressed up to what I do now."

Okay, so that was how Greg got into radio, but perhaps the bigger question was why. After all, radio is not a 9-to-5 job.

"At the time, I was ready for a different challenge and it sounded like fun. It sounded like a good way to make a living. Owning a small business, no matter what you do, is a hard way to make a living, I learned that the hard way."

Indeed. In fact, at the time of this writing, Greg was leading a major remodel of the station. But the hard work, if anything, has spurred him on.

"I got into it. And the more I learned about it, radio was really appealing to me. I don't like doing the same thing day in and day out. Radio is not really like that. It's always something different."

CATCHING THE BUG
Greg actually kind of stumbled into radio when UCM's former play-by-play announcer needed some assistance for a high school game. But once he did that game, Greg was hooked.

"I never had a goal to be a sports broadcaster. I did a game with Jonesy (former UCM associate athletic director Shawn Jones), the Warrensburg Lady Tigers and Columbia Hickman girls in a Christmas basketball tournament. Game one I was the color guy. I was terrible, but I liked it. Then I did a few more and the next thing you know I did Warrensburg Tiger basketball for a couple of years and then I did none until Jonesy came back from working at KU. And then I started in football sideline for the Mules.
I did sideline for quite a while, and then they had some cuts at UCM and everybody was wearing a lot of different hats so I ended up doing color for road games.
"I did home Jennies basketball games, and that freed up other people to do other stuff. I enjoyed it and I got better at it and then ended up doing all the Jennies games. That's when I really felt comfortable and then I started doing football. The very first football game I did, you and I did in Topeka, Kansas, when Washburn and the Mules played in the very last game of the year. That is the very first play-by-play game I had ever done in football. It was me, you and I can't remember who was on the sidelines. So when Jonesy got the job in Arkansas (as athletic director at Henderson State University) I took over everything. It is nerve-racking, but it has worked out pretty well."

TAKING THE LEAD
Given all his experiences before entering broadcasting, it is a bit surprising that Greg can't easily come up with an idea about what he would do other than radio.

"I mean that's a hard question because you ask that question now, I can think about all the stuff that I would have wanted to do. But if you asked me 20 years ago, there'd be a different answer.
"I'd say now I probably would be in the healthcare field (Greg serves on the board at Western Missouri Medical Center). I think I'd be in administration, probably not as a provider—not a doctor or a nurse—but in administration. I'm a leader, Joe (*said with a grin*). I like to lead."

WE ARE THE CHAMPIONS!!
Thousands of college sportscasters go their entire career and never get to call a national title game. In just four years on the job, Greg has gotten to bring the play-by-play for two.

"The (2014) Mules basketball national championship run was by far the craziest thing. Just the way it happened. That was the year no one would do Jennies basketball. I was the only guy that could do it. I'm down with the Jennies down in Arkansas (in the regional tournament). The Mules feel like I've abandoned them as they're playing in Mankato, Minnesota. The Jennies get beat in the second round and the Mules survived on a last-second shot against Northwest (Missouri State) and they move on. I jumped back on board, and of course you know Coach (Kim Anderson) is all, 'Okay! Alight, now you're on board.' And then we end up going to the Elite Eight (in Evansville, Indiana). We beat Southern Connecticut like a dog (98-88) and then we survived Metro State (71-69), and then we win the national championship game (84-77 over West Liberty).

"It was just unbelievable. I mean you roll into the Ford Center in Evansville, Indiana, and you have your sport coat on, you have your equipment, and you think you are big-time. And then you play this game, you win and there's confetti flying everywhere. It's unbelievable. But at the end of the day, you're packing yourself into a car, stopping at fast food and driving home. It's over."

After interviewing Greg the first time, I had to do an update. While I was writing the book, the UCM Jennies basketball team was having a magical season, one that led Greg to Sioux Falls, South Dakota. There Central Missouri ended Ashland's 73-game win streak to claim the 2018 women's national championship. Greg was also on the sidelines in 2002 when the Mules football team, in the last game of the regular season, defeated Pittsburg State in overtime in Pittsburg, Kansas to advance to the national playoffs for the first time in school history. It only seemed natural to ask which of these three events was the most memorable.

"The Mules basketball run was very unexpected, very exciting, just like this one (the Jennies national title). I mean, you lose in the first round of the MIAA Tournament, and then you make the run on the road the entire way. This one (the Jennies' title) was exciting.

The Jennies just played so good. They're just so tough, so mentally strong.

"When the Mules football team beat Pittsburg State, that was getting over the hump. Mules basketball, you know they'd been to a couple Final Fours under Coach Anderson (before winning the title in 2014). They did a great job.

"But this team—the Jennies—you know, 1984 was the last time they won a national championship. It had been 29 years since a Final Four. And then, out of nowhere, they make a run and win a national championship, so this one is very exciting.

"Look, I've known guys who have been calling games for 25 years and have never done a national championship game. I've called two national championship games in five years, and we've won them both. I guess that has to do with being at UCM. There's

As station co-owner at KOKO/KWKJ and Voice of the Mules and Jennies, Greg Hassler has had the opportunity to call action for some of the most historic events in UCM history.

other schools that don't even come close to qualifying for a national tournament. I'm spoiled because we win all the time. You can't expect to go to a national championship game every year, but two in five years? What are the odds of that? Unless you are at a blue-blood like KU or Kentucky, but at Division II, that's hard to do. It doesn't happen very often."

THE CALL

As a former UCM student-athlete and athletic administrator, I watch or listen to a lot of Mules and Jennies sports. As a result, I had a pretty good idea what call stood out most for a Greg. Turned out, I was right.

"This year, the play against Emporia State. (As time expired and it looked like the game would go to overtime, Emporia State threw a pass and tried the old hook and ladder play. But a Mules defender batted the ball away, another Mules defender scooped the ball and raced toward the end zone, fumbled the ball into the end zone at the one, and the Mules fell on it for the upset win over the 15th ranked Hornets).

"The call ended up being on ESPN and on the Bleacher Report, and I had my five minutes of fame right there. I mean, one minute you're settling down thinking, 'Okay let's get this baby into overtime'. The next minute, we win. It's the craziest play, and you're on ESPN. You just never know in sportscasting what's going to happen."

Greg also had a great call just before the half of the 2018 Women's National Championship Game: "Jens by four. Going toe-to-toe. It's Rocky Balboa and Apollo Creed. Exchanging haymakers in the middle of the ring." Where did that come from?

"I watch a lot of movies, so I can draw back on that. It just looked like two heavyweight fighters throwing punches as hard as they could at each other, and neither one of them was moving. They both just stood right there and took it and kept moving forward. At the end of the game, the Jennies just had a few more punches. But that was exactly what it was like."

IT HAS TO BE NATURAL

One thing I know about Greg is that he has quite the self-effacing sense of humor, so I was not really surprised by his response when I asked if he ever practiced for a specific call.

"I'm not smart enough or good enough to pre-think something. My personality is probably a little bit different than a lot of sportscaster's personalities. I mean I laugh during the broadcast, I say things I probably shouldn't say. I have a good time with it and try to make it relatable to people. I'm not a real staunch one-two-three here we go guy. That's just not my thing. I just like to have fun with it."

Of course, he can get away with being a little different; he does own the station, after all. That sparks a new question: Is Greg a radio station owner who happens to do play-by-play or a play-by-play announcer who owns the radio station?

"I'm a radio station owner that does play-by-play. That's just part of what I do. I wear all the hats."

So, *what if somebody were to come along and say, "I want to do play-by-play for the Mules?"*

"Well, now I become the play-by-play guy that actually owns this thing, so that's a no."

LET'S MAKE A DAY OF IT

Silly and playful as Greg can be, when gameday rolls around, he is all business. And it starts early.

"Football is an all-day event. It's up early, it's a cup of coffee while watching College Gameday on ESPN to kind of get your mind right. It's, if you're on the road you, hit the road, get there plenty early, set up your gear and test everything, go over your notes and get ready to go.

"If you're at home you get wherever you're going and you still get there early to make sure everything is set up, everything works. You talk to people and then on with the game. And then after the game, if you're at home, it's usually a celebration. Just have fun with your buddies. If it's a road game, you pack it up in the car, drive six hours home.

"In basketball, you get there a couple hours early, get set up, kind of get yourself in the moment. You go over game notes again and get ready to go.

"Game days are the best part because you've done all your prep leading up to it. Now, if you haven't done your prep leading up to it, it's going to be pretty stressful because you have no idea who anybody is and you have no idea what you're going to talk about, and that's not good."

SPORTS: THE GREAT ESCAPE

When most people think about sportscasters, they simply consider that the announcer is providing information and explaining what is happening during the event. Greg considers himself a servant.

"People need escapes from their daily life. They need that to be able to live happily. So many people do that by paying 500 bucks and going to a Chiefs' game. Other people will turn the radio on and listen to their favorite team. If it just happens to be the Mules, that is their daily escape from all the crap that happened at work, 'Man the Jennies are on tonight at 5:30 at Topeka, they're ranked third in the country, all right!' My job is entertaining them so they can enjoy the next two hours. That way they get their escape."

When I interviewed Greg, he was in his second semester of graduate school working toward a master's degree in mass communication. Now, not only was he using his experience and instincts to call the action. He was using academic research.

"I was reading a research paper from a guy at Northwest Missouri State. He said it is the announcer's job to keep the fan engaged in the broadcast, engaged in the game. This research found that, if there is some controversy, that keeps fans engaged. You don't want to dwell on it, but fans like that. So, if there is a strange call or a strange play, you have to bring that up, to address that controversy—this happened, we'll have to wait and see how it plays out. The fans like that."

A CHANGE FOR THE BETTER
According to Greg Hassler, the internet has been a game changer.

"There's so much more online especially in college. You can get everything you need at a click of a button. And during a game you don't have to wait to get paper stats. There's live stats updated after every play. You can make yourself sound like the smartest guy in the world just by having a laptop sitting in front of you."

Often during the development of this book, I found myself away from my computer with time to kill. Because the work-in-progress was on Google Docs, I could just pull out my iPhone and write. Turns out, Greg has found the cell phone to be beneficial in his work as a sportscaster as well.

"You can do a postgame interview on your phone and email it back to a station. The electronics have changed the whole deal. I can do that on my phone now. I have an app that, for nine bucks, my phone works just as good as a $1,000 recorder and I can cut and paste on my phone. It's got the wav files, mp3 files—I can file share it anywhere I want. It sounds great."

HAVE GAME, WILL CALL IT
During our interview Greg talked a lot about what he liked about football and basketball broadcasts. But which does he prefer?

Greg had an iconic call as the Mules football team upset 15th-ranked Emporia State in 2017. To hear that call, go to YouTube and search "Greg Hassler-The Call vs. ESU".

"Just because of the all-day, gameday atmosphere, football. I like it a lot, but once football season is over I get just as excited to do basketball, and the reason why it's good—and we're fortunate—is because we're good. Now if you're calling a 1-and-10 football team every year and a 5-and-19 basketball team every year, it might not be very fun. It's just all based on winning, and we're good; we always have a chance."

He may favor the sports most often seen on television or heard on the radio, but don't think Greg is averse to calling the less represented sports.

"I did the Jennies softball in the regional and in the World Series a couple years ago, and I really enjoyed that. I thought that was a lot of fun. If it's to the point where we're back in that national championship-type setting, I'd love to be able to do more softball. I've done volleyball and I've really enjoyed that. The thing is that the time constraints are really hard for me to do everything. It's tough. I would love to be doing some Jennies soccer. I don't know anything about soccer, but I would enjoy doing it. It just conflicts with so much stuff we got going on right now."

JOE COLLEGE
Given all he has experienced in his years as a sportscaster, Greg surely must have some goals. For example, he has not done much baseball. Would he like to call more Mules baseball games? As with all the high school and college announcers in the book, I was also curious as to his future aspirations as a play-by-play announcer. Any desire to work in professional sports?

"I've done baseball and I enjoy that. The regionals that I did in St. Cloud were really fun. If Bob (Jackson, current UCM play-by-play announcer for baseball) ever decided not to do Mules baseball I would just go from basketball to baseball and have no problem with it. That would give me something to do in the spring. I think that would be fun.

"Football, to me, is very commercialized in the National Football League. The college game is a little more pure, so I like that. Especially at our level. They are still good athletes, you know, with great facilities. Now, I would like to see a Mules football national championship. That would be awesome. But it's like you're D-I competing at a D-II, so I like that.

"Same with professional baseball. It may not be as commercialized as the NFL, but the college game is still so pure. I prefer that."

SWIM OR DROWN
My dad used to tell a story about the time his uncle put him on an inflatable raft, paddled him out to the middle of a pond, yanked the raft out from under him and shouted, "Swim or drown!" Suffice it to say Dad learned to swim that day.

Greg takes a similar approach to training young broadcasters. Apparently, it too has worked; several young men have come through the station to start their careers doing play-by-play, color and sideline.

"We have to do the high school games. In our size of town, that's what you do and I'm not going to do them. I mean, it's not that I don't want to do them, but I'm busy running the station and doing the UCM games.

"My theory on those guys who do the high school games is, I bring these guys in and show them the ropes and I'm going to teach them how we're going to do it. But once that's done, that's it. It's now their responsibility. I don't even want to hear about high school sports. I don't want to know anything that's going on. I don't want to worry about the board operator. That is your job; you guys figure it out. If you don't get the game on it's on you. If you don't have a board op here, that's your fault. You guys are in charge of high school athletics. Period. I don't have time to mess with it. It's all yours. That's how I handle it with those guys once I show them how to do everything and teach them.

"Now if they have questions about a better way to do something, I'll help them. I listen to the games and I will text them during the games. I'll critique some stuff that they said—shouldn't have said and tell them what they should say. I'll do that. But as far as scheduling and all that kind of stuff, it's on them and that's their job. They have to be responsible and make sure it's done right.

"I've had a guy who just didn't get there early enough. Well, it burned him a couple of times. Well it doesn't happen anymore. He gets there plenty early, so you live and learn."

GIVING BACK

As a single father and station owner who calls the games for one of the most successful athletic programs in NCAA Division II, Greg doesn't have much time to get away. When he does, he says he likes to serve.

"I have passions that I support through the radio station and that I care a lot about, like the Show-Me Christian Youth Home, you know taking care of kids that really don't have a whole lot or a place to go. Battered women programs.

"I think there's just a lot of things that when you can help you go ahead and help. Even though it's not all the time, you can do whatever you can to help.

"I like hanging out with Ally. I try to do as much home stuff as I can because I'm not there all that often during the season."

STRIKING THE BALANCE

Obviously, in order to keep all the balls in the air requires some strict scheduling. Greg says that is not a strength of his, but he wouldn't have it any other way.

"I don't I think I'm a good time management guy. There's certain things at work every day that I have to do; I don't have any choice. I'm able to do a lot of my game prep during the day, and if not, I'll do it at night with my laptop. Basketball is easier to prep for than football. During football season the only thing I do on Sunday is all-day prep. That's all I do all day—both teams—

Greg and Mules head football coach Jim Svoboda visit once a week on the UCM Sports Network.

and it takes me all day. So, when football season is over it feels like Sunday is a vacation. Basketball is not as hard to prep for as football, but there's a lot of basketball games.

"I try to catch up with things around here (after football and basketball season are over), but it's like any coach. The radio guy is invested in his team. When the season is over, there's that empty void and it takes a couple of weeks for that to go away. By the time you get into the middle to the end of summer, now you're ready to go again. It takes a little while; there's that void when the season is gone. You're walking out of that arena for the final time going, 'Man, it's going to be a long time before we're back here. We're not playing a football game until September of next year.'"

ONE WORD: EMOTION

It doesn't take long in visiting with Greg to find out he is passionate—about his family, about helping people and about his job. Being passionate and showing some emotion, he says, is critical for young broadcasters.

"I think it's important for sportscasters, especially if you're doing a game for your team, you're not doing a national game, remember that you are going to be tied to that team. You're going to be emotionally invested in that team. You're going to see things.

"I remember one year we went down to play Rolla (now Missouri S&T), they'd lost 30-some games in a row in the league, and they beat us and it's night. Lights are on, there's not one person around. You're in that press box and you see (former Mules head football coach) Willie Fritz by himself walking across the football field, head down. That just tells you how much goes into it. Same thing when we beat Northwest (Missouri State) up in Maryville. (Former Northwest Missouri head coach) Mel Tjeerdsma, head down by himself in a hoodie, walking across the field, nobody else around. Everybody already gone.

"Those visions you'll never get out of your head, like Coach Anderson and (former assistant coach) Brad Loos jumping up after winning national championship. There's just certain things you will not forget on an emotional, personal level for these coaches and players. A lot of people think well they just show up on Saturday. Not the case. They're pretty invested into it. Radio guys are invested into it, too."

Having witnessed several nail-biters from my post on the sidelines and in the press box, I know the helpless feeling of a biased viewer who is totally invested in the team's success yet can do nothing about the outcome. But while I was forced to keep my emotions in check, the broadcaster has to call the action. I asked Greg how he manages this.

"I don't. I'm up and I'm down. I have so many people tell me they know how we're doing without me even telling them the score. I get really high, I get really low. Sometimes I complain, sometimes I don't. But you know what? When I'm calling it for our fans, do they want me to control my emotions? Do they want me to be excited when their team does something good? Do they want me to be upset when something bad happens? I think they probably do because it's their team, too. That's what they're rooting for. I'm not doing it for a national audience; I'm doing it for us, doing it for Jennies' and Mules' fans.

"I'm an emotional roller coaster during a game and that does come out over the radio because I've had a lot of people tell me that. 'Man, you were really up.' 'Man, you were really down.' 'Man, you were really up.' But that's how they are, too; they're up and down with the with the team. I guess I'm doing my job if I'm conveying over the radio what's going on out there and they're going up and down with me."

Does he ever catch flack from his audience for being so emotional, for speaking so honestly?

"I have people tweet at me, 'Oh, the game's over with five minutes to go? Really?' (Laughs) Yeah, it is. Hate to tell you. We're down about 30 and we aren't going to touch the ball two more times, so yeah it is over. I'm sorry. You know, it is what it is. I don't sugarcoat any of my games. If we're playing bad man, I'll tell ya. We're playing bad.

"I think a lot of radio guys do that. A lot of radio guys in the MIAA do that. They tell you like it is. They don't sugarcoat anything."

Photo courtesy of Mitch Holthus

MITCH HOLTHUS
KCFX - 101.1 FM
KANSAS CITY CHIEFS

Smith Center, Kansas is famous for producing the high school football team that held the nation's longest winning streak (79 games) from 2004-2009. In that time the Redmen also won a Kansas record-tying five state titles. Because of its prowess, Smith Center was the subject of Joe Drape's New York Times Bestseller, "Our Boys".

Smith Center is also famous for being the home of the cabin where Dr. Brewster M. Higley originally wrote the words to "Home on the Range," widely regarded as the unofficial anthem of the American West. The cabin is preserved as a 501.c.3 by the family of one of Smith Center's most famous sons: Mitch Holthus.

Mitch Holthus has been the play-by-play voice of the Kansas City Chiefs since 1994. As such, he is the longest tenured play-by-play announcer in Chiefs' history. He also is an announcer for Big 12 Conference and Missouri Valley Conference basketball games on regional television. And he is an independent contractor who owns his own business, Holthus Enterprises LLC, that features talent, marketing and motivational speaking services. As an entrepreneur, he writes, produces and sells the "Minute with Mitch" radio and television shows that air in-season throughout the Chiefs Kingdom. He also hosts "Chiefs Insider" on select stations in the Chiefs' television network.

Before assuming his duties for the Chiefs, Mitch was the voice of Kansas State Wildcats football and basketball from 1983-1996. Today he is a lead broadcast voice for Fox Sports and ESPN. Mitch has called Big 12, Big 10, SEC and Missouri Valley Conference games, as well as post-season NIT games.

Mitch Holthus' family cares for the cabin in his hometown of Smith Center, Kan. where Dr. Brewster M. Highly originally wrote the words to "Home on the Range".

While at Smith Center High School, Mitch was a multisport athlete who also announced high school games for KKAN, now KQMA, in Phillipsburg, Kansas His list of honors is impressive. He was a 2008 inductee into the Kansas Broadcasting Hall of Fame, is past president of the National Sportscasters and Sportswriters Association (and still serves on its board of directors) and was the Missouri Valley Conference John Sanders "Spirit of the Valley" award recipient in 2007. Mitch has been named Kansas Sportscaster of the Year eight times, the nine-time top play-by-play announcer of the year in Kansas by the Kansas Association of Broadcasters and in 1996 was awarded KAB's Hod Humiston Award of Excellence in Kansas Sportscasting.

A graduate of Kansas State University (degree in journalism in 1979 and in business administration in 1980), he and his wife, Tami (a former KSU basketball player), have two grown children: Brian and Hayley, and two granddaughters.

It took nearly two months of trading emails with Mitch's assistant, Kelly McCabe, and Twitter messages with Mitch himself before he and I were to meet. I was soon to find out why. I don't know that I have ever met anyone with a more chaotic schedule. He finally was able to carve out an hour to visit with me at the Hilton Kansas City Airport before he was to jet off to New Orleans to call action in the Sun Belt Conference Tournament. It was an hour well spent.

I should note that part of Mitch's story told here comes from me being scooped by one of my students, Danielle Sachse. Danielle had a class project to interview a professional in the field she desires to enter. Because she knew Mitch's nephew, Danielle was able to land an interview with him four months before I was while he was speaking at a Minute with Mitch function. Where appropriate, I have noted that it was Danielle, not I, who asked the question (and yes, I have forgiven her for scooping me).

SPORTS NUT, FORENSICS FAN

As an aspiring sportscaster, it was only natural that Danielle would ask how Mitch got involved in sports broadcasting. Of course, this was my first question for Mitch, too.

"I was always a sports nut. I grew up on a farm, and my two brothers, they were great brothers, but neither of them were sports oriented at all, so I was always playing by myself, but I was always using my imagination. Every spot on the farm was a different stadium— Oakland, San Diego. And I would always imagine these games and then I'd play them.

"Then, in high school I was involved in forensics. I did extemporaneous speaking and I did informative speaking. We were too small to have debate. I thought, How do you put speaking together with sports? In a small high school, you can do a lot of different things. There's a value in that."

That desire to use his two loves led Mitch to radio.

"The local radio station, which is in Phillipsburg, Kansas (KKAN, now KQMA) and is our archrival but they had the station, I started doing work with them on a volunteer basis. I actually started doing a school report for my school and recorded it, sent it to them, and they used it as a prototype to do other schools. I just volunteered. I didn't know what I was doing, but I just did it and learned from it. It was a small station, which was great because you can make mistakes.

"There was a guy named Tad Felts, who has since retired. He actually broadcast my games, and I competed against his son. But he was kind of a first mentor. He was a gateway into the business."

THE AMBASSADOR OF CHIEFS KINGDOM

As I was listening to Mitch's interview with Danielle, it became apparent he views himself as more than the Voice of the Chiefs. He is also their ambassador and is really focused on leadership. I asked him to talk about that.

"If you narrow it down to the 'Voice of', whether that is for the UCM Mules or Jennies or for Marshall, Missouri, you are a steward of what is revered in that community, and you are a steward of the message. Because of the impact of the Chiefs Kingdom—and I'll humbly say that I came up with the concept of the Chiefs Kingdom, and it came about after being involved for years of seeing the impact across state lines, across genders, across urban and rural, I thought 'There needs to be something unique that defines it.' And I thought, 'The kingdom!' Well, that stuck and now it's grown very organically.

"What I found, and it's surprising, is the role and responsibility you have as kind of being the gatekeeper of the message. Whether it's the Joplin tornado or working with charities or touching the human fabric of your constituency of listeners. I'm going to start doing some work with Alpha Point, which is for the blind, the visually impaired. There was a story about a young man

Mitch Holthus and BJ Kissel form one of the best gameday reporting teams in the National Football League.

Photo courtesy of BJ Kissel

named Cameron Black, who was blind, been blind since birth. He just loves listening to Chiefs' games. He didn't know much about football; he and his dad have learned together and discussed the game, but he said, 'I just learned so much by listening to you.' That took me by surprise because it is just another example of the impact and the responsibility that you have as a broadcaster, particularly if you are the voice of a team or a director of a department. That goes beyond the obvious of what we do. There are so many examples of individuals, men and women, who are the voice of their community and they become aware of why. It goes way beyond the game. It goes way beyond being a steward.

"Some of the things I do are criticized. I really emphasize the human elements of the game because humans play the game; it's not a digital game. Humans watch it, humans listen to it, humans coach it. And then think of all the emotions involved. One of the things I emphasize is that a lot of things trigger those human emotions. For Chiefs games, I spend a preponderance amount of time on preparation. One of the things I do is try to find the local angle, even if it is for the other team. If they are from the Chiefs Kingdom or have some connection to Chiefs Kingdom in any way, whether they played college ball at the University of Central Missouri or (former New England Patriots offensive tackle) Max Lane from Norborne, Missouri, that's going to weave its way in and be a focus of the broadcast because I know what it means to those communities. We're the largest network now in the National Football League. There was a play where Sam Koch of the Baltimore Ravens had a punt blocked, we blocked his punt. Well, he's from Seward, Nebraska and played at Nebraska. John McGraw blocked his punt, and he's from Keats, Kansas and played at K-State, so it's a Chiefs Kingdom blocking a Chiefs Kingdom. Those are the things that make the game come alive and trigger the human element.

"When you activate those human sensors, the emotional sensors, that opens up the door to things that go beyond life where people have a connection to you and to the team, and that goes beyond football. That's been the most surprising thing in the last 15 years, just the personal and emotional things you get involved with because you are the voice of the team. And I've realized you are a steward or gatekeeper in many ways."

CALLING THE END OF A (BAD) ERA

It might be a stretch to call Mitch Holthus a good luck charm, but he was in the broadcast booth when the Chiefs saw one of the saddest streaks in team history come to an end. That, he says, was his favorite call.

"It would be winning the playoff game in Houston (in 2015). It had been, at that time, 22 years. We hadn't won a playoff game in 22 years. So, my first year was the first year of the no playoff wins. They got to the AFC championship game the year before (in 1994, where they lost to the Buffalo Bills). I told the producer, if it's a blow out, tell me when it's 35 seconds because I wanted to know when it was 22 seconds left on the clock. I said, 'Let me know' because at 22 seconds, I counted down 22 years, and it was a watershed moment because it was an achievement we hadn't had.

"I wanted to honor Coach (Andy) Reid because he brought us that. We were algae on the Titanic when he got here. We were 2-14. People forget that. We're so quick to forget. I just heard a spiritual message and it said we forget what we should remember and we remember what we should forget. He brought us out of the wilderness. That moment was a special moment Chiefs-wise.

"Career wise, my mind has kind of changed on that. Sometimes it's a great game and sometimes it's getting a call in the middle of the night from people in Joplin saying, 'We have to have the Chiefs help.' Well, we'll try to get going, and in three days we filled seven semi-loads with water. And then we took a group down there. Those are moments that are as positive to me as doing a winning game."

THE SIGNATURE CALL

Mitch Holthus is known at Kansas State for his "Big, Big Win" call when the Wildcats had a particularly important win ("It's archived on a page in their media guide that you can gauge how big the win was by how many 'bigs' I say") and for his "Touchdown Kan-SAS CITY" call during Chiefs' games. Danielle, as an aspiring sportscaster and a die hard K-State and Kansas City Chiefs' fan, had to know where those calls come from.

"They happen organically. You can't force them. One of the perils I had in my job is I replaced a very popular guy in Kevin Harlan — 'Oh baby! What a play! and the throaty voice. Still does TNT, so he still lives here. For years I had to hear, 'You're no Kevin Harlan. You're okay, but you're no Kevin Harlan.' And that was okay. But the signature call came because I thought, What can I do that in a sublime way will make people think of us every time we score a touchdown? It's why I'll say 'The sweet nectar of the end zone.' NFL touchdowns are hard to get, so what analogous thing can I do? Well, the sweet nectar. The players laugh about it, but every touchdown becomes a celebration for this whole city. That's why it's Kan-SAS CITY. You're a musician (Danielle is a double major in digital media production and musical theatre). It's the staccato note. When you sing, sometimes, you emphasize based upon the note. Well, it's made to be the staccato note. It's Kan-SAS CITY. And what's cool is little kids are coming up and doing it."

A FAN OF THE ICONS

Mitch's name came up repeatedly throughout my interviews with the other sportscasters when I asked the question, "Who are your favorite sportscasters?" So, who does a fan favorite enjoy listening to most?

"There are guys I admire a lot—Brad Sham of the Dallas Cowboys. Growing up, there were three that had a specific influence on me. Jack Buck, because I grew up rural on the Kansas-Nebraska border. There wasn't an app on my phone (said with a chuckle), and I was a Cardinals fan until the Royals came into existence. So Jack Buck was iconic to me.

"Fred White, who did the Royals for many years. Passed too soon. He did K-State and the Royals. He was a very strong mentor of mine. It hurt when he passed because he was one I could go to for critique. He would watch and I didn't know he was watching, and it would be in an encouraging style, but he would give some helpful hints.

"And then there was a guy, Dev Nelson, who did Kansas State when I was growing up. He was a broadcaster who was extremely articulate, and his delivery was impeccable. He was kind of the old-school broadcaster. Those in particular had a specific influence on me."

THE VOICE OF WISDOM

If you read the chapter featuring Adam Winkler from KNEO in Neosho, Missouri, Adam tells a great story about the time he spotted Mitch at an Ottawa University basketball game and asked Mitch to join him for an interview. That courage is impressive. What is perhaps more impressive is that Mitch remembers the encounter as well. I asked if he has mentored many aspiring sportscasters like Danielle and Adam.

"Countless, really. It's difficult. I'm not in a role in education where I have 50 students in a class, but there are some that I have taken as a mentor. I try to challenge them as much as I can, and I try to be very realistic with them because they have to see a lot of prospective broadcasters—women and men—do it, one, because it sounds fun, and two, because it is their leisure. It is something they enjoy. But when your profession becomes someone else's leisure, that changes the dynamic completely, and that is where the disconnect happens. You're not playing fantasy football anymore. There is a responsibility there and there is a tremendous amount of sacrifice.

"I always tell them there are five holidays in a year; which four are you willing to give up? You get one, but You're going to lose four. And it's time away from family. Your time is not your own. My biggest challenge, and I'm a little busier than most, is that my time is not my own. When Andy Reid says he wants to see you at 3:00, you don't say, 'Well, let's make it tomorrow at 5.' That doesn't work. And the game is scheduled at 'X'. You don't go, 'Well let's move that game next week.' In an attorney's case, they'll file an extension. Well, that doesn't happen. And that's what I try to tell young prospective students. If you can't check that box, it's not going to work. And that's why there are not that many who do it really. That's why so many fall by the wayside."

HYDRATION AND EXERCISE

I watched a video of Mitch calling a game (go to YouTube and search "Mitch Holthus touchdown Kansas City" and you can see it yourself). I'm not sure triathletes burn as many calories as Mitch does when he is calling a game. How, after all these years in the booth, does he maintain that level of energy?

Photo courtesy of Mitch Holthus

Mitch, executive producer Dan Israel, and color analyst Kendall Gammon keep Kansas City fans well informed, not only on Sundays, but also on the Chiefs Kingdom Show.

66

"You try to maximize the time you do have off. My wife and I try emphasize exercise and hydration. I'm not great with diet, but I try to do it. When there is time to rest, you rest. Whether that is getting six hours of sleep or seven hours. The days are so strange. There are days I'll come home at 2 or 3, leave at 2 or 3. But you have to be disciplined to rest when you rest. But hydration and exercise. My wife's sister is a speech therapist, and she's been very helpful as far as breathing techniques and delivery.

"Those games—I was embarrassed by that video, but that's the way it is. When you see it you're like, 'Wow. Okay, I guess I'm that crazy.' But everybody in that booth during the week will say that's what he is. It's not phony. And people will listen to it and say, 'He's gotta be exhausted after those games,' which I am.

"One of the times off during the week are Sunday nights when we have a home game. That's a date night with my wife. You just kind of decompress and have a nice dinner with the wife, but you're tired. It's just kinda the way I'm wired: being prepared, understanding the moment, understanding what it means to 70,000 people watching and one-point-two million people listening. I mean, it's the NFL; I'm not giving a narration of a concert at the Kauffman Center. Those people are hyped up. The people who go to the game, they're excited. So, it's just kind of the way I am, trying to capture the moment. It's a natural reaction of mine, I guess."

FOR THE FANS

In my research for this chapter I also watched an interview Mitch did with Erin Lawless for "Straight Out of KC". In the interview, Mitch said he has a passion for sports, not just because of the sport, but also because of what sports mean for the fans. I was interested in what he meant by that.

"It's the activation of the five senses. It's part of the fabric of our existence. That is excitement, sadness, triumph, tragedy, emotion. Something that is shared with others. You may dislike the person sitting next to you because they are rooting for the other team. But there are very few things we do in our lives that activate those inner fibers of our existence like sports does.

"For those who aren't into sports, maybe that's going to Handel's 'Messiah' that ignites that. But in the NFL, that's like watching the 'Messiah' every week. The anticipation of the event and then it actually happens. That's why I say it is a conduit into people's lives.

"And some people would say, 'Well, then you're giving it too much importance. It has more importance than it should have.' And that could be argued, but I think they're missing the point. The point is, it is activating their fabric of their life and the way God made them because we were creating as beings—like, dislike, love. Because of sports, that's all brought to the surface.

"It's been an interesting study. People will say, 'Why are you so down? It's just a game.' Well, yeah. To some extent it's just a game. But losing that game to Tennessee (in the 2017 AFC Wild Card game), was that just a game to Alex Smith? Losing that game meant, Now what? What does that mean to Elizabeth and his three kids? What does it mean to the Alex Smith Foundation and the work he's done in this community?"

Speculation, and it turned out to be true, was that the loss to Tennessee would be Alex Smith's last game as a Kansas City Chief. He was traded to Washington two months later.

"A fan can sometimes turn a game on or off and then walk away. But if those fans are really engaged in that game, it is more than a game because it is activating the human emotion, the way God created us to be. It's one of the frustrations I have sometimes when I do basketball. I'm going to do the Sun Belt Conference Tournament and I'm not going to feel the emotion. I will convey it because those games are the most important thing to those fans and those kids. They're playing for an automatic berth (in the NCAA Tournament) on national television. But my emotional involvement isn't as intense as a Chiefs game. Walking out of the Tennessee game—first of all it took hours to even walk out of the stadium because I knew what that meant. I knew that was probably the last game with Alex Smith. Derrick Johnson I'd been with for 13 years and Tamba Hali for 12. And it's more than a game when you feel it that deeply because of the human elements that are involved. If I'm playing cards or I'm playing a game of Madden and I lose, it's not the same as losing that game.

"I've learned through the years to see the game beyond the game."

YOU GOTTA HAVE FAITH

Danielle got to work at former Kansas City Royals great Mike Sweeney's baseball camp over the summer. A devout Catholic, she said she had an overpowering moment of faith because of the experience. Having heard that Mitch has a strong Christian faith, she wanted to know if he ever had moments where is faith was really strengthened. A reminder: The Chiefs were in the midst of a 1-6 skid after starting the season 5-0 when Danielle talked to Mitch at a filming of "The Chiefs Kingdom Show".

"Yes, and some can be triggered by an incredibly positive mountain-top experience, and others can be triggered by what we call flash points.

"I was accepted to three law schools—Kansas, Washburn and Valparaiso law—and I law clerked for two years. I was on this path where I was in broadcasting and business, but then decided I was going to go to law school. And it was really kind of this flashpoint that was really getting into the depth of my heart and I was like, Is that really what I want to do? And it was also a faith moment because faith is personal. We can do corporate things of faith; I can walk into a church and sing songs, but that's a by-product of something personal in your heart, I think. My relationship with the Lord is the pebble in the pond for everything, whether it's good or bad. That's been up and down, too. But that's kind of the voyage. There's blessings and there's challenges. That also helps me in dealing with athletes and coaches and fans, and yet I'll get down. But you have a baseline you can go to.

"One of my favorite verses is 'For God did not give us a spirit of timidity but of power and love and discipline. Therefore, do not be ashamed of the testament of our Lord or of me, his prisoner but join with me in the suffering for the gospel according to the power of God.' And that verse goes on and on, but it's something I was lying awake in the middle of the night thinking about it and praying about it because there were a zillion things going on in my mind, and not all of them were good, in fact most of them weren't. But it's dealing with every situation and trying to positively impact lives.

"I have a whole speech I give called 'Making it count: Going Beyond the Mic'. It's more the role of the job than the job itself. I'll give you an example. An Air Force family had a little girl who had inoperable leukemia. She was at Whiteman Air Force Base, right near you. They contacted the team and said, 'We just want to meet with him. He seems like a happy guy. We just want to meet with a happy guy. We've tried all this treatment and bone marrow transplants, and she just needs to be around a happy guy.' I'm not a psychiatrist or a doctor, but I was like, 'Okay, I guess I'll meet with them'. But it was awesome. This little gal inspired me more than I did her. I didn't even know what to do. And then she died, like, two months later. But it got me thinking, 'There's a bigger role here than football or games' because of the impact of what it is.

"We're going to have people lose their jobs because of what has gone on here. So the empathy I need to take to the workplace and my attitude in helping, that's beyond saying 'second and seven'. The more you learn that in your career, the more you become that way, the more chance you have to become that valuable. And the faith aspect comes alive because then it is the life the Lord wants you to have, which is use this life to have impact and influence."

PREP TIME

As I said in the introduction to this chapter, it took several months to connect with Mitch. I made initial contact through his assistant (with the assistance of my former student Derek Haglund) and made another connection through Chiefs reporter BJ Kissel. But it wasn't until I took to Twitter that I was actually able to connect and schedule our meeting. I learned very quickly that Mitch Holthus may be the hardest working man in sportscasting. I was curious what a typical week looks like and how he prepares for a game.

In 2011, Mitch did an interview with Erin Lawless for "Straight Out of KC" in which he discussed his passion for sports. Watch that interview on YouTube by searching "Mitch Holthus interview with Erin Lawless".

"I'm involved in so many things. I try to get from Monday morning to get to Monday afternoon. Monday morning, I do radio hits. Part of what I do on my own as an entrepreneur is I do the 'Minute with Mitch' television series, which is in 10 TV markets. I sell it, market it. The Chiefs let me do it. Hyvee is a sponsor in six of the 10; the other four I've gotta get sponsors that don't conflict with the Chiefs' sponsors.

"I was ahead of my time. I started it 24 years ago. It's a video blog, and it fits on any platform. I'll put it on Twitter, but it fits on over-the-air television platform as well. It's perfect because it gives perspective. It's Chiefs, and people get enough. And it changes. Sometimes it's funny, sometimes it's sad. It's designed to be that way. But I write a video blog. I produce it sell it, market it. But that's Monday mornings.

"Now I'm exhausted. The best thing to do would be to take Monday off and just chill, but I don't. I start with radio hits at 7:00 something in the morning with 101 The Fox. There's two or three others that morning, then I do the Minute with Mitch, then I go to Arrowhead because now the new week is started. That Sunday night-date night after a Sunday afternoon game is the only respite there is because it starts to roll again early the next morning. And then in the afternoon I'll review the game before on video because I interview Coach Reid. And then we have the 'Chiefs Kingdom Show'. So by the time Monday night rolls around, it's about 8 o'clock by the time I start to roll home, and I'm more exhausted.

"Tuesday, I do over-the-air television shows. We do the 'Hyvee Chiefs Insider' show. We have great writers and producers, but sometimes I'll write or produce or edit or help with that. That's a Tuesday approach because we have deadlines to get that done. Tuesday morning there is a glimmer of time that I try to protect for exercise. I've got a personal trainer, and I've got to do that or I just can't exist, and so I try to protect that time.

"Tuesday evening, I start preparation for the opponent for the upcoming week. Now I've been working on them all year long, but now I start to micro in on them, and I start to micro in on the offense of the opponent. I go through every player, every possible story, all the stats. Tuesday night is updating our guys vs. that opponent. What have they done in their career against that opponent, and what are the stories that are there between these two teams or players on our team to the other. If we're playing the Buffalo Bills, what went into the Reggie Ragland trade?

"Wednesday morning, I do eight different radio shows. Wednesday night is usually finish the defense for the opponent. I'll watch video just like a coach, put the individual stories together, go beyond the obvious to prepare. Wednesdays I'm also getting players sound. I'll chase down five or six players; I chart the players so that we're not just getting the same person every time. But a lot of the pregame is, 'Here's what Chris Conley had to say'. Well, I'm the one getting the Chris Conley sound. Not a lot of play-by-play guys do that, but we're on a skeleton crew and have been since I got on the radio side.

"Then it goes into Thursday. Now we're doing another over-the-air television show. I do production at 101 The Fox because we have a game production for every week. Then I'll have interviews that I do with Andy Reid, the coordinators, players.

"Friday there's another snippet of time for a second exercise period. That's all I get is those two periods, but I use them. And then everything starts to come together on Fridays. More radio shows; I do 25 radio shows a week and two over-the-air television shows, television after the game, which is the 'Chiefs Rewind', and then the 'Minute with Mitch' at the beginning of the week. So Friday is bringing it all together. We have a production meeting and we discuss Where's our focus going to be? Usually I'm done by Friday at 4 o'clock, and so Friday nights are a time where I can have personal time. I like to go to high school football games if I can, or I'll watch Smith Center, which has a terrific three-camera broadcast with lower-third graphics, and it's amazing. But that's a time where I can kind of relax my mind.

"Then Saturday I do shows again. If we're on the road, that's travel. If we're at home, there's events going on that Saturday that I'm the emcee for or I am the moderator of a panel.

> *"If you're signed on and you can check all the boxes, you gotta be ready to go, to be unusually passionate, maintain perspective, have perseverance and be willing to do the preparation."*
> ~ Mitch Holthus

"Then it's the game day, and then it cycles. So those are 60 to 70-hour weeks. Friday nights are protected, those two little exercise times, and then home games Sunday nights. That's what you live for."

Listening to Mitch talk about this blistering schedule, all I could think is "Why would somebody put himself through this?" For Mitch Holthus, the reason is simple.

"That's the passion part of it. It's a deep passion. Passion for competition, passion for sport at all levels."

Which, of course, takes a very understanding family. Having kids who played in college and a wife who coached, certainly helps. But, no doubt it is still difficult.

"My kids played at Southwestern College in Winfield, Kansas They've made tremendous sacrifices. So has my wife. My wife gets it; she coached for 20 years and was K-State's point guard. But that doesn't make it easier. I call them steering wheel pounders; the times that you miss that you can't get back, and that's one of the costs. I ask prospective broadcasters, Just what are you willing to sacrifice and give up? My daughter won a state championship in basketball, and my wife was helping coach the team, and I didn't get to see it. I saw the quarters and semis but I had to do a college basketball game, and I drove through the night. I stayed as long as I could and was trying to do as much of my preparations in advance as I could, but I missed that game and I regret it. But that's one of the prices of doing this job."

Photo courtesy of Danielle Sachse

I was so proud that one of my students, Danielle Sachse, scooped me in my effort to land an interview with Mitch.

CHECKING ALL THE BOXES

For those interested in a career in sportscasting, you could do far worse than to take a page from Mitch Holthus. When I asked him for the attributes of a great sportscaster, he shared his personal philosophy.

"I'm going to give you the four P's. Preparation is one of them. But passion, preparation, perseverance, and perspective. If you can't check all four boxes, this is not for you. And it's not for everybody.

"With the passion, you have to understand as a broadcaster the passion of the event. So many prospective broadcasters have no idea about the psychology of sport. I would add a course in your curriculum where it's basically the psychology of sport. Understanding winning and understanding losing, and then put them in a practical laboratory where they experience both. I always recommend and urge them to compete in something because there has to be an understanding of the deep hurt that comes with losing and what that means and the ecstasy of winning and what that means. So that's really the perspective but it also deals with the passion because you have to understand the passion your viewer has. Or that your reader has because we're all involved in writing out for the digital world, whether it's blogs or Instagram, Twitter or Facebook.

"It's not a regular job, and you have to be willing to put in the extra time, and that means having a passion. But that also means understanding, or trying to understand, the passion of your participants of whom you are broadcasting or talking about. It's the most

71

misunderstood and misused element now, I think, in sports. Often prospective broadcasters don't understand that. It's not a game of Madden. It's not digital figures. The great ones are the ones that will understand Romans 12:15, 'Rejoice with those who will rejoice and weep with those who will weep.'

"If you're passionate enough about what you cover and have passion for others, and then you are willing to put in the time, then the perspective kind of bleeds over into that. But in what environment are we broadcasting this game, and who's watching, listening or reading, and what do they want to know, and what does it mean to them? So that goes into the psychology of winning. That's another box we don't check a lot with prospective broadcasters, whether they're young or old or just want to get into the business because it sounds cool.

"Perseverance is absolutely necessary, particularly after you climb. What people see are the end results. They don't see that I was a finalist for the Minnesota Vikings, for the Atlanta Falcons, and the Chicago Bears. There were 300 applicants, and I got to the finals in all three, but didn't get any of them. I filled in for Kevin Harlan when he was auditioning for NBC. I did one game, and now he left and the Chiefs' job was open, and my audition tape was that team. I mean how many times has that happened? I thought, 'Wow, if I don't get this , I don't know what I'm going to be doing'. This is a profession where you lose more than you win, and the losses come in different ways. It takes a mental, emotional, physical, and spiritual toughness to make it in this business. So, if you're signed on and you can check all the boxes, you have to be ready to go, to be unusually passionate, maintain perspective, have perseverance and being willing to do the preparation."

Photo courtesy of Blue Note Productions

JOHN KELLY
FOX SPORTS MIDWEST
ST. LOUIS BLUES

John Kelly is part of a legacy. His father, Dan Kelly, was the play-by-play announcer for the St. Louis Blues for 21 years and is a member of the Hockey Hall of Fame. His Uncle Hal called the action for several teams when the NHL began broadcasting games. John's younger brother, Dan Jr., called the Blues from 1997-2000, and his son, Patrick, a student at Lindenwood University, is entering the profession and covers minor league hockey.

John took over the booth in St. Louis for his second stint with the Blues in 2007 and is now in his 22nd season as an NHL play-by-play announcer. Prior to joining the Blues, he was with the New York Rangers in 1988-89. He served his first tour with St. Louis in 1989-90 and 1991-92 on the Blues' radio and television simulcasts. From 1992 to 1995, John was with the Tampa Bay Lightning doing simulcasts on radio and television, and then he headed to Colorado in 1995 (he was the first play-by-play announcer in the history of the Tampa Bay and Colorado franchises).

Before making his debut in the NHL, he announced American Hockey League games on radio with the St. Catharines Saints (1983-86) and Adirondack Red Wings (1986-89). John has also called baseball, basketball, soccer, Arena Football League games, and from 1993-96 he was the hockey play-by-play announcer at the annual U.S. Olympic Festival.

73

Along the way, he has picked up four Emmys for sports broadcasting and was named to the Parkway School District Hall of Fame.

The Ottawa, Ontario native moved to St. Louis at 8 when his dad got the Blues job. John went on to graduate from Parkway North High School, where he played hockey and one year each of football and soccer. He also tried his hand at baseball "but I realized I wasn't any good at them," he says. Still, he had the ice, playing hockey all the way through Junior B at 19.

John received a degree in communications from Southern Illinois-Edwardsville in 1982. He and his wife, Jennifer, have three children: Patrick, Megan and Grace.

Unfortunately, I did not get to meet John, as trying to schedule an interview with a hockey announcer during hockey season is like trying to nail Jello to a wall with a fly swatter. But he was gracious enough to visit with me for an hour over the phone. Even over the telephone wires, it is clear that John Kelly passionately loves two things: his family and hockey.

LIKE FATHER, LIKE SON

When your father is a hall of fame broadcaster, you can go one of two ways: Either jump in with both feet or run fast and run far. John Kelly chose the former before he could even drive.

John Kelly has served two stints as play-by-play announcer for the St. Louis Blues, from 1989-92 and from 2007 to present.

"Probably the first time was in, maybe eighth grade. I was in junior high school. I played sports as a kid, and like any kid you want to be a professional hockey player or baseball player. Even as a young kid about 14 I realized that was not going to come to fruition. By being around my father, both professionally and obviously as a son, I saw what he did for a living and what an awesome job it was and thought what a great thing it would be for me to pursue.

"Probably the first time I even dabbled in it, I believe I was in eighth grade and our ninth-grade basketball team was playing. We'd take a tape recorder with a cassette and two or three of my buddies and I would announce the game. We would sit in the corner of the gym and we would announce the basketball game into this tape recorder. As a matter of fact, one of the players on that ninth-grade team at Parkway North was a player by the name of Terry Donnelly, who went on to play for Michigan State, and he actually played in that infamous game (the 1979 NCAA Championship game) against Larry Bird and Indiana State."

Given his love of all sports, I wondered if John ever had any desire to call any other sports, or if it was a given that he would ultimately do hockey.

"I never had a great desire to say 'I want to be a baseball announcer or a football announcer.' I think I just assumed I was going to be a hockey announcer because, number one, my dad was and, number two, I was just a huge, huge fan of hockey. I would go to almost every single game, I would watch every game that was on TV. When I was a kid and my friends might be out doing whatever at night, I was at home listening to Sports Open-

74

Line on KMOX with Bob Costas and Jack Buck and then listening to my dad call Blues games at night. And that's what I would do every single night was be a sports junky and a hockey junky. That's what I loved to do, so when I became a professional broadcaster, my goal when I got out of college was to be a hockey announcer. Now, if something else would have come along, because I did every sport in college and in my first job in Pratt, Kansas, I certainly would have taken it. But my main goal was to be a hockey announcer."

KEEPING UP WITH THE ACTION

Radio play-by-play announcers typically provide more description because the audience cannot actually see what is happening. In television, the play-by-play doesn't need to say from where a basketball player takes a shot or which running back is in the backfield; fans can see that. But in hockey, the puck is so small and moves so fast, I asked John if play-by-play for hockey is the same for TV as it is for radio.

"I think that's accurate because, even if you have a fan that knows the game and knows the players, and he has a big, beautiful HD, 45-inch TV, it's still hard to follow the puck and it's still hard to know who has the puck and to know where it's going next. So I do think a hockey play-by-play announcer is way more descriptive than any other TV play-by-play announcer. Because it's so fast and because the arena is so big, especially when compared to a basketball court, you know the puck should be shot across the rink and it could be out of frame for a second, so my job is to anticipate where the puck is going and tell the people where it is and who has it.

"I've done a few games on the radio, mainly in preseason as a warm up, and I'm probably 30 to 40 percent more descriptive on radio than on TV, but having said that, I'm still pretty descriptive compared to other TV play-by-play announcers because of the speed of the game and because of how challenging it is for the fans for follow the game."

MAKING IT TO THE SHOW

Like many hockey players, John started his broadcasting career in the minors. When he got his first job in the NHL, he knew he had made it.

"I had done five years in the American Hockey League, and I got the Ranger job as the back-up to Marv Albert in 1988. I think I had done 40-45-50 games that year. At the time I was 28 years old, and I was living in Glens Falls, New York. I would take the train down from Albany to New York City and do Ranger games.

"It's pretty impressive to think, you know, here at 28 here I am at MSG sitting five rows off the ice, right between the benches, calling New York Ranger games on radio. It was a thrill, it was a great honor to be able to get that position and to be able to travel first class with some of the people. Sam Rosen and J.D. (John Davidson) were the TV announcers and I worked with Sal Messina, who was a legendary broadcaster and a former goalie. So I guess at that point I realized all the hard work paid off and all the long bus rides paid off. Here I was an NHL announcer, which was my main goal. So I guess at that point, 1988-89 was when I first realized my dream."

DID YOU SEE THAT?

When asked how the job of a sportscaster has changed over the years, most of the gentlemen I interviewed responded with something technology based. For John it is more a matter of size, pace and logistics.

75

"I was a radio announcer for that first year (1988-89) and I was a TV announcer when I game to St. Louis. Calling the games is still calling the games. It's still memorizing the players and knowing the story lines and obviously knowing the storylines of the game and the players. But the game is a lot faster now. The players are so much bigger and so much faster now, the broadcast positions are not nearly as good as they were in some of the older arenas. It really makes it difficult to see and to follow the action. In fact, most of them now you are up in the rafters and it's challenging to see at times and to call the games from such a high position. That's the biggest thing I would say technically for calling the game because you're not as close to the game as you were physically. It's hard to see the numbers and the names to tell the players apart."

An increase in media outlets has also had an impact, John says, one that can make the job more challenging.

"The other thing is you don't have as much accessibility with the players because there is so much media around nowadays. The players are great, but there are so many media members at every practice and after every game it's hard to get as much one-on-one time with the players and the coaches because they don't have time for everybody or all they would do is interview.

"When I came to the Blues in '89, there might be one beat writer there, maybe one radio guy and one TV guy after a practice. Now, if you go into a Blues locker room after a practice day, there are easily, just from the St. Louis contingent, 20 to 25 members of the media contingent."

ULTIMATE RESPONSIBILITY

One question I asked all the Show-Me sportscasters for the "Tips and Strategies" chapter was whether they viewed themselves as a journalist, an entertainer, an artist or some other modifier. John's response intrigued me so much I decided to include it in his chapter.

"What makes a really good broadcast is a combination of everything. Our job is to inform, it is to enlighten, but it's also to entertain. I really believe that fans who watch the games, they might have had a tough day, and that two or three hours in front of the TV, they want to be entertained as much as they want to follow their team and their sport."

FROM ST. LOUIS TO LAKE PLACID

I expected John to mention his father as his favorite sportscaster, but that might have been a bit on the nose. Instead, he brought up a couple of other hometown heroes and the originator of one of the legendary calls in hockey.

"I would have to say, all-time, having grown up in St. Louis, it would have to be Jack Buck and Bob Costas. I got to work with both of them as a spotter in football, so I knew them fairly well, and obviously my dad worked with both of them. I still think that Costas is the most talented broadcaster, news or sports or entertainment, whatever, the most talented broadcaster I've ever seen.

"The other guy that I look up to a lot is Al Michaels. I read his book and there's his famous call in the 1980 Miracle on Ice, but at his age (73 at the writing of this book) to be able to be such a great play-by-play announcer in football and to be on top of things …

76

you can watch him do a football game, and the game might take three or four hours and the guy doesn't stumble on a word. He's just flawless. And, again, I don't know how old he is, but I know he's not a spring chicken and to me, as a broadcaster, that's pretty amazing. After all these years and all the games he's done, he's still so sharp and still has it. That's amazing."

LIVING A LEGACY

Until my father passed away in the summer of 2012, he was always my go to for advice. While we were in different career fields (he in insurance marketing, I in college sports public relations), he knew enough about my business to provide frequent words of wisdom. Given as close as we were, I wanted to know what it was like having a father (and now a son) in the same profession.

"It's really, in a way, it's like our family business. It's awesome, especially to be around St. Louis. My father's name is still so prominent in St. Louis, especially among hockey fans. You know, he passed away in 1989. And still, no matter where I go, people come up to me and tell me they loved him and say the reason they became Blues fans was because of my dad. An announcer cannot have a higher compliment than that, that they became fans of a team or a sport because of an announcer. That to me is the ultimate compliment. So it's still thrilling to have people come up to me and say that.

"It's awesome to be around and have the last name of Kelly and my brother was a broadcaster for the Blues for three years and my son is getting into it, so, I guess you could say it is a pretty good family business to be in."

Photo courtesy of FOX Midwest/David Pokorny

John Kelly and his broadcast partner Darren Pang grew up a mile apart in Ottawa, Ontario. Now they share the booth for one of the most storied teams in the NHL.

That brings up another question: Does it bring a little extra pressure? Does John feel like he has a legacy to uphold and to pass on?

"I guess so, but I never think about it in those terms. I know that when I was a young announcer and my father would listen to my tapes, he would instill certain things in me and beliefs. You work hard and you treat people well and you're respectful of the players and the coaches and the officials and the rest sort of takes care of itself. I don't go to the game and think my father did this or that or he's a hall of famer and I have to do a better job. I just try to do the best that I can and try to live by the basic principles that he taught me and that he lived by. I am respectful of the fact that my father set a standard in the Blues broadcast booth, so whether it's me or my partner, Darren Pang, or our production crew, every night I believe we come to work with the intentions of being the very best we can be and bringing the best broadcast to our fans, and that's really all we can do. We can't compare our work or my work to other people, but I truly believe we try and do the very best we can every night.

> "What makes a broadcast is a combination of everything. Our job is to inform, it is to let enlighten, but it's also to entertain."
>
> ~ John Kelly

What is the best piece of advice the elder Kelly gave John, and is it something he has shared with his son? John's advice sounds strangely familiar; my dad shared the same advice with me.

"Don't quit a job until you have a job. And I have shared that with my son."

Knowing the hours and strains of the job, John's father surely tried to dissuade him from a broadcasting career or encouraged him to look at other options.

"He actually did. He didn't pressure me to not become a broadcaster, but he did say, why don't you become a lawyer or a doctor or something like that. I think he did that because he knew how challenging this business is. Broadcasting is very rewarding. A lot of people have good jobs and make good money and a good living as broadcasters, but my father knew it can also be very difficult at times. You can get a new boss and he literally might not like the color of your hair and they want a new play-by-play announcer.

"It's a fickle business at times. My father, for a while, was taken off TV in St. Louis because they wanted to get their own guy on TV for play-by-play for a year. So here was Dan Kelly, who was known as the great broadcaster, every year was doing the Stanley Cup finals, and in his own market he was taken off TV for a year or two. Things like that, I think my father saw it can be at times it can be a cruel and fickle business. So that's why, I think, he encouraged me to be a lawyer and be my own boss. It's not like he didn't help me when I wanted to be a broadcaster, but he sort of said, 'Hey, there are some other options out there; maybe you should consider that.' I guess I considered it, but not for very long."

Did father and son ever team up on a broadcast?

"The only time I did was in the fall of '88. He had been diagnosed with cancer. I was doing the Rangers then, and we had a game in Philadelphia, and ironically enough the Blues played in Philadelphia two nights later. I did not have another game, so he encouraged me to stay around and spend some time with him, go to dinner, and then come to the game with him in Philadelphia. So we did that. We walked up to the broadcast booth, and it was at the old Spectrum. There wasn't an elevator to the booth. I remember it like it was yesterday. He was doing his radiation treatments and chemo and obviously wasn't feeling great. He'd walk up 10 steps and then stop and pause and then walk up 10 more steps.

"We finally got to the top of the building and got into the broadcast booth and he said, 'I'm going to have you do the second period with me' and I was shocked. He had not told me that. So I did play-by-play in the second period in Philadelphia that night and he was my color man, and that was the only night we ever worked together.

"Ironically enough, the Blues won that game and it was their first win in Philadelphia in something like 34 games. They hadn't won there since a famous brawl in Philadelphia back on January 6 of '72. So they had not won a game from 1972 until that November game in 1988, the night I did that game with him."

MAINTAINING ENERGY

As a play-by-play announcer for a team, John undoubtedly puts a lot of heart and soul into the organization. He also covers an extremely intense sport that has a long season and in which the team plays four to five times a week. I asked John how he maintains his energy without becoming completely exhausted.

"You have to love the game and you have to love your job. Even though it's a great job covering an NHL team, the season can get long. You might have four games in six nights and have late nights and cold weather, and you might be sick and whatever it may be. I think that if you truly love the game of hockey, and I do, and you are truly passionate about broadcasting, then you forget about the other things and you try to do the very best you can every night.

"In all honesty, if the hockey season were 11 months long, it would be totally fine with me. If I had one month off every summer and then start training camp in August and play 120 games, that would be alright. Now the players wouldn't like that, and the fans might not like that, but when I say that I'm being 100 percent honest. I love hockey so much that I really miss it in the three months where there are no games. I really wish it were an 11-month sport.

"You never have to convince me when I go to a game that I can't be excited and that I can't enjoy the game and that I have to do the best I can as a broadcaster because to me it's the greatest game there is, and on any particular night you might see something you've never seen. Every game is different and there is drama in every game. You know not every game is going to be a Picasso, but every game is different and every game is exciting and honestly it is a thrill to cover them."

POKER AND GOLF

Still, there has to be something John does to get away from the game.

"Aside from the normal things that everybody does—you know, be with the family or have dinner with the wife or go to a movie, those basic things—I enjoy playing poker and playing golf. Those are the two things I really enjoy. If I'm at a poker table and it's intense and you're playing for money—not that I play for big money—but I'm totally 100 percent focused on playing cards. You're not thinking about things, and it is relaxing.

"It's the same with golf. You're at a nice golf course in the woods. To me golf is the hardest sport there is, and if you are not 100 percent focused, you're not going to do well. For that four-hour round of golf, you're totally engrossed in being the best golfer you can, and obviously if you're playing with some friends or in a charity tournament, for that four hours it's that and it's really nothing else.

"That's why I enjoy those two things is that it takes total focus, and your real-life problems and issues are on the back burner."

MAKING A COHESIVE UNIT

One thing I saw repeatedly when I read about play-by-play is that you have to have that chemistry with your partner or partners. John has worked with several analysts, so he is the perfect person to ask about the subject.

"I've been lucky in my stops in the NHL that I've had really good chemistry with all of my partners, and I think there are two reasons for that. I've genuinely liked the people I've worked with. I've wanted to be friends with them and go to dinner with them. I know of announcers who don't talk to each other away from the broadcast booth and they don't go to dinner and they don't associate away from the rink or away from the football field or wherever. I know people like that. I feel sorry for those people because to me part of being a good broadcaster and a good team is you have to like each other. I've liked my partners, all of them, as friends and I think it carries over into the broadcast booth.

> "If the hockey season were 11 months long, it would be totally fine with me. If I had one month off every summer and then start training camp in August and play 120 games, that would be alright."
> ~ John Kelly

"I think the other thing that makes a good broadcast partnership is if you have two announcers who are on the same page. In other words, they have similar work ethics and they have a similar love for the game and the sport and the team, it is going to benefit you and the broadcast.

"My partner, Darren Pang, and I happen to be from the same hometown in Ottawa, Ontario. We literally grew up a mile apart when we were kids. I didn't know Darren then because I'm five years older, but as it turns out we grew up a mile apart as kids. We both love the game of hockey, and we've always loved it. You never have to twist our arms to go to the rink or go talk to the players or go to practice. It's a passion for both of us, so it's those two things. The fact that we genuinely like each other a lot as people and we both love the game, and I think that comes through on our broadcast. If you listen, the average viewer would say, 'You know John and Darren, they like each other and they're having a good time together,' and I think that comes through on our games."

PASSING IT DOWN

Not every aspiring broadcaster has a father or an uncle who has been in the booth; most need a professional to offer friendly advice and to guide them. John Kelly is just such a professional.

Photo courtesy of Bue Note Productions

The son of Hockey Hall of Famer Dan Kelly, John has been calling hockey action for more than two decades. His son, Patrick, is continuing the tradition in minor league hockey.

"I've always tried to be very helpful. The school I went to, SIU-Edwardsville, they've asked me to come talk to the kids and I've done that. My son's school, he goes to Lindenwood in St. Charles, and I went and spoke to kids. Anytime I'm asked to go talk to kids, especially young broadcasters, I'm happy to do it. At the same time, maybe a couple times a year, I'll have a young broadcaster write me and send me an audition tape, and I've always been more than happy to listen to the tape and then call them back and offer constructive criticism and encouragement.

"I've always liked helping young kids because I was a kid once, and you know, we all need to learn. Most people don't have broadcasting legends as their father like I did. I could go to work with my dad and he might do a Sports Open Line with Jack Buck or Bob Costas. I mean, 99.9 percent of people don't have that luxury, so I feel if I can help someone who doesn't have that or doesn't have a connection, I'm more than happy to do it, and I should do it."

A FORTUNATE MAN

Count your blessings.

My mother used to tell me that whenever I would complain about what I did not have or fuss about having to do something I didn't want to do. Something tells me a young John Kelly was taught the same lesson.

81

"I've been very, very fortunate that I grew up around a broadcasting legend who was also a great father and I had a great family and I have a great family with my wife and three kids. Not many people can say that they love getting up in the morning and going to work and doing what they do and making a very good living. I'm one of the very few who can say that, and I'm very grateful for that.

"I never assume anything; this job can be taken away in the blink of an eye, and I that's why I continue to work hard and do the best job that I can. It's not a right to be an NHL broadcaster. It's not a right I have because of my last name; it's because I work hard and I think I do a good job. That's what I would encourage anyone: Follow your dreams, work hard, and be good to people, and usually good things will follow."

Photo courtesy of Kevin Kelly

KEVIN KELLY
KWOS - 950 AM and 101.1 FM
JEFFERSON CITY, HELIAS, &
BLAIR OAKS HIGH SCHOOLS

I arrived early at the beautiful Zimmer Radio and Marketing Group offices in our state capital, just wanted to be sure I was ready to go. A kind receptionist offered me a cup of coffee and a place to wait. I took that time to review my notes and to look around the office. The first things I noticed were the old microphones, logs, control board, remote amplifier, tape decks, and Magnecord reel-to-reel. KWOS News Radio has been a staple in Jefferson City since 1954. It is a 5,000-watt station by day, 500-watt by night, and features a conservative talk news format with affiliations with CBS Radio, Westwood One, and ESPN Radio.

Now, Kevin Kelly has not been affiliated with KWOS since its inception. But for fans of Jefferson City, Helias and Blair Oaks high schools, it probably feels that way.

Kevin is a member of the Missouri Basketball Coaches Hall of Fame and in 2007 was selected for the Distinguished Service Award by the Missouri State High School Activities Association. He has been with KWOS in Jefferson City for 40 years. In that time, he has called the action for Jefferson City (10 state football titles and one state basketball championship), Helias High School (a pair of state football titles), and Blair Oaks High School. He has won several awards from the Missouri Broadcasters Association for sports reporting and play-by-play.

When he is not providing play-by-play for KWOS, he may be found hosting The Auto Shop Saturday Coaches Show. If Kevin isn't at the station, it's a good bet the St. Louis native is fulfilling his duties as the spokesperson for Missouri Public Service Commission. He graduated from the University of Missouri in 1978 with a degree in journalism and immediately entered the business, first at KFAL/KKCA in Fulton before moving on to KWOS.

Kevin and his wife, Mary, have two sons, Chris and Ryan, and a daughter, Erin.

FROM BLUE DEVIL TO TIGER

Kevin grew up in the basketball hotbed of rural North Carolina but was a fan of all sports. That love led him to the Midwest and a degree at the top journalism school in the country. The goal all along: to be a sportscaster.

"It was something I wanted to do when I was really young. A couple of things I can remember is that when we lived in Greensboro, North Carolina, there were two high schools there—Paige High School and Grimsley High School—and my dad used to take my brother and me to the football games on Friday nights. It was a situation where one

Photo courtesy of Kevin Kelly

Kevin Kelly and Tom Kremer have formed an almost brotherly partnership while calling the action for Jefferson City, Helias and Blair Oaks high schools.

would play one week there at the stadium, then the other team would play there. Then the week before they played each other they would be on the road.

"I just remember him walking us up that hill and you're not seeing a football stadium. All of a sudden that stadium is there and it just explodes on you."

Those evenings with his dad may have sparked Kevin's interest, but it was in the hallway, the yard and the driveway that he honed his skills.

"But I can remember as a kid playing games and doing the play-by-play either to myself or in my head. We had a house where, I had a long hallway and we closed the door at each end and the trim would serve as a basket. We had a little rubber ball go up and down the floor with that and Duke was the team back then that I followed. Duke was playing somebody else every night.

"I remember taking a small football and throwing it up in the air and kind of simulating a game, get on roller skates and grab a hockey stick and ball. What I did most, though, was grab my glove and a rubber ball and throw it against the wall, and kind of having different things like the bare spot would be first base and, you know, throw it against the wall and on a ground ball you would throw against the wall to the first baseman. That kind of stuff. And I'd commentate the whole time."

I had to chuckle as I listened to Kevin relive his childhood because it sounded much like mine. But whereas I went the print and PR route, Kevin wanted to land in a broadcast booth. Coming out of high school he just wasn't sure how to get there.

"That's what I wanted to do. You know the interesting thing about that was, I remember toward the end of my senior year sitting down at a restaurant with a good friend of mine and talking about, okay, what's next? Because you're getting ready to graduate, so you're thinking, What's next? I really hadn't spent a lot of time thinking about it. And he said, 'Well, what do you like to do?' and I said, 'Boy, I'd love to do play-by-play, something with sports.' He said, 'Well, have you thought about going to Missouri because of the journalism school?' So I thought about it, and that's what I ended up doing."

Unfortunately, when he was at Missouri, Kevin did not have the opportunity to do any play-by-play for the Tigers or for any local area high schools; his first taste was not until after graduating. In the 40 years since, all the while covering some of the top high schools in the state, one might wonder if he ever got the itch to work in the college or professional ranks.

"Yes, but I love doing what I'm doing now. I think to some extent you always think about, okay, do you want to try for the next step? But I'm happy doing this. I also value the time that I have with my family. Certainly, that's crossed my mind, but it is probably something that I thought about a lot more maybe 15-20 years ago than I do now."

CARRYING A HEAVY LOAD
That is not to say Kevin is not keeping a bustling schedule as it is.

"This is the schedule we had last week: In a 12-hour time frame I did four basketball games. We did a game here in Jefferson City that started at 7 o'clock, got done at 8:30.

Went home, took a shower, changed, drove to Columbia, and then did the midnight, 2, and 4 a.m. games on ESPN3 from the Norm Stewart Classic. Came home and went to bed for a couple hours, got up and then did a basketball game in Eugene, Missouri Saturday night, and then we were back at the Norm Stewart Classic between Helias and Oak Grove on our station at noon on Sunday."

BROADCASTING THE LEGENDS

Kevin has had the pleasure of calling games for several Missouri coaching legends in both football and basketball.

"It's just been great because I've had the privilege of working with a hall of famer in Pete Atkins, a hall of famer in Ray Hentges, as far as football is concerned, and Jerry Fisher is a basketball coach who spent some time here at Helias. He's in the Hall of Fame. So is David Fox, who is in the Missouri Basketball Coaches Association Hall of Fame. So, you know, it's been a great ride. It really has."

Which, of course, means Kevin has a slew of games to pick from when asked for a favorite.

"When you look at the 1989 state semifinal football game between Jefferson City and Kansas City Rockhurst, it went four overtimes and that was a classic football game. A lot of people still remember that one today.

"When Pete Atkins won his 400th game at Columbia Rock Bridge, that is one I'll always remember. Of course, you know, some of the state championship games with Coach Atkins, too, and how the players responded in that type of situation.

"Ray Hentges in 1998 told his football team at the beginning of two-a-day practices that it was going to be his last year as head football coach, and so it was always special that year. They made it to the state championship game and beat Ozark, so that's one I'll always remember. The thing was, he didn't want to lose 100 games in his career. They lost their first two games of the season, and he sat at 99. So, in order for them not to lose 100 games they had to run the table, and that's exactly what they did. They ran the table and beat Ozark. Just seeing him up on the shoulders of his players, that was pretty special.

"Basketball would be the state championship that the Jays won in 1993. This year is the 25th anniversary. That was special."

MAKING THE CALL

With 40 years experience, several state title broadcasts and a successful radio sports talk show, surely Kevin would say he has made it.

"Do you ever know that you've made it as a play-by-play man? Who would make that decision? When I got out of college, I applied at several places, and there was an opportunity at KFAL/KKCA in Fulton. They were looking for a newsman and a sports person, so I applied, went down, and did an interview with them, but I didn't find out that I had the job until about maybe a week or 10 days before I got married. I really didn't know up until the very end whether we were going to move to Fulton or not.

"One of the things was there was sports and news, and one of the questions they asked me was 'Can you do play by play?' And I said, 'Yeah, I can do play-by-play'."

Remember, Kevin said he had never done play-by-play professionally before.

"The week of the first game, about Wednesday or Thursday, I came down with laryngitis. The guy in the newsroom was a good friend of mine. He ended up doing the game. I went with him and sat and watched him do it and how they put all the equipment together, and I walked out of there and I said I can do this. So then the second game I took over from that point on."

Kevin Kelly has been on the call for 12 state football titles for Jefferson City (10) and Helias (two) high schools.

That is until he joined the team at KWOS.

"I came here in August of '79 to do news and sports. Bob Jackson was the sports director, Ron Medin was the news director, and it was Ron who hired me. I'm always grateful for that because he hired me and brought me from Fulton. Working with Ron, he made me a better reporter and a better writer, and I always appreciated working with Ron because he was very good in the news department.

"When Bob left I became the sports director. Then Ron left in the early '80s to go to the Missouri Network, and so when I left KWOS in August of '83 I left as the news and sports director. Then I came back shortly thereafter and from '83 to early '89 I did a little play-by-play but did mostly color with John McGuire and then with Bill Schuler. Then Bill left in early '89 and I've been doing the play-by-play ever sense."

JUST OFF THE TOP OF MY HEAD ...

In order to really think about and prepare for a call, one has to know it is coming. That's exactly what happened for Kevin in one of his most memorable games.

"I'd say one of the examples was when we started our broadcast of the state championship game the year that Ray Hentges retired (in 1998). I thought in my mind how I was going to do that. The guy sitting next to me doing the game with me, I didn't say anything to him, and they pitched it to us. I started, and I went through the whole thing, and I didn't have anything written down. He just looked at me and he goes, 'I can't believe you just did that'. I had thought about it beforehand, what we were going to talk about, and then when they pitched it to us, I just went."

That got me to thinking whether Kevin usually scripts a pregame show.

"No, I don't script a pregame normally. Now, we'll do something if we've got an intro leading into a break; we may do that here at the station and they run that. But when they come to us live, we hardly ever have a script.

"I would also tell you 90, 95 percent of the time I don't have any questions when I do an interview. I just kind of have in my mind some of the things we want to touch on, but then a lot of it's just basically responding to how they answer certain questions.

"I've never sat down and really written a script down as far as doing something on a live broadcast. Obviously if you're putting a piece together, then you've got the script and stuff that you're working on. But as far as live, I usually don't because for me personally it's easier to just go than to read. I worry about whether it sounds like I'm reading it, and

87

then if you trip over something then you have to get yourself back on track. Sometimes I think if you have that script it can sound like you're reading it, so I don't use a script."

THE MORE THINGS CHANGE, THE MORE THEY STAY THE SAME

One of the things I tell my journalism students is that the internet, cell phones and social media may have changed how we disseminate the message, but the basic tenets of journalism remain. Kevin says the same is true of play-by-play.

"In terms of how we do a broadcast I would say technology. When we first started doing games, all road games were done by ordering a telephone line and doing that. Now we do a lot of our games on a cell phone and the equipment with that is a lot different than when you had it on a phone line.

"In terms of preparing for a game, I don't think it's changed at all to be quite honest. I think the games are different. The games are quicker. Football, for example, there was no such thing as a no-huddle offense, and so it's quicker from that standpoint. I can tell you that the guy that does games with me hates the no-huddle offense; it makes it extremely difficult for him to keep all the statistics. I think basketball is a faster game now. The three-point shot wasn't around when I first started."

One thing that has not changed is that all games are not played at home. That always has required some planning, Kevin says.

"One of the things that we always tried to do—and we didn't do a lot of this at the very beginning but I feel like it's very important that we do it now—is not to assume that a school knows you're coming. We always try to make the contact with the school and ask, Is it alright for us to come and do the broadcast? Here's who's coming; can you set up a spot for us close to an outlet so that we can plug our stuff in? And they've all been real accommodating."

Well, not all of them.

> *"I look at it as every game is its own game. Sometimes I think what you find is that, if the team is the underdog then it's really interesting to do the game."*
>
> *~ Kevin Kelly*

"I can remember one time we did a game, I think at Westran High School while I was at Fulton, and they were supposed to have a phone line put in. They said, 'Yes there's a phone line here for you.' I said, 'Okay, where is it?' It's on the telephone pole, so I say, 'Okay so then what do I need to do?' They said, 'There's the telephone pole, there's where you need to set up to do the game'. Well, the top row of the stands and the pole, it was probably from me to that wall (about eight feet away). I'm having to lean all the way out across the rail to try to snap the telephone outlet into the plug and then having to do it again to unplug it after the game."

Kevin has had to adapt to some other unusual logistics as well.

While at the KWOS studios, I thought it would be nice to catch a picture of Kevin, who has been at the station for four decades, with some of the gear he would have used when he began his radio career.

"Sometimes we have to be outside. There will be schools that will say we don't have a very big press box. Now you guys are welcome to come, but it'll be outside. Two seasons ago at SLU (St. Louis University High School), we knew going up that we were going to be outside. We kept watching the weather forecast and it kept getting worse and worse. It started like a 50 percent chance of rain, and by the time we got to Thursday it was going to probably be 90 to 95 percent chance. We brought enough plastic to keep everything dry, but we basically had to do the first quarter out in a rainstorm under an umbrella. And then we had an associate athletic director say, 'If I can find a tent for you, would you guys want to use that?' and we said, 'That'd be great'. So, we've done that."

THE KID FROM PITTSBURGH
Where most of the subjects talked about some legendary broadcasters from Missouri, Kevin says a pair of voices from his childhood in North Carolina were his favorites.

"When I was a kid, my favorite announcer was Bob Prince, who was the play-by-play voice of the Pittsburgh Pirates. I'm a Pirates, Steelers, and Penguins fan. I remember downstairs in my house I couldn't get it any other time except for when Pittsburgh was out on the West Coast, but if they were out on the West Coast, downstairs in my bedroom

I could get KDKA. It would fade in and out, but I could get that. I would listen to Bob Prince when they were on the West Coast. When we went up to visit my grandparents and aunts and uncles in the summer in Canonsburg, Pennsylvania. I would listen to the games and Bob Prince had them. I think the first baseball game I went to was at Forbes Field in Pittsburgh. I just liked his phraseology, the fact that you could sit and visualize what was going on.

"Mike Lange, who's the play-by-play voice of the Pittsburgh Penguins, is another one that I listen to. He's got all kinds of phrases, and it's just really entertaining."

Of course, Kevin does sing the praises of the voices of St. Louis, along with others.

"When I was growing up in St. Louis, obviously Jack Buck and Harry Carey were two people I listened to quite a bit. Jack Buck was, in my opinion, just a fantastic, phenomenal play-by-play broadcaster. In terms of radio, I'd say those guys because of the way they describe it. I could listen to Jack Buck and Vin Scully on radio all day long. On television, Bob Costas, Curt Gowdy, Pat Summerall, Jim Nantz, Dick Enberg and Jim McKay. Those are my favorites."

SORRY YOUR LATE

Usually when someone says they are going to make you late, it is not a good thing. But that actually, Kevin says, is his intent.

"I've always told people that every time I walk into a football stadium or a gym I'm walking in with a blank canvas, and my job is to paint you the picture with how I describe

it. I tell people those are my brushes and my colors, and my job is to paint you the picture at home as if you were here. If we're able to paint you a Picasso once in your lifetime that would be great. One of the goals that we always have in a broadcast is that, if you were listening to the game on your radio while driving to a meeting and you pulled into the parking lot and you had to go into the meeting but the game was so exciting that you stayed and listened until the end of it ... I'm sorry that you were 10 minutes late for the meeting, but that's what we try to do."

Photo courtesy of Kevin Kelly

For Tom and Kevin, broadcasting is not just a job; it is a fun way to interact and communicate with an audience.

KELLY AND KREMER: TWO DECADES AND GOING STRONG

Two are better than one. It takes two to make a thing go right. Pair of aces. Lots of phrases stress the value of teamwork and solid partnerships. For more than 20 years Kevin has shared broadcasting duties with one man, and that has created an undeniable chemistry.

"I really appreciate the people I work with. Tom Kremer has done games with me for 22 years, and I would say that if you have—in terms of advice—I would say that if you have the opportunity to be able to have who you want on a broadcast, then I would take that opportunity.

"We've had so many people comment over the years that it sounds like too good friends calling the game, and they can tell that Tom and I have a great rapport on the air and that we're good friends, and Tom is a very good friend of mine. It's just been an exceptionally great ride. I've really enjoyed it.

"Some of the people that I've worked with are very good friends of mine still today. John McGuire took my position here when I left on a full-time basis, and John and I worked for maybe four or five years before he left. He's now a professor at Oklahoma State University, and John's like a brother to me. I talk to him and keep in touch, so it's really been special. I've never considered it a job. I really haven't."

As close as Kevin and Tom are, Kevin got a little emotional talking about the person who has meant the most to him in his long career.

"I can't say enough about my wife, Mary, because I've been doing this for 40 years, and it's not my full-time job; I have another full-time job. She has just been great with it. I always tell her, and I said this at the Hall of Fame induction, that you know when you get done with a long week of work, Friday you like to relax and maybe you want to go out to dinner and maybe go to a movie. I owe my wife so many Fridays because I wasn't able to do that. I just appreciate her so much for what she has done for me with regards to being able to do something I have a great passion for."

CALLING THE GOOD, THE BAD AND THE UGLY

One comment I heard several times is that, regardless of the score, a good broadcaster maintains focus and calls the game. Kevin shares that point of view.

"I look at it as every game is its own game. Sometimes I think what you find is that, if the team is the underdog then it's really interesting to do the game. I don't think the approach is different from the standpoint of, do you get more excited if they're struggling, that type of thing.

"I think it's interesting when you go in and sometimes you're not the favorite. We go into a football stadium or a basketball gym, and I don't look at it as, 'Well, this team is struggling,' you know? I think we go in from the standpoint of we've got a job to do and that's to visualize and be the person who's listening at the other end, be their eyes to listen to the game."

91

NOBODY IS PERFECT
Given he is actually the voice for three high schools, I was curious how Kevin Kelly defines "homer".

"To me a 'homer' is somebody who is broadcasting the game and the home team does everything. I try to do a broadcast so that if the other team is doing something really great, it's important that we recognize it. I try to do it the same way; the inflection is the same. To me a 'homer' is someone who is so pro-home team that you don't get the perspective of the entire broadcast. I think people will tell you that, when they listen to most broadcasters, they'll know who the home team is, but I try not to be a homer. I really do."

In Kevin's mind is it okay to critique officials, coaches or players?

"We try to stay away from that. There's a couple things that we always talk about in terms of our broadcast. One is that we recognize that these are high school students, and they're putting on a jersey and they're representing their classmates, they're representing their school, they're representing their community. When they play that standard should not be, Well, would that have been done in the NFL? So we recognize that.

"I think you can make a comment with regards to an official on a call, but we don't harp on it because I just don't believe in it. I don't believe in saying 'They lost the game because of that call.' One of the things that we would talk about on a broadcast that I think is fine, if early in the game there seems to be pushing and shoving and stuff like that, then I would say something to the effect of, 'The officials need to get ahold of the captains or the coaches and get control of this thing because it's getting chippy.' But we are not going to harp on it. They're trying to do their job just like everybody else is.

"The one thing about the coaches, I always tease them when they come out onto the floor. I'll say something on the air like, 'Tom, you know, he's kind of out on the floor, isn't he?' and Tom will say, 'Yeah'. And I'll say 'Whatever happened to the coach's box?' So we'll have a little fun with it on the air. Or we'll have some coaches who don't like to sit on the bench. They're up and down, and we'll mention something like, 'You know, I bet he walked three miles walking up and down the floor.'

"But we don't get on players and we don't get on officials. It happens; I've heard it. But it's not something I want to take part in."

IS THE END NEAR?
Most people who have been at a job for 40 years probably start thinking about hanging it up. Not Kevin Kelly. In fact, he is still setting goals.

"No. I'm still having fun. I would like to get to the 2,000-broadcast plateau. I would like to do a hockey game on the radio before I retire, and I would like to do minor league baseball on the radio. But I still love doing play-by-play.

"Sometimes it gets a little more difficult, and I don't want to say I dislike the road trips, but sometimes it's more difficult with the road trips than it used to be. I said this the other day to my wife, I can have a bad day, but when I put the headset on it all melts away. There have been times where I felt terrible. I was sick one time; I had the flu, and I remember during timeouts—it was like a state semifinal game—I put my headset down, I would go lean up against the wall, and then they would say, 'Okay, 15 seconds.' I'd come back, sit down, flip the switch and off we'd go.

"We'll go to a basketball game or go to a football game, and when we're in the parking lot going to the football stadium we'll have people that are from the school that we're covering, they'll say, 'Hey, I'm glad you came tonight because my mom and dad are at home. They couldn't make the game because of the weather and they're going to be able to listen to the game and listen to their grandson play because you guys are here.' That just makes you feel really good."

REACHING A LARGER AUDIENCE

I teach at the University of Central Missouri, about 15 minutes from Whiteman Air Force Base. We livestream Mules and Jennies sporting events and we cover Warrensburg High School as well as area high school graduations and local dance recitals. We receive lots of "thank yous" from deployed military parents and university families who would not get to see their loved ones' activities otherwise. I asked Kevin if he gets a lot of satisfaction out of covering the teams in Jefferson City, in the state capital, because their parents or grandparents may be away more often.

> "I think the station, in providing the coverage, in covering the games, is a community service."
> ~ Kevin Kelly

"We'll get emails every once in awhile. We had a gentleman who was deployed and was listening to the games on our website and said, 'Thank you. I've been listening to the games.' We've had people who have tagged Tom while we're doing the game, saying, 'We're listening to the game in Florida' or 'We're listening to the game in Minnesota.' The ability to have the games on your website and have people all over the place listening to the game … that's not something that happened several years ago."

We talked about whether Kevin views himself as a journalist or entertainer (more on that in Chapter 16). Given his comments and his full-time job, I was curious if he sees himself as a public servant.

"I think the station, in providing the coverage, in covering the games, is a community service. I don't know that I'm a public servant as that's defined. We'll have people that will want copies of the game they want to give to their son or daughter. It's always fun to have that. For example, I'm sure the Jays will do something to celebrate the 25th anniversary of their state championship. Well, we have the play-by-play of that game. We'll have players from that team, and they'll come in and we'll have a coach's show. Those guys really appreciate that. It's really a fun experience when you can do things like that."

(NOT) WORKING 8-TO-5

More than anything, Kevin says he wants aspiring sportscasters to recognize what the job entails before they take the leap.

"I would say that it's not an 8-to-5 job. Obviously, with games being in the evenings it's not an 8-to-5 job. The thing I would emphasize to them is take as much time as you need to make sure you do the job the best way that you know how to do it. If that means it takes you eight hours in a day to prepare to get to the comfort level that you want to do a broadcast, then do it. I wouldn't worry about it going, well, I've already done this for six hours. I've got to walk away. I think you just have to feel that when you walk in you're prepared and then you do the game. Then when you walk out of the gym you feel like—for the most part—yeah, that went pretty well.

"Be prepared to work some late nights. Let's say Jeff City plays at Kansas City Rockhurst. Rockhurst plays 7:30 football games, so we'll leave here and go do the football game. By the time we tear down the equipment, get in the car, get ready to drive back, and get back into Jefferson City, it's probably 1:30 in the morning. Then I've got the radio show at 7 o'clock in the morning, so I'll come back and I'll spend probably another two to two-and-half hours preparing for the show. So, there may be some nights where I won't go to bed till 4 o'clock and get up at 5:30. Am I tired? Yes. Does it make for a long day? Yes. Am I mad about it? No, because I'm doing what I want to do. I could come home and go to bed at 1:30 and then just go, 'Well, I'll just wing it.' I don't want to do that, and as long as I have control of it I won't do it. I want to be to the point where I walk in to do that show and I'm prepared to go from seven to 8 o'clock.

"The other thing, and I think they realize this, but the other thing to keep in mind is don't come out of college with the expectation that you're going to make $150,000 a year because it's not going to happen.

"A final thought for anyone thinking about play-by-play broadcasting: Do it because you love it, because it is something that excites you every time you put on the headset."

Photo courtesy of Mizzou Sports Properties

MIKE KELLY
KMOX - 1120 AM
UNIVERSITY OF MISSOURI

One cannot write a book titled "Show-Me Sportscasters" and not include the Voice of the Tigers, University of Missouri play-by-play man Mike Kelly. Mike's iconic voice has been heard on Tigers football and basketball broadcasts for almost three decades. It was actually quite humorous; when I got to the Broadway Columbia, his hotel of choice for the Tigers' game against Florida the next day, I asked the two attendants at the desk if he had come down for our interview. They said he had not, but one told a funny story of seeing Mike all the time, not knowing who he was. "And then he spoke to me one day, and I thought 'Oh, man! You're the Voice of the Tigers!'" the attendant said. "I thought he was just a regular guy."

As it turns out, I found Mike Kelly actually is a regular guy—humble, polite, friendly and incredibly engaging. Before we sat down to visit he informed me he was going to have to cut our meeting short because he had to run to Mizzou Arena for an interview with a coach. I said that would be fine; we could schedule a second meeting to finish up if needed.

He said he'd only be about an hour and he would hurry back so we could finish that day if it worked in my schedule. I had to remind Mike that he was doing me a favor, and I was more than happy to wait.

Mike is a native of Dupo, Illinois After graduating from Dupo High School, he attended Belleville Area Community College (now Southwestern Illinois College), where he played basketball for two years until a broken hand as a sophomore and a torn hamstring while water skiing ended his career. He then graduated from Southern Illinois University-Carbondale with a degree in radio and television. While in college, he covered high school sports for WINI in Murphysboro, Illinois and for WDWS in Champaign, Illinois

The first broadcaster west of the Mississippi to do a full season of volleyball (more on that later), Mike also provided postgame coverage and was a fill-in for football at the University of Illinois from 1985-88. After graduating, his journey took him to KMOX in 1989. He became color analyst for Missouri basketball in 1990, took over as play-by-play announcer in 1991, and started football play-by-play in 1994. Mike moved on from KMOX and from 1997-2008 worked full-time at Mizzou while also calling games for the St. Louis Cardinals and Kansas City Chiefs and for the NFL and NCAA for Westwood One. Since April 2014 he has continued to work part-time at KMOX while serving as senior vice president and equity partner with H-M Risk Company in Clayton, Missouri

Mike is a member of the Missouri Sports Hall of Fame (2017) and is a four-time Missouri Sportscaster of the Year (2012, 2013, 2015, and 2016). He and his wife, Laurie, have three grown daughters: Shannon, Shaun and Meagan.

A DREAM TAKES ROOT

Like many young men and women, Mike first started to find an interest in his future profession by spending time with his father. Little did he know that through years of hard work and dedication his dream would become a reality.

"Growing up my father would pick me up from practice, or when we would ever be in the car, he had his radio tuned to one station, and that was KMOX. Through the years of listening to the greats that have come through that station, whether it be Jack Buck or Dan Kelly or Bob Starr, Bob Costas, Mike Shannon, and others, John Rooney certainly, I was always fascinated by the industry. I was doing color in Murphysboro and in Carbondale while I was in college, so I thought I understood sports pretty well. I was doing high school football and basketball, but it wasn't until I got to Champaign then I started doing high school play-by-play. So, I don't know that I really got the itch to try and pursue play-by-play opportunities until I had the opportunity to do some high school sports in Champaign."

Where most sportscasters cut their teeth on the sports more commonly associated with broadcasting-- football, basketball, baseball--Mike took a rather non-traditional route to the college game.

"Illinois' volleyball team was terrific; they were going to go to the NCAA tournament and (former University of Illinois women's sports information director) Tom Boeh proposed to the general manager of WDWS at the time, Jim Turpin, 'We need to do play-by-play'. Jim came to me he said, 'Do you think you can do play-by-play at women's volleyball?' and I said, 'Yeah, let's give it a shot'. I literally learned the sport by having two chairs on the baseline during practice and the week leading up to the NCAA Tournament I was sitting

Photo courtesy of Mizzou Sports Properties

Mike Kelly gets the best seat in the house when the Missouri Tigers hit the turf at Faurot Field. He has seen some of the most bizarre and exciting plays in the history of the program.

with an assistant coach named Don Hardin and Don would walk me through the transition, the sport, and that's how I started. That was my first foray into college athletics, doing play-by-play. That went well.

"They sold the entire season the next year. Ironically, Illinois went to the Final Four in the next season. They won the Big Ten championship, and I ended up doing Illinois women's basketball as well. That was step number two. And then in 1988, when I went to KMOX, there was no guarantee of ever doing play-by-play again. I had two opportunities at the time. I was having conversations with WBBM in Chicago, an all-news station with not a lot of sports activity back in the '80s in terms of play-by-play, so I went to KMOX because it was the station that I loved growing up. When I got into the business, there was one place that I wanted to work, and it was at KMOX.

"So, I'm working, doing a variety of different things, and in 1989 Robert Hyland walks into the sports office one day and he says you're a young guy here, off on Mondays and Tuesdays. Missouri's got this show called 'Tiger Talk'. Bill Wilkerson doesn't want to drive to Columbia. Would you like to drive to Columbia and host 'Tiger Talk'? and I'm like, 'Absolutely! I'd love to.' I started doing 'Tiger Talk' with Bob Stull his first year in 1989. Then (Mizzou athletic director) Joe Castiglione had me fill in a couple of times for Rod Kelly when Rod was not able to do MU basketball. And in the 1990 season Rod said he couldn't do it anymore, so I did color for basketball for a year, and, by God's grace, at the end of the 1990 season Tom Dore takes the play-by-play job with the Chicago Bulls. Joe and Roger Gardner from Learfield hired me to do Mizzou basketball with my first color analyst, Joe Buck. Jack Buck would always tease us and say, 'When are you two fledglings going to start your career?' And I say there's one of us still fledgling; the other one's done pretty well for himself. Then prior to the 1994 football season Bill Wilkerson took the job doing the Phoenix Cardinals, and Joe and Roger came back to me and said, 'Would you like to do football, too?'

"God has a plan. God has certainly put his hand on me and has given me opportunities, and I have been very, very blessed along the way. So, I think the itch came when I started doing high school sports in Champaign. I stepped away from it for few years thinking if it's meant to be it's going to happen, and by this amazing twist of fate it did."

KEEPING THE CHAIR WARM

Given his years of experience at one of the most high-profile sportscasting jobs in Missouri, I wanted to know when Mike knew he had made it.

"I don't know that you ever do. I've said to many people that this isn't my job; I'm keeping the chair warm, and I just try to do it each and every time to the best of my ability. Now, some flattering things have happened throughout the years. Continuing to get contract extensions is one. Being recognized by your peers is another. Being inducted in the Missouri Sports Hall of Fame was something I could have never anticipated for a small-town kid from Dupo, Illinois So, you know, maybe those are tangible signs of sustainability. But I've always said to people at some point in time they're going to come to me, and they're going to say 'You've done a good job. Now we want to go in a different direction,' and that's within their rights. It's within any rights holder's right. It's their job; we're just keeping the seat warm.

"I think with that vision, it's helped me kind of understand that, while this has been a very good passionate hobby, it's also made me focus on trying to find other things professionally to sustain living. Depending on what your quality of life is that you want to have, there are very few play-by-play jobs that can offer you that type of a quality of life without supplementing your income doing something else. So that's what I think helps me to focus on building other aspects of my professional life, which then allow me to dive into my passion during the course of the fall, winter and then the early spring."

THE GREATEST GAME I EVER CALLED

The University of Missouri football and basketball teams have had their share of success during Mike Kelly's tenure on air. Since taking over Tiger basketball play-by-play responsibilities in 1990, Mizzou has made 14 trips to the NCAA Tournament, including berths in the Elite Eight in 1994, 2002 and 2009. The Tigers also have been to the NIT five times during his tenure. University of Missouri football, meanwhile, has won five division titles (three in the Big 12 North and two in the SEC East) and is 7-6 in bowl games. It was only natural, then, to ask about a favorite game.

"That's hard. You know, it really is. The (2007) Kansas game at Arrowhead because of the circumstances that surrounded that game, the fact that they're Number 2 and 3 in the nation, and the fact that college football was focused that weekend on Kansas City and on Arrowhead Stadium and on Missouri and Kansas. Think about how few times that's happened in the lives of those programs where college football on a Saturday night is focused on Missouri and Kansas. So that will always be one. (Incidentally, Missouri won 36-28.)

"The Tyus Edney game is a game that I'm always going to remember in Boise in 1995 because I've always believed that college athletics is about kids making plays. In that particular circumstance, 4.8 seconds to go, that kid made a play that would eventually lead his team to a national championship.

Missouri had just taken a lead in the second round of the 1995 NCAA Tournament; Edney took the in-bounds past, raced up the court and hit a floating right-handed layup as the buzzer sounded to give the UCLA Bruins the 75-74 win.

"The kickball against Nebraska (in 1997 when Shevin Wiggins kicked the ball to Matt Davison for the tying touchdown that sent the game to overtime). You know, you remember quirky things like that. Missouri winning at Colorado in 1997 to secure its first winning season in 14 years. Missouri winning in the Cotton Bowl on a couple of occasions. The Illinois triple overtime game (in 1993). This seat provides you a front row for so many different events, some of which become memorable for the rest of your life. It's a blessing to have that opportunity, so I couldn't just narrow it down to one play or one game or one team because the collective experience has been so memorable."

After seeing him struggle to find a favorite game, I thought I would really make Mike dig back to think of one favorite call. Amazingly, he had no trouble recalling several.

"People will ask, 'How did you call it' or something like that and I have always said I'll let others decide. It's just the way I try to approach it. The 'Ballgame! Bingo' call on the Todd Reesing sack in the end zone during the Armageddon game (Mizzou vs. Kansas in 2007) is one that's gotten a lot of play throughout the years. Shane Ray's scoop and score in the Cotton Bowl with 55 seconds left to secure the win for the Tigers has been one that people have brought up to me.

Mike Kelly began his broadcasting career by calling volleyball for the University of Illinois. He learned the game by sitting on the end line with an Illini assistant coach during practice.

"I think my call of Edney's run to the basket is as good as anybody that did it because from a philosophical standpoint, before I ever did a game Jack Buck said, 'Kid, you're going to do some great games, you're going to do some really bad games. You're going to do some great teams, you're going to do some really bad teams. Call the play. Just call the play.' Because that's all the listener cares about. They don't care about what you think about the officiating, they really don't care what you think about the coaching. They care about what's happening on the field, so call the play. I've always tried to focus on that. Sure, you want Missouri to win but I've tried to do it with the same level of enthusiasm for kids on the court or kids on the field for both sides. And so, you know, when Todd Reesing completed a pass in the fourth quarter a year later (in 2008) to Kerry Meier to beat Missouri, I was, I think, enthusiastic during that call. The same with that Edney run to the basket. So, you know, those are a few that stand out.

"You know, the irony is that before Tyus Edney made the run to the basket there was a timeout after Julian Winfield's put-back basket to give Missouri the lead with 4.8 seconds to go. Going to break I said, 'Oh baby, I love this tournament!' Well, Jim Kennedy was working with me at the time, and we both looked at each other during the break, and we said the same thing: 'Too much time.' It's not over until the buzzer sounds."

TO PRACTICE OR NOT TO PRACTICE, THAT IS THE QUESTION

I heard a story once how Jack Buck really thought a lot about how he would call it when and if St. Louis Cardinals great Mark McGwire broke Roger Maris' single-season home run record. That begged the question if Mike ever practiced a call or think about his wording for a specific moment? Mike didn't have to think long before answering.

> *"This seat provides you a front row for so many different events, some of which become memorable for the rest of your life."*
>
> ~ Mike Kelly

"I don't know that I have. I have thought about tournament championships when Missouri has won a conference tournament championship or in the NCAA when counting down a game. You know, how are you going to capture the moment? But I don't know that I've specifically ever really planned out what I was going to say. And maybe that's to a fault, but I don't know that I've specifically done that.

"But in terms of thinking how I'm going to close out the play, I don't believe I really do. I did read that (about Jack Buck planning what he would say) and I remember Jack saying that. But you know, he didn't do that for Ozzie Smith cork-screwing his hit down the line and saying, 'Go crazy, folks! Go crazy!' or when Jack Clark in that same '85 season hit a bomb in Los Angeles. You know, Clark with a chance to redeem himself after striking out, I think it was in the seventh, and Jack goes through and lays out the situation, and I remember 'Adios, goodbye! And the Cardinals could go to the World Series on that one, folks'. That's a couple of his classic calls. But Jack was the best at framing the circumstances. And I think I learned a lot in terms of that, but also in terms of developing. The respect that I had for him over his body of work in the time that I had a chance to listen to him, I mean just so many different examples of just how good he was at his craft.

EVEN LEGENDS HAVE HEROES

I think I knew the answer to this one before I ever started the interview, but it had to be asked. Given his background in the Southern Illinois-St. Louis area, it was only natural that Mike would have been a fan of the greats from KMOX.

"Certainly I have always loved the work of Jack (Buck), have always loved the work of Dan Kelly. Growing up in St. Louis, Bob Starr was an underrated broadcaster when he did Missouri and he also went on to do the Cardinals and then the Angels. Bob Costas when he did the (American Basketball Association) Spirits of St. Louis as a really, really young guy was terrific. Mitch Holthus is, I think, unbelievably good and I just think he's a terrific person. He's been a great friend. When I did Chiefs preseason games a few years ago he could not have been more kind and warm and helpful to me, so he will always be a guy who I respect and a guy who I've always loved his work."

It was interesting he mentioned how helpful Mitch Holthus had been. The week before, when I was interviewing John Coffey of Northwest Missouri State, John said he wished he'd taken more time with Jack Buck when he had the opportunity. That got me thinking about these professionals as mentors and whether Mike tried to be a mentor.

"You know, I got to KMOX because someone was willing to give me help. I was a young broadcaster from the St. Louis-area working in Champaign, Illinois. The (Chicago) Bears were preparing for the Super Bowl. They were in Champaign practicing under the University of Illinois bubble. There was a news conference at Jumers Castle Lodge in Urbana, Illinois I heard during the course of the news conference this big booming voice from the other side of the room, and I recognized it as Jim Holder from KMOX and I went over to him after the news conference and introduced myself and I said, 'I'm Mike Kelly from WDWS and from Dupo, Illinois and I want to work at KMOX.' And I'll never forget he said, 'Well big boy, next time you come to see the family, let me know. I'll have you over, we'll tour the station, and we'll see what can happen.'

"I followed up on that and eventually came in and met with Jim and with Rob Silverstein, who's gone on to have a terrific career in television. He was the executive sports producer. Rob said, 'We don't have a job, go back to Champaign, Illinois and be our correspondent on Illinois sports. When anything happens--games, postgame wraps, pregame wraps, news events--send us audio, send us voicers. We'll play them. Your voice on KMOX will develop a relationship with the listeners and it will give us a chance to critique your work.'

"I did that for two and a half years and never asked for a dime, not one dime. Then the football Cardinals announced that they were moving to Arizona. There were two sports people related to the Cardinals that worked at KMOX: Bob Mayhall was one. Nancy Drew was the other; she was married to Larry Wilson, the general manager of the Cardinals. So there were a couple of openings. I got a call from Ron Jacober asking if I would audition. I came in and auditioned for the program and did Sports Open Line. Then I got a hold of Holder and said, 'How do I get the job?' He said 'You have to call (legendary general

As the play-by-play announcer for Missouri's flagship institution, one might say Mike Kelly, along with broadcast partners Chris Gervino and Howard Richards, is the Voice of the Show-Me State.

Photo courtesy of Mizzou Sports Properties

manager) Robert Hyland.' 'How do I get of Hyland?' He said to call him, but you 'better call before 6 a.m. because once he gets in, literally just after midnight, and at 6 a.m. he goes to mass, and then at 7 he begins his CBS duties and you'll never touch him until he leaves at 4:30 in the afternoon.' So, for a period of about six weeks on Friday mornings at 4:30 in the morning I would get up from my apartment in Champaign, Illinois and call. 'Robert Hyland? This is Mike Kelly calling from Champaign. I really want the job.' 'We're still looking'--click. And that was as quick as it was in those first couple of calls. Eventually he warmed up, and I knew I had a pretty good chance of getting the job when he would pick up the phone and say, 'Michael, how are you?' So, I knew I had a pretty good chance. But again, it goes back to, had I not met Jim Holder at Jumers Castle Lodge in Urbana, Illinois back in late 1984, prior to the '85 Super Bowl, none of this would have happened.

"It all goes back to yes, we have a responsibility as broadcasters to helping young people get into our business. Not that I'm passionate about the subject, but I might be" (he said with a twinkle in his eye and tongue firmly planted in his cheek).

A DREAM NOT YET FULFILLED

Given all the events he has covered to this point, it would seem Mike Kelly would have little left to shoot for. That is not the case; Mike still has some events in mind he would like to be a part of before hanging up his headset.

"Oh, wow! The BCS Championship game in football or the NCAA championship in basketball for a guy that's got 25-plus years invested into both of those. I mean it'd be neat to see my team get there sometime. Don't get me wrong, as we get older we all get selfish, so yeah, I would love to have that opportunity. I'd love to get the opportunity to call a game from the Final Four. God willing that happens at some point in time, so yeah, that would be one of those dream games that I'd love to do.

"I would enjoy the opportunity of baseball at some point in time. I don't know that it'll ever happen. You know, I never really pursued it growing up and when my kids were younger because I didn't want to be away from my children. That's a six-month season, and I said that's a long season and I just didn't want to be away from my kids that long. That's why I had the perfect niche with football and basketball. Those would be a couple dreams."

Mike got his first job with KMOX by calling legendary GM Robert Hyland every Friday morning at 4:30 to inquire about opportunities.

IT'S A TEAM EFFORT

In doing my research for this book, one thing I read repeatedly was the word "chemistry". Of course, we aren't talking periodic tables or lab experiments. Rather, the chemistry between the play-by-play announcer and the color analyst. Mike has worked with several analysts throughout his career, so I wanted to know how he developed that chemistry, and when he knew it's just not there.

"Hopefully you develop a really personal relationship. That helps with the chemistry. So that's step one. There is a flow to a conversation that you have that hopefully your partner picks up on so they understand when you're going to stop and when you're not. Now early on with a partner it's not uncommon for me to use the tap system. They're sitting next to me, I'm done talking, tap, your turn. Tap, I need it back. So those are techniques that I've used in the past.

"You have to develop that relationship, and when you don't have it then it becomes a crapshoot as to whether you can do your job effectively. Working with Chris (Gervino, his current color analyst), we have got a great friendship on and off the air, and we've known each other for 20 plus years, so that's been good."

WHEN YOU WANT TO GET AWAY

One thing I've read repeatedly is that many of the sportscasters have varied interests far away from what they do as a sportscaster—Kevin Harlan is a very involved parent, Gary Bender is highly into FCA, Bill King visited museums wherever he goes. What does Mike Kelly do to escape the rigors of being a sportscaster?

"My business takes me away from sport, so when I'm not doing a game, when I get up on the road the first thing I do is go to the newspapers—online or whatever—and I read. And then I dive into emails and catch up on stuff on my to-do list. A lot of time is when I just jump back into my business and make sure that I have taken care of things I have to follow up on. That takes me away."

Beyond work, Mike also has a more personal way to recharge his batteries.

"My faith is important to me. One of the things that I really struggle with during the season is I do play-by-play on Saturday and I do a talk show on Sunday morning. I miss a lot of church. How does God feel about that? I feel guilty. I try to read throughout the course of the week. I have my quiet time in the morning where I try to read the Bible each day. Try. There are times I don't get to it. It is not uncommon on an airplane as we're traveling to a game where I will catch up on Bible verses from the week. Time allows me to do it then. I try to, particularly during the off season, have my quiet time. Get up in the morning, have a cup of coffee, I walk outside, sit down on my screened porch and try to have that quiet time with God. I feel guilty when I don't get a chance to go to church. But my faith is important to me. If there's not a God in this world, I'm not doing what I'm doing. He has a plan for all of us, I truly believe that. He's shown great grace and mercy and acceptance of me through all my faults and flaws and all my issues. He's given me the opportunity to not only have a great living but also to do something that's pretty cool. So, it's important to give thanks.

"I'm involved in multiple organizations. I'm on the board of a charity that gives away Segways and a device called an Aly Chair. It's a Segway base that has a seat on it. What we do is we give those Segways and Aly Chairs to service men and women who come back from the theater of battle with huge mobility issues. It was founded by a really dear friend of mine who broke his neck in 1998 in a diving accident and I said whatever you need, just let me know. He reached out and said, 'I want you to be part of this organization.' It's been one of the most remarkable things that I've ever been involved with. We've given more than 1,700 devices, and every time it's the same thing. You thank the servicemen and women for their commitment to you, and they look at you and they say we did our job. We did our job. We knew it was a dangerous mission.

"We have a couple four-star generals on our board, we have a Congressional Medal of Honor recipient who frames it correctly: These young men and women go down to the recruiting station and they put their hand on the Bible and they raise their right hand and they agree to play a road game so we can enjoy our home games. Being involved in that and doing events with them around the state and around the country has been very fulfilling.

"Without question it's important to get away. I think we all take sport too seriously. I don't like when coaches use the phrase "it is critically important". There is nothing in sport that is critically important. Life and death, success or failure in times of battle-- that's critically important. What we do in sport is not critically important. There are no heroes in sport. Other than maybe those guys that have served our country, there are no heroes in sport. I think we have to properly understand what we're doing. It's a game. Yeah, people are well compensated. Coaches are well compensated. Players at the professional level are well compensated. I'm sure broadcasters at that level are well compensated. But it's a game, it's a pastime. There is a reason why they call it the national pastime. I think sometimes that we can overestimate our importance in the whole landscape of where we live, and I think that by pulling away from it and understanding that it is gives you a better perspective."

WORDS OF WISDOM

Mike takes on the air of a father encouraging his child when I ask him for some parting words of advice for aspiring sportscasters.

"Believe in yourself. Always believe in yourself because no one's going to believe in you unless you believe in yourself. Continue to dream. Understand that the path may not always be a direct one, that it may involve stops along the way. But as long as you are living your dream and you're applying yourself to your craft, good things can happen. It's just a matter of if you put in the time to accomplish it.

"Now, we all know that there's limited opportunities. That's why I tell every young person I come into contact with that every conversation you have is a networking opportunity, and the network you build will have a significant influence on your ability to get jobs looking forward."

Photo courtesy of Kansas City Royals

RYAN LEFEBVRE
FOX SPORTS KANSAS CITY &
ROYALS RADIO NETWORK -
KANSAS CITY ROYALS

Growing up in Sedalia, I was a Kansas City Royals fan. But it was not until moving to Warrensburg with my family in 2002 that I became die hard. I bled blue with the Royals faithful through those losing years, including the painful back-to-back-to-back 100-loss seasons from 2004-2006. I cheered on Mike Sweeney and Carlos Beltran, John Buck and Joe Randa, David DeJesus and Mike MacDougal, hoping, praying they would be able to turn it around. I watched as six managers came and went before Ned Yost took over in 2010. Finally, in 2013, the Royals finished above .500. One season later they went to game seven of the World Series before falling to the Giants. Then in 2015, after a 30-year drought, the Kansas City Royals were World Series champions.

Through it all—the highs and lows, the managerial changes, the jokes about Kansas City being a minor league town—Ryan Lefebvre was a constant, calling the action in the press box. Ryan is now in his 26th year in broadcasting, his 20th with the Royals. The Los Angeles native graduated from Loyola High School in 1989. He then enrolled at the University of Minnesota where he was a triple major in speech communication, sociology and American studies. He began his broadcasting career as a freshman when he began working with campus radio station KUOM. Ryan also was a first-team All-Big Ten outfielder for the Gophers as a senior (he was second-team as a junior, and third-team as a sophomore) before being drafted in the 27th round of the free agent draft by the Cleveland Indians. He spent two weeks with the Watertown Indians of the New York-Penn League before deciding his career lay in the broadcast booth and not on the diamond. A job awaited Lefebvre back in Minnesota, and he started doing sideline reporting before moving on to do color and some play-by-play for the Minnesota Twins from 1995-98. In 1999 he joined Fox Sports Kansas City (for television) and the Royals Radio Network.

Ryan won an Emmy in 2016 for the Mid-America Region, received the 2015 Johnson County NAACP Diversity in Sports Award, and was voted one of the "Most Influential People" in the state of Kansas in 2014. He also won the 2011 John J. "Buck" O'Neil MVP award for his commitment to youth in Kansas City and was named the 2006 Boys & Girls Club of Greater Kansas City Role Model of the Year. Ryan is also the founder of Gloves for Kids and the Footprints Foundation.

He and his wife, Sarah, have three sons—Micah, Evan, and Lucas—and a daughter Callie. So dedicated is Ryan to his family that he had to leave our interview early to go volunteer at his children's school. He graciously offered to schedule a phone interview to complete our conversation if I would email him my availability. But when I did so, he showed what a true gentleman he is: He volunteered to drive to Warrensburg to meet face-

Photo courtesy of Kansas City Royals

Steve Physioc, Rex Hudler, Jeff Montgomery, Joel Goldberg and Ryan Lefebvre form one of the most experienced broadcast teams in Major League Baseball.

to-face with some of our students. I gladly accepted and invited some of my Royals-loving colleagues and my youngest son, Grant, who is a blue-blooded Royals fan. Parts of this chapter comes from their questions and Ryan's answers and are noted accordingly.

NOT JUST ANOTHER "DUMB JOCK"

Ryan Lefebvre never wanted to be a sportscaster. His goal from an early age was to be a news anchor, to be one of the gatekeepers providing the information necessary for our daily lives. Lucky for Royals fans, things didn't turn out that way.

"It's a funny story. I thought I wanted to be a news anchor because my mom has always been a news and political junkie, and Tom Brokaw actually started in Los Angeles before he went to New York and ended up on The Today Show and then Nightly News. And I wanted to be Tom Brokaw. There was this stigma, when I was in high school at least, that if you were some dumb jock then you went into sports. Not many athletes were qualified to be in news, so I was going to be one of those guys. I was going to be a news anchor.

"I had some experience at the student station in college. I played in the Cape Cod summer league a couple summers and had an internship one summer at a radio station. But my first internship in Minneapolis was at KFAN Radio. The program director's goal someday was to be a television news director. So, I remember I was sitting across his desk one day and he asked me, 'What do you want to do?' and I said I want to be a news anchor. He said, 'Well, if you want to be a news anchor, you have to be a news reporter first.' And I said yeah, I knew that. So, it was like a scene out of a movie. He leans across the desk, and he says, 'Okay, two kids are playing on the Washington Avenue Bridge and they fall into the Mississippi River and drown. Are you prepared to go with a camera crew to the kids' house and get a statement from their parents?' And I thought I was going to just throw up all over his desk and I was like, Why would I ever want to do that? He says, 'If you want to be a news anchor and you want to be a reporter, those are the kind of stories you have to do'. Before I even walked out of his office I wasn't going to be a news anchor anymore.

"Then I thought I wanted to be a talk show host because that's what KFAN was. At that time, they did the Vikings play-by-play, but it's mostly sports talk. I thought I want to do sports talk. And then I realized I didn't care about all the sports enough. I filled in as a sports talk show host, but I just didn't care enough to study all the different sports. And then I did a little bit of reporting and then I also realized that I didn't really like digging for stories, breaking stories, and it doesn't mean anything to me. That's for someone else. Going into the locker room after a game and talking to players after the game, I didn't want any part of that. Having been a college athlete and growing up with my dad (former Major League player and manager Jim Lefebvre), I just know that's a volatile time, a very sensitive time.

"So, I think over time and really having an empty canvas, my personality and play-by-play just really seemed to match. But I didn't go into it wanting to be a play-by-play announcer. This kind of evolved over time. Just looking at everything, I think I realized this is what I'd like to do, and then when I started to listen to Vin Scully as an adult, you know he was the voice of my childhood. But I didn't realize how good he was; he was just the Dodger broadcaster. Then when I really started listening to him as an adult, the storytelling part of it, I thought I would enjoy that because people interest me.

"My favorite part about doing a broadcast is when I have what I feel is an interesting story about a player that I can share with the audience that humanizes them, makes them sound more like a regular guy, taking an extraordinary person and making them seem more ordinary—I really enjoy that. I really enjoy watching documentaries on TV about people. Then having played the game, having some knowledge of the game, and having some interest in numbers, I think you put all that together, that's why I landed in play-by-play."

A NONTRADITIONAL ROUTE TO THE BOOTH

A quick check of the math and I realized something: Ryan literally went straight from college to a cup of coffee in the Cape Cod League to a broadcast booth in Minnesota. In short, he didn't take the traditional route.

"No, I didn't. Funny story—I've told the story a hundred times—but when my dad was managing the Mariners, I used to sit next to him in the dugout and drive him crazy second guessing him, this cocky teenager. So, we're at old Cleveland Stadium in these tiny dugouts and he was looking for a reason to get me out of the dugout. I was majoring in broadcasting in college, and he sends me up to the booth to sit with the Mariners' broadcasters, and I sat with Rick Rizzs. He was doing radio that day—they had a three-man team and the two play-by-play announcers would switch after four and a half innings. Before the game begins I'm up with Rick Rizzs. He's doing his prep, we're chatting, and the game begins, and he just launches into the weather and how the Mariners are doing and how the Indians are doing and how the starting pitcher's been doing and then the game starts and he's weaving in the stories and I remember sitting next to him thinking, 'Well I'll never be able to do this; I can cross this off the list.' I went into it actually thinking I can't do this. I just couldn't believe how he just kept talking and he didn't have a bunch of notes in front of him. So yeah, being a play-by-play announcer was not my original plan."

MAKING IT BIG

Making it to the majors in what seems like record time, one might think Ryan would feel safe and secure in his present position, that he has arrived. One would be wrong.

"I went into it with kind of like a survival mode, and I don't know if I've ever gotten out of that. I mean, this would be my 20th year with the Royals, but it still feels new to me. I don't know if I'll ever get over being the guy sitting in (legendary Royals broadcaster) Fred White's chair because that was such a big deal when I came to town.

"First of all, I was the benefactor of circumstance. In '93 Fox got the rights to the NFL and instead of hiring all the NBC guys, they hired Joe Buck and Tom Brennaman, just young announcers, and the whole industry was in shock. What are these guys doing, hiring all these kids in their 20s, you know? It was all these grandfatherly guys in their 50s and 60s. Maybe 40s. I mean that was young. Now here are these guys in their 20s. In '94 they got the rights to Major League Baseball. Same thing: Joe Buck, Tom Brennaman, Chip Caray, Josh Lewin, all these young announcers.

"So, there was a trickle down from the networks to the regional networks and some of the regional networks started thinking, 'You know, maybe we should add a young person,' and that's really when baseball started to become afraid of 'it's an old person sport, how do we get younger'. So, the Twins, like everybody else, thought, 'Well, let's add a young guy' and I mean you talk about being in the right place at the right time. I had just finished my baseball career at Minnesota and had been successful. Gopher baseball wasn't super popular in Minneapolis but it was popular enough where, I wouldn't say I was a household name, but for true sports fans they knew who I was. And, of course, my dad being in professional baseball, so I had that. I did have broadcast experience. I wouldn't call it qualifying for the Major Leagues, but I had some experience. I had a baseball name, and I had been interning and doing some work for the television station that covered the Twins. If I had been anywhere else five years earlier or five years later, I might still be doing minor league baseball, but it was like, 'Here's Ryan. He's young, he's got a name, he's got some experience. Let's give him a shot.' That was 1995. I'd love to tell you that I was the best 24-year-old in Minnesota, let alone anywhere else, and that they had to give me a job because I was just so talented and that I had paid my dues and all that, but it's just not true. I was in the right place in the right time."

YOU GOTTA HAVE THICK SKIN

I teach sports reporting in college, and it seems that people are always eager to pounce on students learning sports broadcasting. I can only imagine what it's like for the Voice of the Royals.

Ryan Lefebvre won an Emmy for sportscasting in 2016. He also is the founder of Gloves for Kids and the Footprints Foundation.

"I don't care what anybody says, that's hard to get over. Early on, even today, I don't ever want to hear someone criticizing me. It's probably a human flaw that when someone says, 'Hey, you do a great job' or 'I really like listening to you' or 'That was a great broadcast or a great call', it's kind of like, 'Oh, gee thanks.' But when somebody's like, 'Gosh, I can't stand to listen to that person', that's the one that you pay way more attention to. I've gotten better at that over time, but yeah, that's another thing about getting to this level. You do a college game or minor league games, not many critics out there. When you get to this level, and especially when you come in after a legend, they're looking for reasons, they're looking for flaws."

YOU CAN MAKE THIS STUFF UP

In 2014 the Kansas City Royals had a magical run from the Wild Card game to game seven of the World Series. In 2015 the run continued all the way to the World Championship. That excitement lent itself to some great calls. It is only natural to assume, then, that Ryan might have practiced his potential calls.

"The only time I really did that was the game in Chicago when they clinched going to the playoffs. I just I agonized over that because we had no idea they're going to end up in Game Seven of the World Series, so my whole thinking was 29 years of no postseason and that might be it. They could lose a Wild Card game and then that's it. When we go to Fan Fest the next year this is the call to say, 'Hey, you know, the Royals are off the hook now. They don't have the longest drought anymore', and so I spent a lot of time thinking about it. I wouldn't say that I scripted it, but I thought a lot about it.

"The Chicago game was really good, even though we're all taught don't script it. But it was my first big moment as a broadcaster, and it was a huge moment for Kansas City and the Royals. I just thought, 'Don't mess this up'. How do you summarize 29 years? And I said too much. You know, it's been played back many times, but they edit it down to the best parts and it sounds pretty good when they do it that way. But that was just 'trust your instincts' and just do the basics.

"And you know, obviously the Wild Card game, well that highlight gets played a lot. There's no way to prepare for that. Salvi's (Salvador Perez) base hit, the 'Fair ball! Fair ball!' thing, and then the final out of the World Series I had the same thought: Don't try and say anything clever. Just say the basics so that when they use it on the video and all this stuff, just make the point the Royals are World Series champs. Because I remember Herb Carneal, his call when the Twins won in '87, and he just said, 'The World Champion Minnesota Twins', and I think I said the same thing.

"I remember the Jack Buck thing, too (about practicing his call if and when Mark McGwire broke Roger Maris' home run record that started this question). Jack Buck said something about 'on his way to planet Maris' or something like that. That's where you don't try and be clever; just make the point. The part that everyone remembers from the World Series one is when I said, 'Strike three called' because he kept fouling off pitches. It was like 'When is this thing going to be over?' and that's what people remember. I can't script 'strike three called' you know? I remember saying, 'Strike three called. It's over!' because that inning just went on. But for the first time, every other celebration for every other time they clinched it was at home, and there was a huge roar of the crowd, which is the best thing to have as a broadcaster. It's like broadcasting with an orchestra. And I remember going, 'Strike three called!' ... and it just went silent. And I said, 'It's over!' and then I remember thinking, 'It is over, right?' Like, why is it so quiet? Because we had never experienced that, and then I see the gloves in the air, and this is just me being ultra-critical, but I say 'It's over' and there's this awkward kind of, they've done it and I think it was me just telling myself they've done it, and then I kind of got back into the Royals are World Series Champions."

As a Kansas City fan, I pray it won't be another 30 years before Ryan and the Royals get another crack at postseason glory. Having been through the experience, then, does Ryan have an idea of what he would do differently?

"If I ever get a do-over, there's two things I learned: The worst way for a game to end is a strikeout. And the way worst way, the worst of the worst ways, is a called third strike. Because when the ball's put in play you can kind of build-up and then hit the punch line. But (with a strikeout) it's over, there's no build-up. And then I remember, because of the silence, I could have been calling that out in the parking lot or here at Whistle Stop (in downtown Lee's Summit, where we met for coffee). If you listen, there's nothing behind me, it's like I was in the studio.

"I listened to Joe Buck's call, and he's done so many World Series, and I've never asked him this question, but if you listen to his call it was quick and to the point. And I've always wondered, Does he prepare himself differently for a road call? Of course, Fox had mic's everywhere, so there's a little bit of crowd noise on the Fox call. But he just says, 'The Royals: 2015 World Series Champs.' That's really quick. And then I've heard him call final outs when the home team wins and he strings it out a little longer. I just wonder if over experience, since he realized on the road you don't have crowd noise, just make your point and get out. If you took my World Series call and filled the gaps with the roar of the crowd, I think it would sound better, but there was no crowd there. It was just shocking to me because it sounded like we just won the World Series and nobody cares and the stadium just went silent. Because the fans were cheering leading up to it, hoping that (Wilmer)

Flores would get on and get something started, and then I'm trying to call this big moment in Royals history with no ambient noise at all. It was really awkward."

TELEVISION VS. RADIO

One of my colleagues, Dr. Wendy Geiger, came to class the day Ryan visited with our students. She was interested in Ryan's perspective on television vs. radio, and particularly in which he prefers.

"I feel like I have a completely different mindset on radio vs. television. What I never want to sound like is a radio guy on television and I never want to sound like a television guy on radio. When we do the game on radio, it's obviously a lot more description and a lot of review. When I started in television, you didn't know what the score was and you didn't know what the inning was and you didn't know where the base runners were and you didn't know what the count was. Every now and then we'd bring in the count and the score. Now on Fox, we have this thing we call the Fox Box, where you turn a game on TV, and it's all there.

Ryan, here with color analyst Rex Hudler, has seen the lows (three straight 100-loss seasons) and the highs (back-to-back trips to the World Series, including the 2015 Championship).

"You can never say the score too much on radio because I never know when someone is tuning in. And for me, if I'm going to listen to a game on radio, there's three things I need to know: What's the score, where are we, and how did we get there? Mitch Holthus is great at repeating the score and the time all the time. But if I turn on a Chiefs game, what's the score? Where are we? What quarter are we in and how much time is left? And then how did we get there? If Mitch tells me it's 7-7 in the second quarter, I'm like okay, a couple touchdowns. But if he tells me it's 21-0 and we're five minutes into the first quarter it's like, dang! What happened? You have to let people know. Even if it's 0-0 in a baseball game in the eighth inning, well then, man! Somebody was pitching! So every now and then, it's 'Royals and Twins, no score, top of the eighth inning, Jason Vargas threw seven scoreless innings, and Phil Hughes threw seven scoreless innings. Now it's in the hands of the bullpen.' Alright, now as a listener, I'm caught up. I know what's going on. Now I can just concentrate on listening to the game.

"So, on radio, there's a lot of resetting the action. On television, especially today, my microphone could go dead and you don't need me. When I think I'm so important calling the game on television, I remind myself how many people are watching this game in a bar right now with no volume. And they can follow everything that's going on. Maybe I'm complementing the thing, but on radio, you turn it on and I'm not saying anything, you have no idea what is going on. Television is more conversational, and I feel like everything I can bring to the table as a play-by-play announcer is taken away by the Fox Box. I might say the score every now and again, I might review. But it's my job to keep my analyst explaining, complementing what you just saw. Here's the names and numbers. Why is that important? Here's a replay. Why is that important? One of the things I was taught early on in baseball on radio was don't miss a pitch. The pitch is important. Television, a routine ground ball to second base, I don't need to say anything; everybody can see it. Foul ball, you can see it's a foul ball. There's not as much description; there's more conversation.

"I feel like television does not get enough credit. Everyone thinks radio, those guys are the real artists. They have to paint the picture and describe, and that's true, but if you take away all the resetting from me on TV, you better know the game because if I can't say, 'Two balls and one strike, runner at second, one out, Royals lead 3-1' a few times every inning ... if you take that away from me, I better have things to talk about with each player and with the team and have a conversation. I have to know more about the teams and the players on TV than I do on radio. On radio, if you really wanted to, you can just get through it by describing and resetting everything."

So, if he had to choose ...

"I came at the tail end of just about everybody doing radio and TV. When I was with the Twins, I would actually do radio and TV in the same game. I would do television in the first three innings, I'd do radio in the middle three innings, and come back and finish on television, which was great because I got to talk to both audiences in the same game, and I got to do two different broadcasts in one game. And I really like that. When I started I was encouraged to do both; don't ever limit yourself so I could only apply for radio jobs or I could only apply for television jobs. I really like both of them, and the Royals have been great to allow me to do both. I fear the day when they come to me and say, 'Look, you have to pick one or the other'. That was one thing I asked for when they asked me to move over to mainly television. I asked if I could still do radio and they've allowed me to do that."

> *"I never want to sound like a radio guy on television and I never want to sound like a television guy on radio."*
>
> ~ Ryan Lefebvre

STATS CHANGE, BUT THE GAME REMAINS THE SAME

Weighted on-base average. Batting average on balls in play. Wins above replacement. Such sabermetrics have made tracking success in baseball much more detailed and complex. And while the new complexities haven't altered how he prepares, Ryan says technology, coupled with the new data, has made it more of a challenge to provide new information to fans.

"Fans have more access to what we have access to because of the internet. The hardcore fans can look up the numbers on their own, so when we share something that we think is interesting, there's a percentage of our fans who are already aware of that. I think the expectation of a certain segment of our fan base is more demanding because they have access to the numbers and the stories, but I think by-and-large, the fans who are on Twitter, you know the hardcore fans that really study the Royals, is still a small percentage.

"I think for the vast majority of fans we're still informing them, and we're still sharing stories and numbers and why this is important. I know there's a push to do more of the advanced numbers because a segment of our fan base is into that. (He notices a group of gentlemen visiting and drinking coffee). You know, like I see there's a table with five guys over there, and they're just chatting. Two guys have their Royals stuff on. I'll bet none of them know what WAR is or care what WAR is. They just want to know are the Royals going to win tonight, and if they are how are they going to win and why are they playing well and why aren't they playing well or why is this player playing well or why is he not playing well. Then they have their own opinions about it, but most fans are not going to dig into it. It's so much like politics, too. The most vocal is usually the minority; it's the same in sports. Most fans like the Royals, but they still rely on us for information."

DON'T BE TOO CRITICAL

Sport is, by nature, competitive. So it would stand to reason that all who are around sports have a competitive nature with their counterparts. While guys like Denny Matthews, Vin Scully and Joe Buck may be personal favorites, one of our students, Bailee Daniels, wanted to know if any of Ryan's counterparts had practices or techniques that he just didn't like.

"One thing I learned really early on is don't be critical of other announcers. I just think it's bad karma. I remember my first couple years with the Twins, my mentor was a guy named John Gordon, who did radio for them forever. He retired a few years ago. I remember my first couple years we were doing games on the radio and I'd ask him, 'Hey do you think so-and-so is any good?' And he'd say 'Yeah, I think he's good.' We'd be sitting there and I'd say, 'What about this guy? Do you think he's any good?' Because I was young and I was listening to everybody. 'Yeah, I think he's pretty good.' 'Well, what do you think about this guy?' And finally, he just stopped, and he goes, 'Ryan, let me tell you something: I think everybody's good. Because if you broadcast at this level, you're good. And if you start getting caught up in who's good and who's bad, it doesn't matter because they have the job.' He was kind of scolding me at the same time, and I just never forgot that."

FAITH COMES FIRST

One thing I heard over and over about Ryan was that he is a devout Catholic and a devoted family man. Those don't always go together in the high-pressure world of professional sports. But somehow, he manages to find the balance.

"The easy answer is that who I am as a person, which is a follower of Christ, a husband, a father, and a friend, is way more important to me than what I do as a broadcaster. I'm able to separate the two. I love my job, I feel extremely blessed to have this job for as long as I have. I can't tell you that I deserve it, but here I am, and I hope that I've demonstrated that I appreciate it. But it's not who I am. If you gave me the choice between my wife calling me and telling me while I'm on the road that it's been a great day at home and the kids had a good day at school, and I could choose between that and being on the MLB Network because I called a game-winning home run, I would much rather take the family part. So,

113

it is a job, I enjoy it, and it's how I support my family, but it's not really who I am.

"It didn't always used to be that way. I'm not as concerned with how that may come across, and just being able to separate those two makes that easier. I don't have to worry about what someone may think. My responsibilities as a man and how I carry myself is more important than how people may perceive me as a broadcaster."

THE BEST ADVICE I EVER GOT

While most of the students in our program are interested in the production side of sports broadcasting, one of my students, Danielle Sachse, is an aspiring talent (if you read the chapter about Mitch Holthus, you'll remember her as the student who scooped me and got to Mitch first). She was really interested in what Ryan had learned as far as covering for errors on the broadcast.

"The biggest mistakes I've made were ... I was driving home and I started thinking, 'What were you talking about?' And usually that has happened when I couldn't think of anything to say and so I just started talking. I've been doing this long enough that every-once-in-a-while I'll try an experiment and just not say much for an inning or two, and nobody has said anything to me about it. I'll go back and listen to it, and I realized I'm the only one who noticed it.

"It happens to all of us. There is really no way I can tell you what to do other than experience. First of all, I would tell you go back and watch your broadcast. It'll never be as bad as you think it is. It also, unfortunately, is never going to be as good as you think it is, either.

"The best advice I ever got came from John Gordon, my mentor in Minnesota. I was doing minor league games in Minnesota on the radio in the Minneapolis area, and I wanted to be a Major League broadcaster. I met John Gordon in spring training, and he knew my dad and knew I was playing at Minnesota and he said, 'Hey, I heard you got in the business' and I said, 'Yeah, if I gave you a tape of my play-by-play would you listen to it?' And he said, 'No.' And he says, 'I'll tell you why. You're just getting started. There might be a time I'll give a listen to it, but now is not the time. Here is my advice for you'—best advice I ever got—'when you're done doing anything, radio or television, when you're done, go and listen to it or watch it, and then think of three things that you can do better next time. Just three.'

"Now, when I was starting, I could have thought of 27 things that I could have done better when I listened to it. But if I'm thinking of 27 things that I could do better, I'm not going to concentrate on what I am doing. That was like gospel to me. I did a minor league season that year. Eighty games, and it was all by myself. I don't know if I listened to every game, but it was pretty close. I don't know if I improved on 240 things over that summer, but I tell you what, if I played you the first tape and the last tape, I was a lot better. And it wasn't just because of experience; it was because I picked two or three things every game that I wanted to get better. Maybe I wanted to slow down a little bit, maybe I wanted to say the score more, maybe there was this crazy play and I couldn't find the words to describe it. But let's say I knew that play was coming, how would I say it next time? So, critique yourself. Watch yourself."

Photo courtesy of Mike McClure

MIKE McCLURE
McCLURE BROADCASTING, ESPN+ & ESPN3
MISSOURI SOUTHERN STATE UNIVERSITY &
MISSOURI STATE UNIVERSITY

I had three interviews to do in Southwest Missouri, so I decided to spend some time with my wife's family and cover them all in one shot. It was a rather cold and drizzly day as I drove to Mike McClure's house from my in-laws' home in Clever, Missouri As I traveled west on Highway 60, I thought about all my interactions with Mike. He actually had me on as a halftime guest once while I was working at Missouri Southern. Ever the gentleman, he welcomed me into his home, offered me a drink, and shared his story.

In the roughly 20 years I have known Mike McClure, this may have been the first time I ever saw him sit still. And that was before he started McClure Broadcasting in the summer of 2009. Through his business, Mike and his associates cover high school sports in Monett, Mount Vernon, and Aurora, Missouri

But that is just the tip of the iceberg. Mike also works with Fox Sports Radio Joplin to broadcast Missouri Southern football and basketball games; with ESPN+ and ESPN3 for Missouri State men's and women's basketball, men's and women's soccer, baseball and softball; and with Mediacom for Springfield Lasers tennis, high school football and basketball in the Springfield area, and Drury baseball and softball (Mediacom is a cable television and communication provider with offices in Springfield).

He has been in the broadcasting business for 34 years, but he did not take the typical road to the broadcast booth. Rather, after graduating from the University of Arkansas with a degree in accounting, he began working at Mercantile Bank in his hometown of Monett. But one year into his career at the bank, he was asked to provide color commentary for Monett Cubs games. After five years at the bank, Mike joined Monett Communications—KKBL and KRMO—where he remained until 2003 before starting McClure Communications.

Mike was inducted into the Missouri Basketball Coaches Association Hall of Fame in April 2017. He and his wife, Angie, married in 1988 and still reside in Monett.

BANKING IN

Mike got started in broadcasting almost as a favor to a friend. He was working at the bank, was asked to provide color, and realized this was what he wanted to do when the station called.

"I probably realized this is what I wanted to do when they made the offer. It wasn't a great salary, but I thought this is something I can probably do for a living. Up until then it had never even crossed my mind. I was happy doing the banking thing and then doing some sports and it just evolved. Sometimes it just finds you."

And if he weren't in sports broadcasting?

Photo courtesy of Mike McClure

On November 26, 2016, on a foggy day at Plaster Field in Springfield, Mike got to call Monett High School's 27-18 win over previously unbeaten Maryville. Monett has won three state football titles, and Mike McClure has been at all three, two as a child (in 1971 and 1977) and in 2016 while broadcasting for his alma mater.

"I'd probably be a CPA because that is what my college degree was for."

McCLURE BROADCASTING

For some, "making it" is an elusive goal. Can anyone really say when they have actually made it to the top of their game? Mike, though, had a pretty concrete idea that this was working out when he decided to start McClure Broadcasting. Of course, that decision did not come without some trepidation.

"You pray about it, you jump into it and you hope you're doing the right thing. It's been beyond my wildest dreams as far as a success. Even when I was at the station, I would think 'Yeah, I'm doing it, but will I ever be able to move on or will I be doing high school for the rest of my life?' There is nothing wrong with that, but I always wanted to do the college thing and I think whenever Mediacom hired me to start doing college sports was when it kind of clicked that maybe the hard work is finally paying off."

The founder and owner of McClure Broadcasting, Mike McClure has called more than 3,400 games for ESPN+, ESPN3, Monet Communications, Mediacom and Fox Sports Radio.

That is when he started to get the itch to develop his own broadcasting business. And having worked in both business and radio, Mike had the perfect blend of experience.

"I think you have to have the radio station and sales background to understand how it all works. I was really fortunate that I was the sports director from '89 through '03, and from '99 to '03 I was also the sales manager. I was in charge anyway of getting advertisers for the games, but now I had extra incentive to make sure it is done right."

When Mike left Monett Communications in 2003 and began freelance work, he had some time to think about his next move, to carefully develop his business plan before launching McClure Broadcasting. That has made him really appreciate the advertisers that helped the venture succeed.

"I've done 3,400 games, and every one of them has had broadcast sponsors. Those are the people that have a special place in my heart. I am nothing without those people. Those people pay good money to advertise their business, and I cannot thank every place of business I've ever solicited business from. Those are the people I will never be able to thank enough.

Finally, in 2009, it was time to launch.

"I knew how to do it. I knew how to sell it and I knew how to do the play-by-play. I just needed some technology help to do it. And I waited for the technology to get a little better, to figure out what streaming companies are good to do high school sports. You know, you want the ones that sound clear but are affordable. I talked to my friends who were still in radio and asked what equipment they were using and if I could still use it for an internet broadcast because at the time nobody was really doing it.

"I still had my foot in the door with Mediacom and some freelance work, and again I was still waiting for the technology to catch up. But as far as getting back into it full time, it just came when I had done my homework on streaming and I decided I could make a go of it."

IF HE HAD TO CHOOSE ...

Mike has had the unique opportunity to call high school, small college and major college sporting events. He has also had the chance at some professional work, thanks to the Springfield Lazers tennis team. He's worked in radio, television, and online. So you'll excuse him if he can't limit his favorite game to just one. But if he had to choose ...

"Probably the first time I got to do my alma mater, when I did a Missouri State-Arkansas baseball game. That would have been around '04 with Mediacom. High school literally has happened within the last year: when Monett won the state football championship in Springfield in November 2016 and Monett softball winning the state championship in October 2017.

"I had to leave the softball game; I got to do an inning and a half and then had to go to Joplin because there was a Missouri Southern football game at 3 o'clock on a Saturday, so Don West and Dave Beckett finished up the softball game for me. I suppose if I had said something that Missouri Southern would have been fine; they would have said, 'Yeah we can have you covered till you get there,' but I just didn't make an issue of it because I knew I had great backups.

"I need to mention the Missouri Southern football team winning at Number 6 Pittsburg State, 35-21, on November 16, 2013. It was the final game of the regular season and the loss knocked Pitt State out of the D-II playoffs. It was the first win by Missouri Southern over Pitt State in football since 1993 and the first win by MSSU at Pitt State since 1983. It was also my first season covering MSSU on the radio.

"March 9, 2014 MSSU beat Central Oklahoma 84-72 to win the MIAA Postseason Tournament at Municipal Auditorium in Kansas City. It was MSSU Head Coach Robert Corn's 25th and final season at MSSU and still part of my first season covering MSSU on the radio.

"Fifteen days before MSSU upset Pitt State in football, the MSSU men's basketball team played an exhibition game in Fayetteville, Arkansas. The Razorbacks beat the Lions 99-82 on November 1, 2013, but what a thrill it was for me to broadcast a basketball game at Bud Walton Arena since I graduated from the University of Arkansas. Two days later I was back at Bud Walton Arena as the MSSU women also played Arkansas and lost. Again, this was all part of a magical first season of broadcasting MSSU football and basketball games on the radio."

Sometimes it's not the game itself that is memorable. Mike shared a heartwarming story that could serve as a reminder to all who get into the broadcast business why it is they do what they do.

"I had a mom come up to be during a high school game, and she tapped me on the shoulder, and I'm going to change the name, but she said, 'Hi I'm Susan's mom, and I just wanted you to know that her step dad will be listening tonight.' This was on McClure Broadcasting, on the internet. I said, 'Oh, is he working?' She said, 'Yeah. He's in Afghanistan.' I mean my jaw just dropped. So she gave me his name, we did the starting lineups that night, mentioned Susan, and I said, 'A special shout-out to Susan's stepfather (mentioned his name), who is serving our country in Afghanistan. Sir, thank you for your service to our country, and we hope you and all your people get back soon.' Almost a year to the day I got a tap on the shoulder, turn around and I see a guy I've never seen in my life, and all he said was, 'Hi, I'm Susan's step dad.' I'm not kidding you, the hair stood up on the back of my neck. 'He just said, 'Thank you for the shout out during the ballgame. You didn't have to do that.' And I just said, 'Sir, if for two hours I took your mind off what you were doing over there, then I did my job.' You never know who's listening or who's watching and the impact you'll have.

SHUT UP AND LISTEN

One of the unique challenges for any broadcaster is knowing when not to speak. That can be especially difficult when a key moment happens. Mike said he had just such a moment, and that non-call may be his favorite all-time moment.

"I did the last out of Missouri State's baseball game when they clinched the Missouri Valley Conference championship. We were doing that on ESPN3 and I just let the moment speak for itself. The best part is shutting up and letting the crowd roar. It's hard because you want to be excitable, but at the same time you just have to go, 'Swing and a miss, strike three, and Missouri State—for the fifth time in school history—has won the Missouri Valley Conference baseball regular season title'. The Missouri Valley Conference used that clip and put it up on their website. That's pretty cool to see.

"Another one, I apologize but I don't remember the player's name; you do 3,400 games sometimes you forget. Missouri State was playing Mizzou and we were doing the game on ESPN3. The Missouri State right fielder made a diving catch, just sprinting toward centerfield and that was the number-one play on SportsCenter's Top 10. Now, they covered up my audio, but I knew it was there. You could barely hear it because their anchor was talking over that, but I mean that was kind of a unique thrill for a kid from Monett."

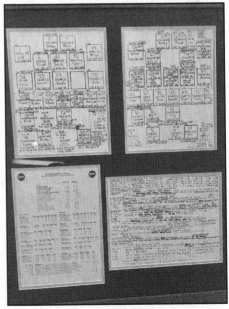

LET THE MOMENT BE THE MOMENT

Speaking of the moment, in all those 3,400-plus broadcasts, there must have been some key moments when Mike wanted to get just the right wording. Does he prepare for those calls beforehand?

"You do. Sometimes it plays out like you anticipated it will and sometimes it doesn't. I'm not one of these guys who comes up with catchphrases. I just kind of let the moment be the moment. In March of 2003, boy's basketball state championship, Verona (32-0) beat North Shelby 65-47 in Columbia.

Mike shared his spotting boards from the 2016 Missouri State Championship game with me. Most play-by-play announcers use a similar approach in creating their boards.

119

Verona's entire senior class that year was made up of 18 students. One of those seniors was JJ Tauai (pronounced TWY). JJ went on to play at Bradley University. His older brothers all played on great Verona basketball teams, but they never could quite get the job done and win a state championship game. So at the end of the North Shelby game, as we knew Verona was going to win, I said, 'If at first you don't succeed, Tauai, Tauai gain.'

When Monett softball won the state title, that call would have been 'The queen of diamonds in Class 3.' But again, I just kind of let the moment be the moment and try not to botch it. That can happen when you're trying to make it more about you than what the moment is for those kids."

THE HAY IS IN THE BARN

Play-by-play can be a seven-day a week job, or at least six days. While the fan sees or hears the broadcast, it is the research, analysis and memorization during the week that makes the games flow for the sportscaster. Fortunately for Mike, the grind is still fun.

"Game day is the easy part. It's those four or five days before the game. After 33 years of doing this, the prep work ... it's just like coaches, you know? It's like watching film; it just it never stops. I'm sitting here on a Monday and the kitchen table is covered with prep work for Missouri Southern-Pitt State football. Friday will be our first Missouri Southern women's basketball broadcast. That's also on the table. And our first Missouri Southern men's basketball broadcast will be that same night, Saturday, after the football game. Fortunately they're both playing at Pitt State, so that's also on the table.

> *"This is year 33 for me, and it has never seemed like a job to me. Ever. Does the prep work get longer? Yeah. But, boy, on game day, that's as good as it gets."*
> ~ Mike McClure

"I still do everything by hand. I just retain it better. I know a lot of the younger announcers type up their spotting boards or their basketball score sheets or baseball scorebooks; it's all done on the computer. But I just retained it better when it's me writing it down. There's not a right way or a wrong way. If you've got a hundred broadcasters in front of you, you find a hundred different ways that we all do games.

"Literally, for the next five days, that's what I'll be doing is prep work. But game day, that's the easy part. That's when, again, it's kind of like coaching. The prep work is done. On game day, you take your team to the field and you go play. I'll go take the equipment to the broadcast booth and I broadcast. There's always stuff to check on—name pronunciations to double check on, last minute injuries, try to talk to the coaches a little more in detail when you can, get a little more information about the teams. But by game days the work is done."

A NEW DAY IN COMMUNICATION

No hesitation when I asked Mike how sportscasting has changed since he began: Social media, the internet and email.

"I can still remember going to the schools and getting numerical rosters when I started in January 1985. For football in particular because of the 70-man rosters. Just trying to get that roster and getting starters, heights and weights, positions—all that stuff. We didn't have the internet or email back in the '80s; you just had to go to the schools or they stuck it in the mail to you. You would call them all and say, 'I'll be covering your game in week six or week 10 or whatever' and they put a roster in the mail. Or they may have faxed it. But we didn't have the social media or the internet back when I started."

HARD TO PICK JUST ONE

While all sportscasters have a style of their own, they no doubt are going to have their favorites. Or perhaps two. Or three. Or ... well, Mike had a hard time naming just one.

"Vin Scully is the absolute best. Obviously growing up it was Jack Buck and Denny Matthews. I still have a lot of respect for the way Mike Kelly and Art Hains do it at the college level. In the early 1990s I went to Manhattan, Kansas because Mitch Holthus was putting on a sportscaster academy, and I was two years into my full-time position, and got named the best sportscaster at Mitch's play-by-play school. We've always kept in touch since then. He's been a mentor, Art's been a mentor. But man, listening to Vin Scully was magic. Just magic. I would have loved to have listened to Ernie Harwell with Detroit because he's of that same era."

In his 30-plus years as a sportscaster, Mike has seen and heard hundreds of play-by-play announcers. I asked him what is it, in his mind, that makes them stand out.

"Their pace, their delivery, their storytelling, but they still let you know what's the score, who's ahead, and where we are in the game. There are great storytellers out there, but one of my biggest pet peeves is turning on a radio broadcast and for five minutes or 10 minutes or longer, they never tell you the score, or who's ahead or how much time is left. As a listener and as a sports fan, that drives me crazy.

"Mitch Holthus ingrained that in me. He said you set up every play. Missouri Southern 10, Pittsburg State 7. Seven minutes to go in the second quarter. Pittsburg State has the football, first and 10 at their own 27-yard line. John Roderique is the quarterback. I mean every play. Now, you're not going to do it just like that every time because of the flow of the game, but you constantly tell me what the score is and where you're at in the game because people are tuning in all the time during the game, especially with social media. They've got the phone on, they're in their house or driving in their car, and they want to know what the score is, so tell them."

AH, TEMPERATURE CONTROL!

When I asked all the sportscasters what is their favorite sport to call, I expected to get their response and then learn it is because it is the game with which they are most familiar or it is one they played or it is because of the pace. Mike had a more practical reason for naming is favorite.

"Basketball (again, no hesitation). It's 72 degrees, indoors, no wind, no rain, and I know how to dress every game."

I couldn't help but grin at that, and I assumed I would know the answer to my next question which was, What would be your least favorite sport? I was not surprised when Mike didn't actually have a "least" favorite sport. But it was interesting to hear about the challenges faced in others.

121

"It's not the least favorite, but it's the hardest for me to broadcast and it's football because everything is so far away and you have 22 players and you're trying to get jersey numbers. Let's face it, at my level you don't necessarily have spotters every game, and I don't want to rely on the PA announcer to have to tell me who made the tackle. It's just football is the hardest just because of the logistics and where you are up in some of the broadcast levels. Volleyball is hard to broadcast and soccer is hard to broadcast. They're not my least favorites, but they are difficult because of the pace. That doesn't mean I don't enjoy it because I do.

"Typically, when people ask me what is my favorite sport I just say whatever is in season. Basketball is my favorite because that's what I've done more than any other sport, and the flow of the game is conducive to having a good broadcast—when the officials don't interrupt it every 30 seconds with a whistle (said with a grin)."

THE DREAM: CALLING THE MASTER'S

Mike had the most unique answer of anybody in the book when I asked about a dream event to call. When he responded I was a bit surprised I hadn't heard it before.

"The one event that I hold dear to my heart is the Master's, so yeah, put me on the 18th tower. Jim Nance has got the best job in the country. He does the NCAA Final Four, hops on a plane and goes to Augusta, Georgia for the week. I've been really blessed. I've made five trips to Augusta to see the Master's. TV doesn't do that place justice. It is absolutely the most beautiful place on Earth. I've never gotten to call golf. I've played it; my senior year we were state runner-up, but never got to call it."

HIGH SCHOOL VS. COLLEGE VS. PROS

Mike owns his own internet broadcasting business and does a lot of high school games. He is the Voice of the Missouri Southern Lions. He covers Missouri State sporting events on television and he assists on telecasts for the Springfield Lasers professional tennis team. I asked him which he prefers and if he ever had a desire to go full-time in professional sports.

"If God wants me to go pro, it'll happen. I've been blessed beyond my wildest dreams to be where I am. I guess I prefer college because of the higher level of play (compared to high school), and the information is more accessible because of the internet to be able to look up player bios, stats, or whatever you need to do a really good broadcast. As you know, we're a 'we need it yesterday' society; we can't wait for information. We need it right away."

SPENDING TIME WITH MRS. McCLURE

Like any smart spouse, Mike is quick to give credit to his wife, Angie, for his success and to devote as much time to her as possible when he is not broadcasting.

"We'll go to concerts, go visit different places when we have the time. I've been married almost 30 years, never had children, so besides my family she is my life, and she has been unbelievably supportive through all of this. It's worked. It's not her cup of tea, and that's okay. I've never forced my love of sports on her. Obviously my schedule, from August through May, there's not a whole lot of time but when we do have time, we like to go to concerts and go to movies and just be a married couple.

Mike and his long-time broadcast partner, Dave Beckett, wait out a weather delay in the Monett at California football game on August 18, 2017. After two lighting delays, the game finally ended at 12:15 a.m., proving anything can happen in sports.

IT'S NOT ABOUT "US"

One thing I know about Mike is that while he considers the broadcaster a part of the team, he does not believe the broadcaster has an impact on the game. As a result, he is not a fan of interjecting himself into the event.

"I think a homer is someone who constantly uses 'we' or 'us' and I'm sorry, you're not out there involved in the game. That's one of my pet peeves is when the broadcasters do that. I mean people listening know who you're covering. You don't need to be saying 'we' did this. Yeah, people know when I'm covering Monett or when I'm covering Missouri Southern, but when the other team makes a great play I'm still going to talk about that. I'm going to say something positive about it, whether it is somebody from Pittsburg State or somebody from Mount Vernon that made a great play because it's part of the broadcast. I'm not going to downgrade what they did just because they were from the opposite team. You lose credibility that way. I want to be credible. People know that I'm covering both teams. That's the old-school in me."

BROADCASTER FIRST, TEACHER SECOND

One of the things I've always admired about Mike is his humility. He is not shy in pointing out that he had a lot of help along the way to achieving a successful broadcasting career. He is, therefore, keen to give back and he expects others to do so as well.

"I hope other professional broadcasters mentor because we all got mentored by somebody, so yeah pay it forward and pass it on. I'll have high school kids and younger that will come sit in with me and ask questions and watch, and usually by the end of the night their jaws are dropped. They don't realize there was that much work involved. They don't realize the hours of prep. We all have an interest in something, and if their passion happens to be sportscasting or broadcasting, then yeah I'm going to do everything I can to help them. If they're willing to work at it to get good at their craft, it's good for our profession."

One of my jobs is to supervise our interns as they go into the field to gain hands-on experience. I could not, therefore, miss the opportunity to pick Mike's brain. Does he take in interns or provide feedback on demo reels? Does he hire people part-time?

"I do hear tapes, and honestly everybody that's still with me, they're not my employee but rather they are independent contractors. They've all worked college. My two Mount Vernon football guys are John Miller and Ray Meyer; they both do Drury University basketball. I have Don West, who is the lead play-by-play voice for Missouri State football, basketball and baseball with Mediacom, ESPN+ and ESPN3. Dave Beckett has worked the NAIA Division II National Basketball Championships at College of the Ozarks. Perry Phillips has worked the NAIA Division II National Basketball Championships at College of the Ozarks. Corey Riggs is currently doing not only play-by-play but also producing of college sporting events. So everyone I've had who has worked for me, they've all worked college because I'm really picky about who gets on McClure Broadcasting. All it takes is one bad broadcaster to totally spoil what I've tried to do for 33 years."

I pressed further and asked what Mike expects from prospective employees when they come up.

"I expect them to be professional. I expect them to not criticize the officials or the opponents. I expect them to do their homework, and I expect them to give the score and the time and where we are in the game. I do not want to have to wait. And don't make it about them; it's about those kids on the field."

Sensing an opportunity for my students, I finally dropped the last question in this line: How do they get on with McClure Broadcasting?

"They have to prove to me they're worthy. Again, by me going back and listening to tapes. Fortunately, with all these people I've told you about, I've been able to listen to their tapes at work in colleges. I've had a couple send me some stuff who don't have the college experience, and I just kind of politely tell them it's not necessarily that you need the college experience, but you need more work at the high school level doing games, whether it's make-believe games that you recorded for the American Legion in the summertime or whatever. If you go work at it and bring me a tape and let me listen to it again, here's what you need to work on. If I see that you've worked on it, I'll find a spot for you."

SEEING VS. HEARING
Mike McClure is one of the rare broadcasters who has the opportunity to provide play-by-play on radio and television. Naturally, I wanted to know which he prefers and why. His answer surprised me a bit.

"Television. You talk 50 percent less and let the pictures do the describing. You still have the informational nuggets, but you don't have to set everything up as you do in radio. In radio you set everything up. In TV it kind of sets itself up, and even though you still describe the score and the inning, it's pretty much on the screen the entire broadcast. So you still mention it, but not as much. You just have more time to tell the informational nuggets and to tell stories, again depending on the sport. Baseball is conducive to storytelling. Basketball, maybe not so much. Football, you have a little bit more time.

"The old-fashioned part of me says radio because that's what I grew up on, but I really like all the work that goes into the TV side. I appreciate all the camera people and the technical people, the audio people. They do all the grunt work; the announcers just kind of show up at the game, put the headset on and do their thing and then walk out and don't have to tear down. It's really grown on me. I didn't think I would, but I've really enjoyed it, and I've worked with some really talented producers. I've been with ESPN3 and ESPN+ for three years and with Mediacom since the late 1990s. Again really, really talented people. The Mediacom people, they'll go to Arkansas to work an SEC game or a CBS game or go to Kauffman Stadium to work a baseball game or Arrowhead to work a football game. These guys are so good at what they do."

While they are obviously different, I did want to know which Mike finds more difficult—radio or television.

"I guess radio is more difficult just because you're having to talk more and describe it more. But that's okay because when I was younger, just getting started in this business, a broadcaster told me, 'Pretend you're speaking to an audience of one person, and that person is blind. And I want you to be as descriptive as you can to this blind person that can't see. I want to hear about the green grass or the blue jerseys with the gold pants or the white helmets or describe the uniforms or just be as descriptive as you can for this one blind person that is your audience.' And 33 years later, it's still stuck with me."

GIVING THANKS

Again, Mike is incredibly humble and grateful for the opportunity he has been given. So when I asked him for final thoughts, I was not at all surprised he took the opportunity to show his appreciation for those who have helped his business thrive.

"I want to thank all the advertisers and the people who buy ads, whether it is high school or college. I want people to know how appreciative I am of that and how appreciative I am of getting to do this for a living. I mean, holy cow! I get paid to go to ball games.

"Love what you do. When you love what you do it doesn't seem like a job, and I know you hear people say that all the time. But this is year 33 for me, and it has never seemed like a job to me. Ever. Does the prep work get longer? Yeah. Do the bus rides get longer? Yeah. But, boy, on game day, that's as good as it gets. That is not a job."

Photo courtesy of FOX Sports Midwest/David W. Preston

DAN McLAUGHLIN
FOX SPORTS MIDWEST
ST. LOUIS CARDINALS

When most people are 23, they are starting that entry level job just a year or two out of college. Not Dan McLaughlin. He was calling his first Major League Baseball game. Since 1999 fans who tune in to Fox Sports Midwest to watch the St. Louis Cardinals have had the joy of listening to Dan McLaughlin on the call. In that time, he has won a pair of Emmy awards for sportscasting and received the prestigious Burmese/Broeg Award from the Missouri Athletic Club for his contributions to the city of St. Louis through sports. He also covers Saint Louis University basketball for Fox Sports Midwest.

The St. Louis native got his start at St. John Vianney High School in Kirkwood before attending Lindenwood University on a baseball scholarship. While at Lindenwood, he also worked at the campus radio station, KCLC, and it was there that his drive and ambition were first noticed.

"I was taking a class through Lindenwood at KMOX," Dan explains, "and I got pulled out of class and the guy said, 'Hey I heard you do a lot of sports. You were recommended by the folks over at Lindenwood to potentially become an engineer to run the board for various shows and games.' So I was actually hired there."

After graduating from Lindenwood in 1996 with a degree in mass communication (emphasis in radio and television) and a minor in psychology, Dan began his speedy climb to one of the most coveted broadcast booths in all of professional sports. Along the way he has done about everything a sportscaster could imagine. He provided play-by-play for the NFL on Fox in 2006. He has also covered college postseason baseball for ESPN and Fox Saturday Baseball and been studio host for St. Louis Blues hockey on both radio and television broadcasts. He has called college football for ESPN and FOX College Sports and for a decade Dan served as the television play-by-play voice for the University of Missouri men's basketball team, as well as ESPN's basketball coverage of the Big East, ACC, Big 12, and Missouri Valley Conference Game of the week.

He and his wife, Libby, are involved in several St. Louis-area charities, including the Dan McLaughlin Golf Tournament to benefit special education. They also stay busy with their four kids: son Luke, daughter Avery, and twins Olivia and Barrett.

IT STARTED WITH A PLASTIC BAT AND BALL

Being a baseball announcer was almost a foregone conclusion for Dan McLaughlin. He loved the game and he grew up in St. Louis. He says as a small boy in the yard he was already practicing for the booth.

"It probably started when I was playing wiffle ball at the age of 3 or 4 in my backyard in south St. Louis. I always wanted to do this. The kids in the neighborhood, and especially myself and my brother, we always played wiffle ball in the back and I would always announce. I loved playing sports. That's what got me to college and through college was a scholarship to play baseball at Lindenwood. I've known I wanted to do this all along."

From those early beginnings to sitting in one of the most coveted seats in all of sportscasting. Surely Dan believes he has made it, right?

"I don't know. Everybody's parameters on making it are different. I treat every day as though I never had the job before and I just continue to keep going. I never really ever say I've made it. I've done some neat things, I did some things I never thought I'd have a chance to do, but I never said, 'Hey, I've made it now'. I'll never do that."

Fair enough. Besides, to Dan it is not awards or accolades that determine how successful a broadcaster is. It is time and an ability to relate to the audience, whether that is through baseball or through life in general.

"Longevity. A connection to a fan base where they feel like you're family. Being well-rounded so when things happen in the world and you're in the middle of a game— which I've had happen multiple times—you can address it so you're not just focused solely on what I guy does on a 3-2 pitch. Studying backgrounds. Reading. All of those things are enormous, I think, in trying to do the job that we do."

MATT HOLLIDAY'S FINAL AT-BAT

St. Louis fans have been called the best in baseball because of their knowledge of the game and for their loyalty. Dan is first and foremost a Cardinals fan, so when a beloved member of the team is wrapping up his time in the Gateway City, it stands out.

"I think my favorite call was when Matt Holliday a few years ago was a free agent-to-be, and he had been injured. We're going into the final weekend of the regular season, and I knew the Cardinals wanted to give him the right send off in front of the fans. He came up to pinch hit and it was like storybook: He hit a home run.

"I got the chance to know Matt a little bit on a personal level, and he is a tremendous guy. To see him go out in what we thought was his final at bat in St. Louis—consequently he had another at-bat—but we thought that was his last one. He was battling back tears in his eyes, he knew that this is probably going to be it, and he hits a home run. It was just an amazing moment. That's something in this job that you get. You develop those personal relationships with people and you pull for certain guys, and he's one of them. To get to see that was really cool."

OFF SCRIPT

While he is covering the team once covered by Jack Buck, and while he surely has studied the legendary broadcaster, Dan says he has not prepared for a call the way Buck did when thinking about Mark McGwire's home run record.

"Never. I never script anything. I just go off the emotion of the moment. I always equate myself as being a fan in the booth. I'm doing my hometown team, and I do try to be fair on both sides, good or bad, but we're going to a hometown audience, so you're obviously going to favor the Cardinals a little bit, so I do it off the emotion of the moment and that's how I make the calls."

Photo courtesy of FOX Sports Midwest/David W. Preston

Dan views it as his job to set up color analysts like former St. Louis Cardinals All-Star Jim Edmonds so the analyst can provide fans with the stories within the games.

Okay, let's imagine he could write out his ideal scenario: What would be Dan's dream event to call? What would cap his broadcasting career?

"I would love to call game seven of a World Series. I've never had a chance to do a postseason game. But that would be my dream. To do postseason or a World Series game. Once the regular season ends, we're done because the networks take over then. It'd be pretty cool to get to do that."

PHONING IN

Dan agreed with many of the subjects I interviewed that social media and the internet have made a difference in sportscasting. But he points to the cell phone as the greatest advancement.

"It's changed a lot. The fact that when I travel I have a cell phone now, that's kinda cool. For the longest time, even late '90s, early 2000s, just trying to get on the internet in a hotel room was difficult. Just simple things that you think about now that you take for granted. That was the biggest. I remember traveling and I had a card that allowed me to make calls that was prepaid because we didn't have cell phones. Those were things that really changed to make the travel a little better. The fact that there's access to stories and things now that you can research and search that you just didn't have back then.

Dan McLaughlin was enrolled at Lindenwood University when he was recognized for his efforts and was hired at KMOX.

That begs the obvious question for those of us who are trying to find a way to unplug: Does it make it difficult to get away?

"No, I think the more information you can get the better, the more we can educate ourselves—the fans included—maybe the background of a player or trying to figure out sabermetrics and terms like WAR and WHIP and things like that, the more that you can do research as a fan, the better. So no, it doesn't make me feel like I can't get away from it. I live and breath baseball 24/7, 365 days a year, so whether that was around or not, I'd probably be doing the same thing I'm doing now."

CONTINUING THE ST. LOUIS LEGACY

Listening to and cutting his teeth as a young sportscaster at KMOX, Dan McLaughlin grew up in the hotbed of some broadcasting icons. Not surprisingly he has a list of favorites.

"Growing up here, Jack Buck would certainly be on that list. I grew up listening to Jack Buck. I grew up listening to Dan Kelly, long-time hockey announcer here in town. Ken Wilson was a long-time Blues announcer who I enjoyed listening to. Mike Kelly on basketball for Mizzou. I used to love listening to him. Still do. Randy Karraker, who is a sports talk show host here in town, I used to produce shows for him and eventually made it on the air with him at KMOX. All those guys were great listens and great background for what I tried to do and what I try to emulate in many ways."

The St. Louis Cardinals are one of the premier teams in all of professional sports in America, so I asked Dan, as play-by-play announcer, if that brought with it a certain extended level of responsibility?

"No, I would like to think if I were doing any other team I'd do it with the same preparation, care, emotion because I think you owe it to the fan base you work for to give them the best that you have. The one thing I think we've gotten away from in our industry is that this is entertainment. It's not life or death, this is entertainment. This is meant to be fun. This is meant for some guy or girl to come home, flop on the sofa, open a cold one, and get away from everyday life and enjoy a baseball game.

"It resonates with me that I'm doing the Cardinals, but it doesn't add any pressure. The Cardinals are a historic franchise and brand, and to do your hometown team is a big deal, but I don't think it adds any extra pressure because I put a lot of pressure on myself for any team I was doing or any broadcast I was doing that I'm giving them everything I've got in those games."

CALLING THE HOMETOWN TEAM

That was a nice segue to my next question: What is a homer, and is that appropriate?

"I think it's okay to be one. I personally try not to be that way, but I will say this: I work for the Cardinals, I'm going to Cardinal fans, so when I'm doing a game the emphasis of my broadcast is to be fair on both sides and show the color of both sides of the players—you know the background, who's doing well, who's not—and point out when they're not doing well and to be honest on bad plays. But I always do the broadcast with an emphasis towards the Cardinals' fans, so if I'm doing the game you're going to hear a lot more about the Cardinals than you are the opposition. You're going to hear about the opposition, but you're going to hear more about the Cardinals, so that's not necessarily being a homer. It's just I'm tailoring the broadcast to the people who are tuned in and that is Cardinals' fans, by and large. That's why I feel it's more important to tailor to the Cardinals' fan. Not necessarily say every call against the Cardinals is bad and these guys are all great. I don't do all that. I just do the game. I'm honest during the game, but there's going to be more of an emphasis on Cardinal baseball than there is the opposition."

Dan mentioned being honest. Knowing broadcasters who have been called out and even fired, I wanted to know if he had ever been accused of being too negative on the Cardinals when things were not going well.

"I think most players, because I show my face non-stop and if I say something the night before that may not be real complimentary of a play that might be construed as negative, you know we can talk about the next day. I think every broadcaster has gone through that where it's like, 'Man you were a little negative on this' and I'll respond, 'Well, I'll tell you why I said what I said.' But if players hustle, I don't rip them because we're human beings, and everybody makes mistakes. The mental errors are a little rough not to point out, but my broadcasts will never be negative in terms of harping on the poor aspects of a player or a game. I just don't do that. I don't think the people want to hear that stuff. I think if somebody makes a mistake, you point it out, you talk about it, and you move on."

GRINDING IT OUT FOR THE HOMETOWN TEAM

As the play-by-play announcer for the Cardinals, Dan undoubtedly puts a lot of heart and soul into the organization. And he covers a team that plays 162 games in 187 days. That made me ask how he maintains his enthusiasm and energy.

"I go into every game and right before the first pitch I kind of look out—especially when we're at home—and I see all these fans and I think, 'Man, I am really lucky to do what I do. This is a dream job. You're in your dream job, so go for it.' And so, I don't ever let fatigue come into the broadcast.

"I always say, look, no matter how tired I am—and there are times you do get really tired, especially if you got home late the night before and there's a day game—fans don't care about that, nor should they. I don't ever let me being tired affect how I do a game because I owe it to the fan base to give them the best I got. So if I can't figure out how to do it and be the best I can be for three hours, then shame on me. I shouldn't be in that seat."

Photo courtesy of FOX Sports Midwest/David W. Preston

Calling the action for his hometown Cardinals is a dream come true for Dan McLaughlin. Getting to share the booth with former Redbirds like Rick Horton is an added bonus.

DADDY'S HOME

In visiting with Dan McLaughlin, I was struck that, here is a man who is a master at compartmentalizing. When he is at the ballpark, he blocks everything out, focuses on the task at hand and calls the game. But once he leaves the park, he is in full-on daddy mode.

"I have four little kids, so taking care of them is the number one priority. My escape is that I become the daddy driver. I take my kids everywhere. We have practices, we have school, we have all kinds of stuff. I do a lot of that, as much as I can when I'm home."

When pursuing one of his other favorite pastimes, Dan places his attention there, too.

"I play a lot of golf. That gives me some escape, too, which I really enjoy. Just the three or four hours of playing golf. A lot of times I'm playing with guys that are involved with baseball, so we talk baseball anyway. I like to fish and hunt, so I'll fish and hunt a lot in the offseason to get away."

The fact, though, is that Dan really does not require much of a break.

"I really don't like getting away from it that much. I'm kinda different that way, and I understand why people would (want to get a break), but I really enjoy all the nuances of the game. I absolutely love baseball. I love the downtime of the offseason and what happens in free agency, I love learning what organizations are doing, and I enjoy just talking about the game and some of the things that are changing with the game. I think it's fascinating. I get away plenty. I shut my brain off with it, but I really enjoy it. I just find the whole thing fascinating."

CHEMISTRY IS SPELLED R-E-S-P-E-C-T
Turns out Aretha Franklin was on to something. In order for any relationship to work, those involved must trust one another. According to Dan, that includes sportscasters.

"I think you develop chemistry by having a mutual respect, number one, for each other. You may not always agree, especially in baseball, with what the other one is saying, but you can talk about it. You say, 'Yeah, I get what you're saying, but how about this way or that way.' And having a respect for one another where you don't talk down to each other is important.

"It also develops by going to play golf together or having dinner together or just hanging out. You're on planes and busses all the time and you're chit-chatting about life and about the game and what's happening, and that always develops chemistry, too.

"We probably spend more time with each other than we do with our own families for about seven months. We're with each other non-stop, we go through the ups and downs with each other on a personal-life side of things, we see what's happening with each other. So that's chemistry, and my feeling has always been I want to take care of my partner. I look at it as, if we are a team and we are truly a team doing the best we can for each other and helping each other out, then the broadcast is better. So I've always tried to be a guy who has taken care of my analyst, of setting up my analyst. I can probably tell you 99 percent of the time what they are going to say, but to give a good broadcast, I always set them up. The role of the play-by-play guy is of course to call the game, but also to tee up your analyst because he's really the star of what is going on, so put it on a tee and let him knock it out of the park."

> "No matter how tired you are—and there are times you do get really tired—fans don't care about that, nor should they."
> ~ Dan McLaughlin

I decided to press Dan a bit and asked if he felt comfortable naming an analyst he really enjoyed working with.

"I've worked with so many guys. I'm probably in the hundreds of guys that I've worked with. There's not one that I'd say is above another with chemistry because I've always gotten along with all of them. Whether it be the guys I've worked with in baseball or the guys I did stuff with in football—first time only, one time only, some guys I've worked with a hundred times. I've always gotten along with them because I try to just tee them up. I'm not trying to upstage anybody. I don't go in there with an ego, ever. I just go in with 'Hey, let's do the best broadcast we can because if we're good as a team they're going to like us, and so there's always been good chemistry with just about everybody I worked with."

VERSATILITY IS KEY

I tell my students who want to be on-air talent that they also need to learn to direct, run a camera, set up the gear. From now on when they doubt me, I am going to have them read the advice Dan had for them.

"You have to be well versed. Just because you want to be an announcer doesn't necessarily mean that's how it's going to turn out. I've seen so many guys who started out in front of the camera and then wound up being behind the camera, and vice versa. You have to be able to roll. It's an industry that's constantly changing because of the technology, and you have to keep up on it, so learn to edit both radio and TV.

"Get involved as much as you can with any kind of internships, write informational letters, pick up the phone and start immediately when you start your college career or you're going to get left behind. And any opportunity that you have to call a game—and I don't care what it is, I don't care if you're going to call cards—do it. That's how I did it. I was sleeping in my car to go call football games, just to get experience. And then the next day getting up and doing a wrap-up show for free. And I did that non-stop. I did those kinds of things just to get on the air.

"What got me noticed at KMOX was I was setting up a remote for Ken Wilson and Joe Micheletti at Scott Trade Center for a Blues game, and there was a protest going on at city hall. I always carried a recorder, and I went and covered the protest and sent it down the line and gave them the lead story in the news. And they were like, 'Well, who is this guy? Who is this producer guy?' That's how I got noticed. I made it on the air when I was 20 years old doing sportscasts on weekends. And that doesn't happen unless I was aggressive and trying to cover those things. My advice is get as involved as you can and just get experience."

Photo courtesy of Jacob Woerther

GREG SCHMIDT
KMMO - 1300 AM and 102.9 FM
GAME OF THE WEEK

Just off of I-70 sits the small town of Concordia, Missouri, population a little over 2,600. And tucked away in the newest neighborhood in Concordia lives a man whose name has become synonymous with high school sports in Midwest Missouri. I had the opportunity to sit down at the kitchen table with Greg Schmidt, his wife Ruth and the family cat sitting nearby in the living room, as he began to tell me his stories of more than 45 years in the sports broadcasting industry.

He has been the voice of more than 4,900 sportscasts, just under twice as many games as there are people in all of Concordia. In his more than four decades on the air, Greg Schmidt has covered all of the schools in the I-70 Conference, I found Greg to be energetic, excitable, eager to tell his stories and share his experiences. He's been called descriptive yet concise, an artist who paints amazing word pictures. The walls are full of photos, souvenirs and knick-knacks, a testament to his farming background as a youth. His office is lined with photographs and mementos from the many schools he has covered.

He began his career as a newspaper man while a prepster at Santa Fe High School. There he wrote for the Santa Fe newspaper from 1970-74. After graduating, he attended CMSU (now the University of Central Missouri) where he majored in mass communication and worked for the campus radio station, KCMW, from 1974-76. In 1976 he went to KMMO in Marshall and from 1976-84 he worked for KLEX in Lexington. After two more years at KMMO, he went back into the newspaper business with The Concordian (1986-91) and the Higginsville Advance (1991-93). From 1993-96 he served in the private sector, and then from 1996-2005 he worked for the Carrollton Democrat before returning to the Higginsville Advance from 2005-08. He has worked steadily as a play-by-play announcer for KMMO since 1986. The Alma, Missouri native has covered 26 total high schools along the I-70 Conference. He also covered Missouri Valley College football for 23 years and Central Missouri State University athletics for two years while in college.

Greg has provided MSHSAA Show-Me Bowl Football championship broadcasts for 15 different teams and Show-Me Showdown basketball championship games for 38 different schools. Throw in state baseball championships for 19 teams and state volleyball broadcasts for seven schools, and you start to get an idea just how accomplished he is. Of all the awards he has won (and there have been many), Greg says he is most proud of the MSHSAA Distinguished Service Award, which usually goes to coaches and administrators. While Greg and Ruth have never had children, they say they've adopted all the kids Greg has covered.

THE CALLS THAT ALMOST WEREN'T

Greg's streak of calling games was almost cut short in 2006, but thanks to a quick-thinking school administrator and a new medical device, Greg was able to tell the tale.

"I had sudden cardiac arrest May 15, 2006. I was not broadcasting at the time, but I was writing for the newspaper in Higginsville, Missouri, and I had sudden cardiac arrest in the middle of the Higginsville—St. Paul playoff game at Barstow High School. I fell over and they did the defibrillator thing on me. They had just gotten a defibrillator (at Barstow) as a gift from a doctor about a month before. And just the week before the staff had been given instructions.

> For much of his career, Greg Schmidt was both a newspaper sports writer and a play-by-play announcer for schools all along I-70.

"I guess I went into a coma because it happened about 6 o'clock on a Monday night. Next second it was 6 a.m. Wednesday morning; 36 hours later I woke. They didn't know if I was going to have any brain damage or anything. I woke up and the cardiologist said, 'You didn't miss much; the Royals lost two more games. 'They were really bad back then. I asked how many days it had been, and the cardiologist said, 'May 15th you went down.' I said, 'George Brett's birthday'. The cardiologist looked at Ruth and said, 'He's going to be fine.'"

"After the heart attack he was told he would never broadcast again," Ruth said. "But the Lord blessed him."

136

Photo courtesy of Kaleb Nierman, KN Photography

The man whose voice has become synonymous with high school sports along I-70 from Marshall to Higginsville almost had his career cut short by a medical emergency. But thanks to some new technology and quick-thinking school administrators, his legend lives on.

Greg fell so hard, face first, he had to have two vertebrae fused, but the doctors had to go in through the front, past his esophagus and vocal cords.

"I had to sign a waiver absolving the hospital of any fault if they clipped a vocal cord. I thought, 'Oh, that's nice!'

Today Greg and Ruth are huge proponents for defibrillators.

"If you Google or go to YouTube and search, 'Greg Schmidt, KOMU News,' they did a story on me and how the defibrillator saved my life. Doesn't really say much about me as a sportscaster, but they tell the story about how the principal at Barstow used the defibrillator.

"They put a pacemaker defibrillator in me, and I'm on certain types of medication, but I'm doing fine."

THOSE WHO CAN'T -- CALL

It was in high school that Greg Schmidt realized his future was going to be in the press box, not on the field or court.

"I discovered I wasn't good enough to play at the next level, so I figured, if I want to be involved in sports for a living, maybe I better find a different avenue. I wrote newspaper articles and sports stories in high school, but when you work at the local level you're writing for a weekly or a biweekly paper, and the game story comes out the Thursday after a Friday game was played. People want to see the game story. They want to see their names or their kids' names in print. They want to see how many yards Johnny gained or how many yards Billy passed for and stuff like that. But when you work for a weekly paper or a biweekly paper—two issues a week—you find out that it's old by the time you write

137

Greg has "lettered" for more than 20 schools. While I was visiting with Greg and Ruth, he was happy to share the plaque he received following his 4,000th broadcast in February 2013.

the story on a Saturday night or a Sunday night after a Friday game. It doesn't get printed until the following Thursday. It's old, so I didn't enjoy that aspect of it.

"I enjoyed being able to report on the here and now, and 40 years ago the here and now was radio. Forty years, I mean now we've got instantaneous online coverage over newspapers. We didn't have that 40 years ago. Forty years ago the here and now was radio being able to describe something as it happened."

ALL ABOUT THE GAME

It took a microsecond for Greg to think about what his career would be if he were not a sportscaster: "Sportswriter" practically springs from his mouth. After all, much of his career he doubled as a sportswriter for local newspapers while moonlighting as a play-by-play announcer. But a newer development in sportscasting also caught his interest.

"Looking back on it now, I don't know if these avenues were open 40 years ago, but if I had to do it all over again at Central Missouri State, I'd have liked to have probably gotten into some aspect of sports administration. By and large I see now at the schools like Central Missouri, Missouri Southern, maybe Northwest Missouri, some of those guys—if not a lot of those guys—are also employees of the college. When I was growing up, the guys at Warrensburg, the guys at Maryville, the guys at Cape Girardeau were all news directors and sports directors of their particular station. Bill Turnage was news and sports director at KOKO (in Warrensburg) at the time. Maryville had their news and sports guy, and he did the play-byplay. If I'd have known this business would evolve into that, I probably would have tried to be in sports administration more and become a college employee because by and large it's college employee people now that are doing the play-by-play."

4,000 GAMES, ONE CALL

It would seem to be difficult to pick out one specific call that stands out for a man who has called the action for more than 4,000 games. For Greg, though, there is one that clearly stands above the rest.

"I think about the game here in the '90s between St. Paul Lutheran and Concordia in basketball over here in the St. Paul gym. Concordia was down by a few points with a couple of minutes left and they rallied and they tied the game. They got to within four, and I think they hit two free throws or hit a basket late to tie the game. St. Paul came down and had the last shot of the game for a district championship down here. It was the fifth meeting of the year between the two schools and Concordia won three of the first four.

"St. Paul's star player, Josh Dahlke, shot from the corner to try to win the game in the waning seconds and the ball deflected off the side of the backboard into a Concordia kids hands. He threw the ball half the length of the court to another kid who made an out-of-bounds catch, almost like a wide receiver keeping his feet inbounds at the timeline, and then he flipped it back over his shoulder to another Concordia kid standing under the bucket. He scored a layup at the buzzer to win.

"That was after St. Paul had the ball on their end of the floor and was looking for the last shot. If anything, the St. Paul kid might have shot a couple seconds too early, which you do hoping for an offensive rebound and a stick back, but the ball grazed off the rim and went to a Concordia kid. I don't remember exactly what I said, but that call is one people remind me about all the time."

THANK GOODNESS FOR THE CELL PHONE

Radio stations are now producing video. Twitter, Facebook and Instagram have greatly changed the way we communicate. Offenses are more complex. But to Greg Schmidt, the major development that has most affected broadcasting will fit in your pocket.

"The biggest reason why I've been able to do as many broadcasts as I do in a given year, is the advent of cell phones. When I started this business in the '70s, everywhere you went you had to put in a phone line. You had to have a phone line installed everywhere you went to broadcast, whether it be a road game or a home game. It's evolved into where you can do most of the games through a cell phone, which has given you freedom to go different places and do more things.

"You couldn't go to a lot of places maybe to do a lot of games you wanted because it did cost stations so much to put in phone lines to do the broadcast. If you tried to do all the ballgames I'd do, the station would go broke, or you'd just stop doing sports. But now that there's cell phones you can do more games of more teams and more places simply because you're free to do it."

Interesting and unexpected, but I had to know if Greg is involved at all with social media.

"No, I am NOT a social media guy. I am not even one of those guys that broadcasts through the computer. I hate that. I'm a cell phone guy. Now, when cell phones started, there were pockets of places you could not go because cell phone reception was terrible; there are still some places you can't go. But the advent of cell phones has enabled us to do more games for more teams and more places so that's the reason why I do 140 basketball broadcasts a year now. I'm working every night because I can go everywhere."

> "I arm myself with as many stats, as much history on the teams as I possibly can going into every game."
> ~ Greg Schmidt

Of course, when technology is involved, there are bound to be challenges. Greg, fortunately, knows how to adapt.

"Back in 1989 we were broadcasting a conference tournament at Grain Valley. I was working at the newspaper in Concordia at that time. I told somebody from KMMO to pack

139

up the equipment, bring it to the Concordia office, and then I'll take it with me and drive down the interstate to Grain Valley and broadcast. That way I wouldn't waste almost two hours driving to Marshall.

"Well, they brought me the equipment, but they didn't bring me everything I needed. In those days we set up to broadcast from the gymnasium, short waved the signal to an existing phone line, and then we had a connection of some sort that hooked up to the phone in somebody's office. It went down the line that way. But, the people that packed the equipment up for me at KMMO didn't pack everything I needed, and that connector that received the signal from the gym and in turn then sent it down the phone line, it wasn't sent along."

Enter Ruth.

"She sat in the gymnasium and called me and told me, 'Number 15 has the ball, passes on the right side to 25 to 35, etc.' I sat in the principal's office with the receiving thing in my earpiece and I could hear what she was saying. I had a program in front of me and would say, 'Meyer passes right side to Johnson, puts it on the floor, gives it down low to such-and-such, etc., etc.' I was talking into a phone and it was my voice they heard down the line, but I was hearing her voice and you really called the play (he said looking to Ruth).

"She was in the gym transmitting it to me. I became the connector because I was listening to her shortwave it to me from the gym and I did the play-by-play of a game I wasn't even watching."

Photo courtesy of Kaleb Nierman, KN Photography

In February 2016, Greg reached game number 4,500 in his broadcasting career. He is now over 4,900 with a goal of 5,500.

NOBODY LIKE KEVIN HARLAN

I asked Greg what he does to escape the rigors of the job after all these years. His answer surprised me as he says he watches and listens to sports. And for his money, there is only one man for calling football action.

"Football coverage by Kevin Harlan on the radio is wonderful. We went to a Royals game one night and watched the

Royals back in September, and then we turned on the radio and we heard a Westwood One broadcast of Kevin Harlan. I think he was doing a Monday night game from out on the West Coast. We were listening to it off the Kansas City station while driving home, and he was so good, and so descriptive, and so tremendous. He was describing every little nuance of every play--which way they were going, left to right, what the wind was blowing like, the uniforms they are wearing--that type of thing. And she (Ruth) kind of shook her head and said something like, 'Golly, how does he do that?' and I said to her, 'As broadcasters, we should all be half as good as Kevin Harlan on the radio.'

"The TV doesn't do Kevin Harlan justice because when you call TV, you let the pictures do the talking. When he's on radio, whether it was the old days when he was doing Minnesota Timberwolves basketball for the NBA or when he's doing the Westwood One radio broadcasts. He's as descriptive and is informative and as entertaining as they come. Like I said, we should all as broadcasters strive to be half as good as Kevin Harlan. That's a guy I'll listen to any time on the radio, day or night, any sport."

GREG SCHMIDT: CONCISE AND DESCRIPTIVE

Lots of things I read said Greg is "concise and descriptive" and talked about him as having "vivid description and attention to detail". Is that an accurate depiction of your style, I asked.

"Probably. I do a lot of prep stuff. I mean, I arm myself with as many stats, as much history on the teams as I possibly can going into each and every game. I tell people sometimes at least half of what I take into the game with me I never get to use because the flow of the game takes me a different direction.

"A teacher did color for me one year on a couple of football games and he couldn't believe the amount of game prep stuff, notes and stuff that I had written down. I had a handwritten form on a legal pad to go over and talk about coach A did this, coach B did that, this player did this, that player has done that. I told him the shame is the flow of the game takes you a different direction and a lot of what you take into a given broadcast you don't get to use. He told me the same thing happens when he teaches. He prepares for a given hour of teaching, and a lot of what he has prepared for that certain hour he never gets to use either. So, in essence, maybe broadcasting is a little like teaching. You prepare because there's a lot of times I'll drive home after a game and I'll say to myself, 'Oh, I didn't say that, I didn't use that' because I either didn't think about it or the flow of the game took me elsewhere."

THE COUNT IS ON

4,776. When we visited, that was how many games Greg had called (that number had reached 4,954 by the fall of 2018). Surely there would be an end, but when? When will he know it is time to hang up the microphone?

"People are asking me when 5,000 is going to come. If I get to keep working at the same pace that I have in the past, 5,000 will probably come in January of 2019. Next year will be my 45th year in the business. The goal is to get to 5,500.

"There was a guy at Missouri-Rolla who did Rolla Miner football. His name was Tom Colvin. I was sitting at home on a terribly hot day in July of 1999 listening to the Cardinals. The Cardinals were a God-awful team in 1999. All they had was (Mark) McGwire hitting home runs, and I was sitting at home listening to the Cardinals one day and I heard Jack

141

Buck say, 'The affiliate we're honoring today on the Cardinal Radio Network is KTTR out of Rolla, Missouri, station general manager is such-and-such, station news director is such-and-such, sports director is Tom Colvin, who this past winter celebrated his 5,000th sports broadcast during the month of January calling Rolla Miner basketball.' And I thought, well fine, gosh, 5,000. That's an awful lot because at the time I was still under 2,000. But now, somehow, over the last 17 years or so, that number has increased to 4,776.

"Tom passed away about three years ago, I think. I punched up his name and found his obituary, and in the obit it said during his radio career Tom called more than 5,400 sports broadcasts. I'm sitting at 4,700 now, so the goal is to get to 5,500 because I don't know if he did 5,401 or if he did 5,499. I don't know, but the goal is to get to 5,500 and surpass him, if I can stay healthy. But to do that will probably take six or seven more years."

Photo courtesy of Southeast Missourian/SEMOBall.com

ERIK SEAN
RIVER RADIO
SOUTHEAST MISSOURI STATE UNIVERSITY

He may be tucked away in the Missouri Bootheel, but Erik Sean has not gone unnoticed as the sports director for River Radio. River Radio is home to 13 stations in Poplar Bluff and Cape Girardeau, Missouri and Carterville, Illinois. Erik spends the bulk of his time with SEMO ESPN, Southeast Missouri's ESPN radio network. The play-by-play announcer for Southeast Missouri State University football, men's and women's basketball, and baseball, Erik was on the call as the Redhawks won the 2007 Ohio Valley Conference women's basketball title. He has also called the action for a SEMO baseball team that has won four OVC regular season titles, three conference tournament crowns, and advanced to a pair of NCAA Tournaments (in 1998 and 2016). And he finds the time to host a local daily sports talk show, The Sports Huddle, with Jess Bolen (weekdays at 9 a.m.). For his efforts, Erik is an 11-time winner of the Missouri Broadcasters Association play-by-play award and a three-time winner of the MBA sports award.

Erik has been at River Radio since July 1997 and has been in broadcasting for 24 years. A U.S. Navy veteran and die-hard Chicago Cubs fan, his journey began at WJPF in Herrin, Illinois in 1994. From there he moved on to WEBQ in Harrisburg, Illinois, where he covered El Dorado High School football and basketball, along with Galatia, Gallatin County and Carrier Mills.

Aside from the fact that he works for one of my alma mater's rivals (or at least they were when I was playing football for the Mules of Central Missouri State University), I'd have to say we are kindred spirits. He was born in Macomb, Illinois, as was I, and we are both members of the Class of '88, he from Macomb High School and I from Smith-Cotton in Sedalia, Missouri

A three-sport athlete in high school (he played football, basketball and baseball), Erik spent four years in the Navy out of high school, stationed at Key West, Florida, as an aviation environmental technician. He graduated from Southern Illinois University-Carbondale in 1996 with a degree in radio/television. He now resides in Cape Girardeau with his daughters Josie and Chloe and his son Christian.

I KNOW A GUY

We talk all the time in college about making connections. While I don't totally agree with the idea "It's not what you know, it's who you know" (I know a surgeon, but that's not going to get me into medical school), it is important to get to know people in one's field. That's how Erik Sean broke into the business, and it happened in the least expected of places.

Photo courtesy of Southeast Missouri Athletics

As the Voice of the Redhawks, Erik Sean not only calls play-by-play, he also hosts The Sports Huddle, a daily sports talk show where he interviews the likes of Southeast Missouri State head men's basketball coach Rick Ray.

"My first radio job right was nothing involving sports at all. One of the jobs I had while I was going to college was working at Wendy's. I happened to be working next to a guy, and we got to talking, and he said that he was a radio broadcaster. I thought, you gotta be kidding me, and he actually did play-by-play for a little town near Carbondale, Illinois called Carterville. He was the play-by-play guy there for football and boy's basketball, and he was also the news director for WJPF radio. I'm telling him I'm a radio/television broadcaster, so he became my best friend. I just started following him around all over the place because I wanted to do what he was doing.

"So one day he came into work and said, 'Hey, we had a guy quit at the radio station', and so I'm immediately all, 'Can you get me an interview? Can you get me an interview?' He said he could get me an interview, but I'm just going to have to wow his boss, the guy who owned the radio station, who is this old Italian gentleman named Bob Ferrari. How's that for an Italian name? So I went in one afternoon to interview with him, and I'm nervous, and I'm sitting out in the lobby, and I'm talking to the receptionist. Just asking a couple of questions because I didn't know much about Mr. Ferrari or anything. I did know that they were a Cardinals radio affiliate—they had Cardinals pictures up out in the lobby. She told me that his grandson was a minor league baseball player and she thought he was in the Padres' organization. Well, back then I followed things pretty closely in Major League Baseball, so I knew a lot about the Padres even though they're a West Coast team.

"As I went into his office for my interview, I saw a picture of a baseball player sitting up on his file cabinet, and I say, 'Hey, is that your grandson?' And he says, 'Yeah, yeah.' I wanted to start some sort of a conversation that was non-employment related, so we got into a brief discussion about his grandson. He was a closer in the Padres organization. I happened to know back then who the closer was for the Padres. That was kind of the guy who was standing in his way from making it to the Major Leagues as the Padres' closer, so he had a good conversation there.

"He played my tape that I made at school, and it was awful. I mean I'm listening to that tape, and I thought, 'There is not a human being alive that would let me open a microphone on the radio.' It was just awful, but he sat there. I can't prove it, but I think he fell asleep during the interview. We were talking and he eventually says, 'Okay, here's the day I need you to start, here's what you're going to do,' and I don't even know if I heard anything after he said 'here's the day I need you to start'. I mean, I don't even know what he said after that; I was just so excited that I got a radio job."

And that's when the Erik Sean story took off.

"My first job was working on Saturday night. This is as a college kid on a Saturday night, you know. Saturday night, college kids are usually out having fun. Well, my shift started at 6 p.m. on Saturday night and it went until 6 a.m. the next day where I was getting the church services ready to get on the air. So I was the babysitter for the equipment overnight, and back then you used to have to change satellites at the top of the hour to go to mutual news and then flip it back over to whichever station—one of the stations was a talk station and the other was an FM music station. So I was just basically there to flip satellites and kind of look over the equipment. I didn't get to talk on the radio for the first few weeks.

"Then he wanted to train me to do the afternoon shift. We had to read the senior citizen's menu, the lunch menu, and the obituaries and some public service announcements and things like that. No sports. But in that building they did two different high schools, Herrin High School and Carterville High School.

Which is when Erik met the third person who would kick-start his career in sportscasting.

"I got to know the guy who did the Herrin High School games, and his name was Mike Murphy—you may have heard of his brother, country singer David Lee Murphy who did a song called 'Dust on the Bottle' and 'Party Crowd'. He had some success in country music, and so immediately he just kind of took me under his wing, and when I would get off with my shift on a particular night where there was a basketball game, I would race to whatever little town in Southern Illinois where the basketball game was. I wouldn't get paid, but he let me put a headset on and sit and do color work for him. And man, the first couple of games that I got to do that I was absolutely hooked. The owner, Bob Ferrari, wasn't exactly thrilled about me trying to get into sports—he thought that I should do other things in a radio. He wasn't a big fan of sports, but that's what I liked, and so that's how I got started doing sports.

"Then one night I got a call that Ray Gruny, the guy who I used to flip burgers with at Wendy's who got me the job interview, came down with laryngitis and wasn't going to be able to do the Carterville basketball game that night, and they needed somebody to go do the game. At that time, they were just doing sports on their AM station, so what they would do is do the Herrin High School game live and then Carterville would be on tape delay. The way that it was done, they sent me with a tape recorder and four cassette tapes, and each quarter I would change out the cassette tape. Then I would drive the cassette tapes back to the radio station, and they would play the game on tape delay because Herrin took priority and they were live.

"I did the first game; it was Carterville and Anna Jonesboro in 1994 on Valentine's Day. That was the greatest thing! I finally got to do my first game as play-by-play. It was fantastic! I got to drive back to Carbondale in time so my girlfriend and I at the time could sit and listen to my game because it was on tape delay. So we sat and listened to my game on the radio on Valentine's Day, and I was so excited that I got to do my first game."

TAKING THE NEXT STEP

So that was how Erik got into radio and made his entrance into sportscasting. But I was curious how he began to make a career of it.

"I'm going to say in the late summer of '95, I approached Mr. Ferrari and said, 'Hey, I'd really like to do some sports work here at the radio station', and he basically said, 'We've got Herrin, we've got Carterville and we've got two guys doing those games, so really we don't have any openings, any extra radio signals. I don't think there's really going to be any opportunities to do sports here.' So then I started looking around to I find my own play-by-play job, and there's a little town in southern Illinois called Harrisburg. I applied there, they called me in for an interview and interviewed me. I said I'll get back to you, and so I'm driving from Harrisburg back to Carbondale, and that's probably a 40 minute-drive. By the time I got home, there was a message from the general manager at that radio station on my answering machine saying that I got the job. So I was fired up, called my mom, and told her I got my first sports job in radio.

"I was there for a year doing El Dorado, which is a town right next to Harrisburg. I did El Dorado football and basketball, and they also did these other little surrounding high schools—Galatia, Gallatin County, and Carrier Mills. They tried to do as many games as they could so they could sell sponsorships out of those towns. They had me just sell all the advertising. Well, you know, I was young and fired up. I sold it out, so we had sponsors for all those high schools. During basketball season it seemed like I had a game probably four or five nights a week. One night I'm doing Gallatin County, the next night I'm doing El Dorado, and then Galatia has a game the following night, and then there's a tournament, so I'm running all over the place. But I'm loving it. I'm getting my feet wet as a play-by-play broadcaster, learning the ropes, learning all the technical aspects.

A sad turn of events then led Erik back where his radio career started and ultimately to his present position.

"After a year of working there I got a phone call and the gentleman I was flipping burgers next to at Wendy's that got me my first interview, Ray Gruny, he had gotten struck by a car while riding his bike and died. It was just shocking. He was a great guy. He had two kids and a wife, and so all of a sudden there was a job opening back at the WJPF where I first started. Mr. Ferrari asked me if I would consider coming back and taking Ray's place, and I said absolutely and put together this whole package. I was going to try to sell myself and, you know, here's the amount of money that I wanted, and I thought I had some negotiating leverage.

Before enrolling at Southern Illinois-Carbondale, Erik Sean spent four years in the Navy, stationed in Key West, Fla. as an aviation environmental technician.

"Two minutes into my presentation with Mr. Ferrari he's like, 'No problem. Done. What else?' So I got everything that I wanted to come back there, and while I was working there, Mr. Ferrari sold his two radio stations to a company called Zimmer Broadcasting. Four brothers, all with the last name Zimmer, and they were based in Cape Girardeau, but they had radio stations in Kansas, in Columbia, Missouri, in Jefferson City. They were just purchasing these properties in Southern Illinois, and they acquired the two stations that I worked with, so I worked for them for about a year. Then they asked me to come to Cape Girardeau and sit down and have a meeting, so I went over to Cape, had a meeting with all of the Zimmer brothers, and they said we would like you to come over to Cape Girardeau and be our sports director. At the time I was interested in doing play-by-play. Well, they did Cape Girardeau Central High School, and there was a guy already there doing that. I said it sounds like a really nice offer, but right now I'm doing play-by-play for two high schools—Herrin and Carterville—and I would only be interested if there was play-by-play broadcasting involved. So they made the decision, 'Okay if that's what it's going to take to bring him over here, we'll do either Jackson High School or Scott City High School. The way we decided which school they were going to do was wait until it got dark and then we just drove around and listened to the signal, 1220. Did it come in better in Jackson or did it come in better in Scott City? Each town is about eight miles from Cape. Well, it came in better in Scott City, so we did Scott City sports, and I went and sold all the advertising.

"I did those games for three years, and during that time I would help with SEMO a little bit. I was the sideline reporter during football games and in '99 I got to do a couple of SEMO baseball games, but that was about the extent of it. Well the guy that was doing the SEMO games ended up getting a job at Western Kentucky University to be the play-by-play guy for Western Kentucky. So he moved on there, and I got the job in 2000 to do SEMO athletics, and I've been doing that since 2000."

CALLING A DIAMOND DANDY

In 1990 Southeast Missouri State made the jump from NCAA Division II to Division I, then I-AA and now FCS in football. Like most programs that make that transition, the Redhawks have had their struggles. But Erik still has found joy in calling SEMO games.

"SEMO hasn't been the most successful entity in the Ohio Valley Conference. They won one football championship in 2010, the two years before I started doing the games. They won an OVC men's basketball title, but I didn't get to call those games. They won a couple of championships in women's basketball that I got to broadcast, and we went to two NCAA tournaments, one in Denver and one in Austin, Texas.

"The baseball program, now, has been really successful. They won four OVC titles and just came off a stretch where they won three in a row and the coach got the job at the University of Missouri. Southeastern Conference, I mean, that's how good he made the program here.

"I would say probably the first OVC championship that the baseball team won in 2001 was one I remember. The Ohio Valley has the automatic berth to the NCAA, so they went to Tuscaloosa, Alabama and played the Crimson Tide at Sewell Thomas Stadium. They had never lost a postseason baseball game there, and so SEMO went down there and they beat them. Handed them their first ever postseason loss, and that was a thrilling game.

"First pitch of the game our third baseman tripled into right-center, and we thought, 'Oh, they may get something done here tonight!' That was a really good team. Had a couple of 10-game winners on the mound and an All-American closer, so they were really good. Just going to Alabama and winning a postseason game there, that was a big highlight. That was fun."

BON VOYAGE!!

Some broadcasters practice how they'll announce a significant event, others don't. Some have a signature call, others avoid those like the plague. While Erik says he does not script his work, he has no problem with a good catch phrase.

"You know, sometimes you think about certain things that may happen in a game. I heard Jack Buck talk about the fact that he was disappointed with his call when McGwire hit number 61. He said something about McGwire's home run ball, number 61, headed for planet Maris. It didn't sound like Jack Buck, and he said he regretted pre-scripting a call.

"Two of his most famous home run calls were when he called Ozzie Smith's home run in '85–'Go crazy folks!'—and then he's doing the national broadcast for Kirk Gibson's home run in '88–'I don't believe what I just saw!' I mean he didn't script any of those.

"It is obvious to me when a play-by-play guy scripts something, and I don't like it. I'm not a fan of it. I don't like to do it.

"That doesn't mean that you can't have certain catch phrases that you use as a broadcaster. That's fine, but I don't think that you have to be rote with the way that you call a particular sporting event. Like I've got a home run call that I crafted a long time ago, and I don't use it on every home run. I use the phrase 'bon voyage'. I've never heard anyone do that. I wasn't going to steal anyone's, I wasn't going to copy anyone; I wanted to come up with my own. But I don't use it on every single home run.

Tat, Erik says, requires a vast vocabulary and a firm grasp of the English language.

148

"One thing about being a broadcaster is the diversity of your calls, the diversity of what you are using in terms of your terminology. You have to have a very diverse vocabulary if you're going to be a good play-by-play broadcaster. You can't call the same play the same way every time. You just can't.

"There are different spots on the floor in a basketball game where a guy is on the right wing, or he is on the wing, or he's on the right arc, or he's on the right side of the floor behind the three-point line. There are probably 10 different ways to describe when a guy is on a basketball court in a certain spot, and you diversify the way that you call that as often as you can. Guy hits a three-point shot you don't just say 'good' every time. How many different ways are there to call a made basket or a made three-pointer? I could probably just off the top of my head come up with 15 different ways, and you need to rotate all of those each time. Diversify your vocabulary, diversify your call, and when you script something ahead of time it just sounds a little forced.

"One of the things about sports is emotion, and a good broadcaster will let the emotion go and just see what comes out of your mouth."

Play-by-play announcers often become local celebrities called upon to help with charitable events. Here Erik serves as emcee for a sports trivia contest.

Photo courtesy of Southeast Missourian/SEMOBall.com

GOING DIGITAL

Since he got started, Erik says the biggest change has not been the caliber of competition he sees, the internet or even the advent of social media.

"Equipment is the biggest thing. The equipment that we've got now is just light years ahead of what we used to have. I mean now I travel with a piece of equipment where I can broadcast on a phone line—a regular phone line—that turns the sound into digital quality sound and there's no way anybody can tell you're on the phone line. Now, back in the day when you were just using a phone line and you were using equipment that did not have a capability of digitizing that phone line you could tell. You listen to a talk show and they get a caller on the line, you can tell that caller is on the phone because of the sound quality. It's limited. Well that's what our games used to sound like. Unless you were using a Marti setup, and that would be basically for home games, on road games you were on the phone line, and that quality is so limited. Now I've got a piece of equipment that can take a phone line, turn it into digital, and there isn't anybody that can tell you're on a phone line. You've basically got a computer modem on your end, you've got a computer modem back at the radio station, and that phone line connects the two, and basically, it's like old-fashioned dial-up internet. Remember those days of AOL and connection sound and all that? It turns it into digital. So that same piece of equipment I can plug an Ethernet wire into my port and I can get a very high connect rate, all digital sounds.

"If that is unavailable, I've also got a Verizon router that I've had for the last couple of years so it operates on the Verizon network, and it is a regular router with three hard-line ethernet outputs. So I can run three different things out of that router—I can run my tie-line, my broadcast unit, I can plug right into my laptop so I've got internet for checking emails or doing Twitter and updating scores—you know keep it all right there. So technology and the way that we can broadcast, just all of the upgrades and equipment and technology that is the biggest change in our industry."

Naturally when Erik discussed the advancement of social media I had to ask if he tweets during ballgames and, if so, how?

"I do before the game gets going. Say we're doing a basketball game. I'll pull up the ESPN Top-25 scoreboard and I'll pull up the Ohio Valley Conference scoreboard so I can keep people updated on what's going on with the teams in our league and then what's going on in the Top 25. What's Duke doing? Hey, I know that Kansas was playing Florida and that's a big match up. What's going on in that game? People care about that stuff. So I keep those pages pulled up.

"We take emails for all of our broadcasts, so I keep an eye on emails and then we keep an eye on Twitter as well if somebody is going to post a notification. We try to stay involved there."

> "There's one thing about being a homer, and it's obvious what team your broadcasting for, but you can also walk a very, very tight line about being very respectful, giving plenty of praise."
>
> ~ Erik Sean

The global reach of sports also has added a layer of excitement, Erik says.

"It is so fun—talking about the big changes to the industry and the technology—the fact that people in every corner of the world, if they want to listen to a Redhawks game they can. SEMO obviously isn't just exclusive to that, but that's the technology. We now have phone apps where if people just download our app and they've got their smartphone, they can listen to the game anywhere they go. When I was young, they had the transistor radios. Now, you got one; it's your smartphone. You just log into our app and you don't have to miss a play ever for any of SEMO sports. You can have it on your phone, you can get it through your computer, and then obviously you can listen to it on the radio.

"It's so neat when we get emails from other places. We have a football player from New Zealand. We have baseball players from Australia. And we just had a basketball player from Slovenia, and the time difference is there. Relatives will stay up, and it's like two in the morning there, three in the morning there during the time that we're broadcasting the game. I will get emails from them that they're listening overseas. It's really pretty cool getting those emails. We read all the emails that come in on the air because there's a lot of downtime in sports. Football, between plays there's all kinds of downtime. Basketball, you've got time outs and you've got when the game stops for free-throws and there are times when basketball moves slowly. And in baseball, I mean, that's the slowest pace of play of any of the sports, so there's no problem doing that one."

VIDEO CHANGES RADIO

Gone may be the days when radio people resented video. Today many in radio embrace their visual brother.

"The other big advancement is the video, at least for us at SEMO. The Ohio Valley Conference mandates that every home football and men's and women's basketball game is streamed live with video on their digital network, the OVC Digital Network. You're mandated to do this, and the technology is great. It looks like you're watching an ESPN game with all the graphics, shot clock, replay—everything. They just plug into our radio broadcast so you reach so many more people that way because, let's face it, if free video is available versus just listening to the game on the radio I think a high percentage of people are going to turn on that video, watch it and they are hearing us. They're hearing the radio."

The addition of video and the fact that now audiences outside a radio station's coverage area can follow the action, Erik believes, has also changed what is considered "homerism", the broadcaster who only covers his or her team.

"Especially now with the video stream, you get a lot of the visitors tuning in because they're following their team, and even though you're the Redhawk broadcaster, that's what they get if they tune in for the video. They log on to watch the video, they're getting SEMO's radio crew, so we try to be as professional as possible.

"There's one thing about being a homer, and it's obvious what team you're broadcasting for, but you can also walk a very, very tight line about being very respectful, giving plenty of praise and not being homers and slanted one sided for your team. Boy, every call goes against you, and all those things. But knowing the entire time you're broadcasting you've got a pretty nice contingent of people from the opposing fan base that are tuning in. And the emails; we get to hear from them as well."

As a professor who teaches sports broadcasting, I had to ask how the video gets produced. I was thrilled with the answer.

"The school's video department and its students do the video streaming; it's on-the-job training. This is real-world training for them—running cameras, doing production, doing the producing, running the instant replay, and all that. It used to be our local television station took charge of all of that, but then they kind of cycled out. The university wanted to implement their communication's department and so it's mostly students and it's headed up by two non-students—a professor and then another guy who is the head of video services."

Of course, play-by-play announcers present their broadcasts differently depending upon the medium—more description and detail in radio, more setting up the play and tossing to the color analyst in television. I asked Erik if the addition of the livestream has changed how he does his radio broadcast.

"You want to talk to both fan bases that are listening. You've got the radio people and you've got the people watching. So you have to acknowledge replay of a particular play: 'Okay, if you're watching the video right now, you're seeing the replay. Here's what we're seeing'. And you're describing that for the radio people, which is not much different than if you've got a straight radio broadcast.

"Let's just say you're listening to the Cubs and the Cardinals. It's a radio broadcast. Well, because replay is such a big thing, they're telling you what they're looking at in their booth as far as the replay. Is there going to be a replay challenge? So that is already implemented in a straight radio broadcast. If we're looking at the video, you're talking to people who are not only just listening to the radio side of it, but they're watching it and they're watching that video replay right along with you as you're watching, so you're really able to talk to both entities."

HARRY CARAY ALL THE WAY

You have to remember that Erik was born and raised in Illinois. So while his favorite sportscaster called some action in Missouri, he is probably best known for his time as the iconic voice of the Chicago Cubs.

"Harry Caray. He's probably the biggest reason that I became a sportscaster. I just loved Harry Caray when I was a kid. Before I was born he was the longtime Voice of the Cardinals on radio. He had the falling-out with the Bush family and did the interview upon exiting with the Schlitz beer can in his hand, and I've heard him interviewed saying he regretted that. He went out to Oakland to work for Charlie Finley for one year after he left the Cardinals. And then he went to White Sox, and so that's where I first heard him. In Macomb,

you could obviously get the Cubs games on WGN, but there were also ways to watch the White Sox games. There's a station called WFLD out of Chicago, and I would tune in to watch the White Sox. Because the Cubs games were in the daytime, a lot of the Sox games were at night. Wrigley Field didn't have lights, so at night, if I was watching a baseball game, it would be the White Sox. And here's this guy who was just loud and bombastic and exciting, Harry Caray.

"For a long time, his sidekick was Jimmy Piersall. I mean that guy was literally crazy. So those two in the booth, as a kid I just thought, 'Man they're having so much fun!' and I just loved listening to Harry Caray. Then all of a sudden, one

Photo courtesy of Erik Sean

If Erik has one dream it would be to someday be the broadcast voice of his beloved Chicago Cubs, to occupy the seat once held by his hero, Harry Caray.

year, he gets the job to do the Cubs games. My team. All of a sudden, this guy that I just think is fantastic, he's doing the Cubs. So I was a huge fan of Harry Caray.

So enamored with Caray was Erik that he spent all night making a tribute to the man who inspired his career.

"When he died in 1998, I was a sound rat. I had all these cassette tapes of just sound bites, play-by-play clips, interview clips. I used to hoard all these things on cassette tape. I had so much stuff, and I remember the night that he died I was watching television, and it came across ESPN that he had passed away, and I was just devastated. He was my guy. I mean, I know he was getting old, but he was just so fantastic. Hall of Famer, different style than the normal guys.

"I remember going into the radio station, it was probably 9 or 10 at night, and I was in there all night. I put together this feature about Harry Caray. I typed up all the facts about his life and his career, and I had so many sound bites that I had to go through. I had all these cassette tapes that I had hoarded, like him calling Stan Musial's 3000th hit, him calling Stan Musial's last hit of his career, and he's walking off the field and him saying, 'There he goes', and when he's at the plate, 'Remember the stance. You're never going to see another one like it.'"

To hear all of Erik's moving package about his broadcasting hero, go to YouTube and search "Erik Sean: A Tribute to Harry Caray".

"Then I had some sound bites of him with the Cubs. And then I had several interviews with him. I interviewed him once at Busch Stadium when the Cubs came to town, and that was in '97, so it was the year before he died. I still have that interview. It's just fantastic, and I got him talking about being a part of three generations of sports broadcasting. When he got up to make his Hall of Fame speech, he was thinking about being a part of three generations, all doing Major League Baseball at the same time—him, Skip and Chip—him, his son and his grandson. I had other interviews with him about what it was like to broadcast the Cardinals because he was a St. Louis kid, and him saying, 'One of these days the Cubs will win the World Series, and maybe somebody he'll think about me and say, boy it's a shame Harry wasn't here to see it', which ended up being the case.

"So, I put together this little tribute to Harry Caray, and it won a Missouri Broadcasters Association Award, but I just remember going in like 9 o'clock at night, and I was there until my shift started at five in the morning. I just finished that thing up, and so we played it on the radio all that morning. But Harry Caray he's my guy; he's my favorite baseball announcer of all time because he was the guy I listened to growing up as a kid.

"I think the best baseball broadcaster now is John Miller for the San Francisco Giants. I really don't think it's that close now that Vin Scully has retired. But John Miller is my favorite. My favorite football guy, he used to do the Bears, now he does the Green Bay Packers and his name is Wayne Larrivee. He is just an outstanding football broadcaster. He's probably my favorite football guy.

"But Harry Caray was my main man. He was probably the reason I wanted to be a sports broadcaster."

A FAN OF THE SILVER SCREEN
On those rare occasions when Erik is not in full-on sportscast prep mode, he says he is totally into his children. And movies.

"I like hanging out with my kids for one thing. We are movie buffs. We really like movies, so I always try to stay up on the latest movies, and if I'm on the road and we get an opportunity to go to a movie, I will always try to go. I try to go to the little local shops in some of the cities that I travel to. That's always fun."

Granted, in Erik's role, as with all sportscasters, that escape time is limited.

"Believe it or not, I do spend a lot of time in my hotel room preparing for the broadcast. I just spend a lot of hours doing it. When we go on the road during conference play, there'll be doubleheaders, the women will play and then 40 minutes later the men will play. Well, I have to be prepared for four teams—two SEMO teams and then two teams from the opposing side—and I have to have all of that. It may be a Thursday—Saturday turn around, and so Friday when we get there I'm spending most of my time in the hotel getting everything ready for a doubleheader the following day where I haven't been able to prepare ahead of time because I just had a game Thursday. So, because of that schedule I don't get out as much as some of the other people do just because I'm focused on how the next broadcast is going to go. But I definitely like to go to as many of the local things that there are in the particular towns. I get on websites of the towns that we're going to quite often and just see where the tourist attractions are, what is this city known for, what are some of the cool things. And maybe my family's traveling with me. We make a point to go check that out. And, of course, I watch a lot of sports in my off time. I love sports."

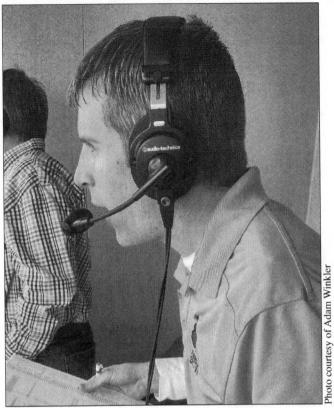

Photo courtesy of Adam Winkler

ADAM WINKLER
KNEO 91.7 FM
WEBB CITY HIGH SCHOOL

"But someone will say, 'You have faith, and I have works.' Show me your faith without works, and I will show you faith by my works"

James 2:18

When Adam Winkler graduated from Ottawa University, a non-profit Christian-based university, his mission was to share his faith while working in the profession he loved: sports broadcasting. That passion and drive led him to KNEO 91.7 FM, a 14,000-watt contemporary Christian radio station in Neosho, Missouri that covers a 65-mile radius in the four-state area (Missouri, Kansas, Oklahoma and Arkansas). There he covers the Cardinals of Webb City High School, one of the most successful high school athletic programs in Missouri's history.

When I went to visit Adam, KNEO's offices were in a building little bigger than a trailer. It had rained, so I was careful to wipe my shoes so I did not track mud; though the offices were small, they were tidy and neatly organized. Part of the mud outside came

155

because of an active construction project. I soon learned that KNEO was in the process of an expansion and new headquarters (since completed). Adam greeted me and escorted me to his small office in the back of the building where, though he describes himself as shy, he treated me like a long-lost friend who was eager to share.

The director of operations at KNEO, Adam covers Webb City football, basketball, softball and baseball. He has been on the call for eight state football titles, as well as state championships in baseball (2006), softball (2007) and women's basketball (2010). The station also covers Seneca, Diamond, East Newton and McDonald County high schools, and has broadcast some Crowder College sporting events.

Adam is now in his 13th year at the station, having started at KNEO just two days after he graduated from Ottawa, where he ran cross country and track, worked on the campus radio station, and graduated with a degree in professional communications. Adam and his college sweetheart, Jill, have three children: daughter Bruynnlea and sons Jaden and Logan.

NEVER ANY DOUBT

The average college student changes majors about six times. Adam Winkler was not the typical college student. In fact, he says being a sportscaster is all he ever wanted to do.

"I've always loved sports broadcasting, but it was pretty much when I was in high school. I knew that I wasn't going to play professional baseball, and so it was automatically, 'Let's go into sports broadcasting.' There was no hesitation or question. This is the only thing that I wanted to do; there was no other option for me."

So he knew from an early age and had no back up plan. That made me wonder what Adam did to prepare for the field and what advice he would give young people who know they want to get involved in sports broadcasting but because of their youth or circumstances can't take classes or get any formal training.

"You hear this all the time, but the best advice I give to people if they're thinking about getting involved in this is, number one record yourself doing it. Turn down the volume on the TV and sit there with your phone and broadcast the game. And just listen to guys do play-by-play. That's where my love and passion grew for it, listening to Denny Matthews and Fred White, Bob Davis and to Mitch Holthus. That's where my love and passion came from. I would just sit in my room all night long I listen to those guys. You listen to how they do things, and you have to have your own style, but you remember how those guys do things and how they handle themselves in certain situations and how they call a certain play and then adapt your own style to it.

Not only is Adam Winkler the Webb City High School play-by-play announcer for KNEO, he is also the director of operations.

"Again, practice and listen. To be honest with you, I actually never did the turning down the volume and recording myself thing, but I just listened to somebody broadcast.

"I knew this was what I wanted to do from an early age, and my freshman year at college, first football game

I was on the radio. That was my first time ever doing it, but it was just one of those things because I knew that's what I wanted to do, and I'd listen to so much of it I just had the knack. Now I would tell people that you need to practice and record yourself because I kind of took the unconventional path the way I did it. But people can tell if you've practiced.

"I've tried to train people who say, 'Oh yeah, I can do that', and you realize two pitches into an inning that this half inning can't get over fast enough. The ability to process information and have it come out at the same time is tough."

IN SEARCH OF PERFECTION

If this has been his dream since he was a child, and if he spent so much time training and preparing, surely Adam believes he has made it as a sportscaster. Not so; in fact, the desire to achieve perfection is what drives him.

"I don't know if you ever know that. When I got the first job I was ecstatic. Just the longevity; being able to do this for 13 years and being able to hold down the same job for that amount of time and people appreciate it. You realize that once you're in, don't rock the boat. But when did I know I made it? I don't know if I feel like I've made it because there's always room to improve. It's just one of those things where I don't know if I'm ever good enough; I've never called the perfect game. I had a fairly good instinct in college that I knew that I can do this for a living and everything because it was just something that came easy to me."

CALLING A SHOOTOUT

Webb City High School has been one of the most successful athletic programs in Missouri high school history. As a result, Adam had a large sample from which to pull when asked about a favorite game. It didn't take him long, though, to pick one.

"It would probably have to be the 2011 state title game for Webb City. The Cardinals were playing MICDS (Mary Institute and St. Louis Country Day School), and it was a shootout, back and forth. Two great teams—two great defenses against two great offenses. It ended being a 56-42 shootout. It was tied; the Cardinals couldn't stop the opposing quarterback, Thomas Militello. He'd throw into double coverage and they'd catch it. But Webb scored the final two touchdowns. It was the most exciting game I've been a part of.

"The 2011 state semifinal game was exciting, too. Webb City was down 24-3 at halftime and came back and tied the game and then won on the last play of the game on a touchdown run. So those are probably the two that stick out to me the most."

GETTING IT DONE

Little surprise Adam's favorite call came from that state title game.

"I have a lot of favorite calls that I thought would happen but didn't. Probably the Phoenix Johnson touchdown run to win the Savannah game in the 2011 state semifinals was the most exciting call I've had. It was it was fourth and goal from the one-yard line, and they ran it off the left side and he got into the end zone by a yard and a half.

"That was just one of those things where the whole place was in euphoria. No one thought Webb City—they knew they could come back, but it was one of those games, 24-3 at halftime. They were on the ropes, and then the last play of the game, state title is on the line ... to go there and get it done, that was pretty special."

THE CALL THAT NEVER WAS

For Adam, one of his most memorable calls, one that he was gearing up for, actually didn't happen.

"It was two years ago in the 2015 state title game. Webb City was playing Kearney. Webb was on the one-yard line, it was the final play of the game, 10 seconds were left, and there was a timeout called. I'm sitting there thinking I'm going to call a touchdown right here and they're going to win the state title on this play. But with 10 seconds left, Webb City fumbles the handoff into the end zone and automatically you have to flip from 'this is going to be the one of the most exciting moments of the season' to 'how do you describe this?' and get it into words.

"You have to pull the emotion out of it. That was one of those you're like, 'I'm getting ready to call the greatest call my life right here.' They're going to win a state title on the final play of the game, which is everybody's dream—to be able to call a play like that. And then they fumble the ball into the end zone and Kearney recovers. So from the highest of highs to the lowest of lows. That was one that sticks out the most to me."

GAME DAY!!

For anybody involved in athletics, be they a coach, an athlete or a broadcaster, game day is something special. But while fans may see the product on the field or hear the game over the air, they don't necessarily notice what happens before the first play.

"We're a little different since we're kind of a smaller station and we cover a couple different teams. Usually I get in and I break down the coaches show that's recorded earlier that morning by our sideline reporter. He also does a halftime interview, so I break that down and get that ready to go, and I put together all our special features for that night, whether it's an interview with another coach in the school district or I have an interview I do with a former athlete, kind of find out where they're at in life. So it's a lot of production early in the morning, making sure my board's ready to go and watching film the night before and at times throughout the week, just to make sure I'm ready to go for the broadcast.

"We get to the stadium about 4:30, haul all the equipment up, get it all set up and ready to go for pregame at 6 o'clock because we do an hour pregame show, which is kind of odd for high school. We do a six to 7 o'clock pregame show. We do ours live. We have a pre-recorded coach's show and some other special features, but the first 30 minutes is live and then we have the special features. Then we're back about 6:50 to get ready for kickoff.

"Fridays are usually pretty much of a blur because it starts at 8 o'clock in the morning and usually you're done about 10:30 at night.

"Basketball is a lot of the same. I'll email the coaches, get the roster and starting line ups to make sure I have all that set to go before I get to the gym, make sure everything production wise is good here for the game, make sure our board op is set and good to go for the broadcast to make sure everything runs as smoothly as possible.

"Basketball is pretty easy because you get into a groove and there's so many games per week that it's a lot easier. It's just kind of getting into that routine—this is what I have to do and get it done—just making sure you have everything from the opposing team that you want. Usually with high school it depends on if they get you stats or not. Opposing coaches are different; some coaches are really good about getting you information, but some coaches think that you're going to tell everybody in the world that you got these stats and they don't want your coaches to find out about it.

Photo courtesy of Adam Winkler

Here Adam is performing his primary job—providing play-by-play for Webb City High School. But as technology has improved, he now often may be seen with a camera in hand providing a video livestream as well as audio.

"Baseball and softball are pretty much the same. The coaches at Webb City are great. They give me access to all the stats so I can get all that stuff on my own. I don't have to bother them with that, so I have all that ready to go. I'll make sure I have the line-ups and usually get to the game site about an hour before broadcast time just to make sure everything is set up and ready to go."

FROM SIMULCASTING TO VIDEO

I went to a Broadcast Education Association conference recently, and one of the most significant developments in radio, they said, was the inclusion of video—video spots on the stations' websites, video news packages, and especially streaming of live events, like high school football. Adam said KNEO in Neosho, Missouri is following that trend.

"We were doing simulcasting when I first started, and you had your radio broadcast and then your internet audio webcast. But with the explosion of video, people expect that now. They want that with the high school broadcast. It adds a whole other element, a whole other dimension to the broadcast.

"If people peek behind the scenes there's a lot more going on than just the play-by-play. I got a color guy up there and he's doing stuff, I have a sideline reporter, but I'm sitting there running video spots. During basketball season I'm running the camera while doing the play-by-play and then run video spots because that's what you do with a small station. But the advancement in technology with video, I think, is the biggest change that I've seen in the profession. It's just going to keep on changing. We have people who cut highlights of the games. They watch the games and cut them and then they share them on social media."

159

Given the demand for audio and video content, another development that has been a benefit is the ease in which broadcaster and coach may communicate.

"The advancement of information right now is another big thing. You can communicate with coaches via email and have them send you stats and things. Another is the advancement of being able to watch video on Hudl and those types of things, being able to break down film. You don't have to get a copy of a DVD from a coach and then take it home and pop it in. Hudl is right there; everything is broken down for you, so you can go back and watch games from three years ago and see what happened on this play and if there are any tendencies that they might have this year that they had last year.

"To me that's the coolest thing—being able to watch a game in 30 minutes and not have to go through all the process again. I mean, I can sit down on a Monday and start watching film for the following week, and even earlier than that if I wanted to. But you don't have to wait for coaches to drive two hours to swap film, get it back on Saturday, break it down, and then it's finally available on DVD."

SPEAKING OF VIDEO ...

When the play-by-play voice also has full-time programming duties, game prep can be an enormous challenge. Still, Adam says video study is essential.

"Each week's kind of different depending on what's going on. Since we're a smaller station, if there's things pressing beginning of the week, if there's other stuff that has to be done, sometimes that prep gets pushed back. But you should always get the roster early on in the week, and make sure you go through the roster and make sure you know how to pronounce everybody's names. If you don't know how to pronounce everybody's names, make sure you get with someone who does because there's going to be opposing fans listening; not everyone has a station covering them, and if you know how to pronounce a tough name on the team, even though you're not for that other team, people are still going to appreciate what you do. We simulcast online. You have video and audio, so there's people out there listening.

"The biggest thing would be to sit down and watch film, especially during football. Basketball, you see so much action throughout the week, but for football it helps if you sit down and watch film.

"Here it's a little bit different because I'm also trying to help run the station. Throughout the day you have productions you have to do. You have to help sell, and so I have to fit that film watching into different times where I'm not actually doing other things. For me it's a matter of finding time to do that with a wife and three kids and working here 40 hours a week and then ball games on top of that, but I'd say film study is the biggest thing for football because that's where you're going to learn the most. You need that information that you can pull out in the middle of the ballgame so you can say, 'Well, they did this last week, so watch out for this'. And that really helps with your pregame prep as well. If you don't sit down and outline your pregame show then you're pretty much sunk because you're just throwing the line out there hoping to catch something."

FOUR FAVORITES

As a Kansas City native, it's not too difficult to guess Adam's favorite sportscasters. A hint: They all wear red and/or blue.

"I'd have to say there's four of them. Growing up in Kansas City, some of my earliest memories, I mean, Denny Matthews, obviously, is right there at the top. Growing up listening to Royals games, just sitting on my bedroom floor looking at Royals notebooks and listening to Denny and Fred (White) call play-by-play are still some of the great memories.

"Bob Davis (the Voice of the Kansas Jayhawks) had a huge impact on why I got involved, just for his excitement of the game and the way he called it, and just the enthusiasm. Those are some of the earliest memories, too. Listening to him on a Saturday afternoon with my dad as were doing remodel projects at our house.

"And then Mitch Holthus. Man, what a great guy he is. A cool story about Mitch: His kids played at Southwestern College while I was at Ottawa, and Mitch was at a basketball game at Ottawa one year. I saw him over there, and I'm like, 'Man, that's Mitch Holthus!' I got the gumption up to walk over to him and say, 'Hey would you be willing to do a halftime interview?' He says, 'Sure, no problem.' Came right over, sat down, and at the half we talked Chiefs football on a campus radio station. He didn't have to give me the time of day, but he did that twice while I was at Ottawa. Just the most humble person that I've ever came across, and he has a good, solid foundation.

"Then I have to throw in Ryan Lefebvre in there, too. I love the way that Ryan and Denny interact when they do a radio broadcast together. Ryan's the ultimate professional. He just has the ability to bring you into a game. So those four are Kansas City guys, but that's where my heart is."

> "This is the only thing that I wanted to do; there was no other option for me."
> ~ Adam Winkler

THE MAKINGS OF A LEADER

As director of operations at KNEO, it stands to reason that Adam would mentor young men and women who enter the station. That is a responsibility he does not take lightly.

"Yeah, we have a new guy that we just hired a couple of months ago. I've been really reading some books on leadership lately, and that's something that is really pressing on me. You're here to make an impact in people's lives, so whatever I can do to help him become better than I am at what I do, I'm going to do that.

"There's so many people who have talent in this industry, and you're blessed because you get a chance to be involved with it. So anything I can do to help him out—to show him the ropes and teach him the things that I've learned and then give him opportunities to thrive and succeed and build a confidence and be able to take the next step, I'm going to do.

"I had that with the people in Ottawa. Gary Bateman and Brad Howard of KOFO Radio up there in Ottawa, they gave a college guy a chance to go broadcast an NAIA National Tournament in basketball up in Sioux City, Iowa. They didn't go up there; they said, 'You can do it. We trust you.' So those are the things people do, giving you those opportunities to do those type of things. That's was pretty cool."

FOR LOVE OF THE GAMES

Webb City High School is known across the state for its dominant football program, so it might surprise people to learn Adam's favorite sport to call is basketball.

161

"Just because of the pace of the game and the ebbs and flows. It's the smoothness of a basketball game; there's not a lot of breaks. And the excitement involved in it. I just like the faster play. Basketball was probably my first love when I was at Ottawa. Calling that, just being able to get behind the mic and call it as the team's going up and down the court and being able to describe something and coming up with different words because there's so many shots in a game, there's so many different things that can happen but you're not saying the same thing over and over again. Coming up with different calls that give it a different feel to each and every single play, ya know?

> "Who knows where God is going to lead in the future, but I know this is where I am supposed to be, and I really don't have any desire to change unless God would change that desire."
> ~ Adam Winkler

"Baseball I always thought would be the toughest thing to call, but I've fallen in love with calling baseball. And even high school softball—the pace of the game of high school softball is so much fun. Obviously, it's a lot faster than baseball. Baseball was the toughest one learning just because of the pace of the game. To be able to fill, especially when you're doing a broadcast by yourself in high school. Being able to fill seven innings of continual play-by-play, and yeah, the crowd noise helps out, but it's tough. Denny (Matthews) and Ryan (Lefebvre) do it so well, just being able to space out your words and changing the inflection in your voice depending on where the ball is hit. It's a love of mine; I love baseball, but basketball probably came to me the easiest."

While basketball may be his favorite sport to call, Adam says his dream event would be on the diamond.

"Probably game seven of a World Series. There's nothing that gets better than game seven of the World Series, in my mind. Even when it was the Dodgers and Astros (in 2017), there's something about it. It's special. It has that feel to it. There's nothing like it in sports. I know Super Bowls are great, and Final Fours are awesome, but game seven in baseball is still to me the purest there is, and to me that would be the ultimate thing to do."

IN GOD HE TRUSTS
Adam does not hesitate when asked how he got to Neosho. In fact, he is quite bold in sharing his faith and how it guided his journey to KNEO.

"I did my internship with Sports Radio 810 up in Kansas City, and the desire was to be this big sports guy, and my senior year at college I just kind of felt my heart change, and I wanted to get into Christian radio. It's just where my heart was leading me. I felt like God was leading me to it, and I'm like, 'How is this going to work out? Christian radio—sports broadcasting. It doesn't work that way. My wife still had a year left to school down here at Ozark Christian College and one day saw that there's a job in Neosho. I'm like, 'Where's Neosho?' I never heard of the place. Never heard of Webb City. Didn't know anything about it. She's like, 'That's 14 miles from Joplin'.

"I applied, and really this has been everything I've wanted it to be. I'm at complete peace that this is where I'm supposed to be. I love it here, I love covering Webb City. I feel like I've been blessed and given opportunities in my life that I never thought would be possible. I'm covering the best high school football team in the history of the state of Missouri, covering the best coach in the state of Missouri in John Roderique, and an incredible fan base and incredible community. Who knows where God's going to lead in the future, but I know this is where I'm supposed to be, and I really don't have any desire to change unless God would change that desire."

Given that KNEO is a Christian station, I asked Adam why they don't cover Ozark Christian College athletics.

"You know our whole philosophy has been, How can we make an impact in public schools? So that's why we do what we do, and God has opened doors for us to cover more state championships than any other station here in the area, whether it be basketball, football, baseball. We've gotten to cover all that, and so God has blessed us for being obedient to him.

"Ozark, I've always thought about it, but there's just not enough hours in the day, there's not enough personnel to get that done."

I pointed out he'd have to sell it, too.

Photo courtesy of Adam Winkler

As announcers for Webb City High School, Adam and his broadcast partner Scott Boudreaux have the pleasure of calling some of the finest high school sports action, not just in Southwest Missouri, but in the entire Show-Me State.

"Webb City sells itself; everybody wants Webb City football, and we've been blessed to have it for, what? Seventeen years now, and so they're committed to us, we're committed to them, and people ask us, Why aren't you covering Neosho? Well, Neosho had a station when we got into this, and Webb City opened up and that's where we're supposed to be right now."

WHO IS ADAM WINKLER?

When most people think of media personalities, particularly those who speak for a living, they expect that they are highly extroverted and comfortable in a crowd. But that is not always the case; in fact, many of the gentlemen I interviewed are comfortable behind the mic because they are not in the crowd. Adam is just such a sportscaster.

"I'm an introvert. After a ball game I'm completely happy to go home and just hang out with a family. Don't need a large group of friends; I have a large group of friends at church, but I don't need that. I'm fine to sit in the room all day and do my own thing, which is kind of weird.

"A lot of sports broadcasters are extroverts, and they want to get out there, but this is who I am. I'm happy just showing up, doing my job and moving on with life because I realize that sports broadcasting is what I do, but it's not who I am. I want to be known as a man of God first and I want to be known as a good husband, a good father and then a good sports broadcaster. I'm a little bit different than many other people in this profession, but that's who I am in a nutshell. I'm a quiet guy, and I'm okay with that."

TIME TO ENERGIZE

In his down time there is one place Adam says he likes to go to recharge his batteries: Home.

"Obviously family is huge for me, so spending time with my wife and kids and just enjoying life because it goes by so quickly. You look back on stuff that pops up on Facebook, your memories from four years ago, and it's like, 'Man, that's been four years and they've grown so much!' So obviously that's what I try and invest in.

"Running is another outlet for me. I love to run, and so the ability to just go out and run and clear your head. A lot of times I use time when I run to pray, just to kind of work through things in.

"And then church is another thing. We're highly involved in our local church and spending time with friends and just relaxing and having fun together as a group of people."

START SMALL AND BUILD

Many young people come out of college with big dreams. A few have visions of calling the Super Bowl or working for ESPN or Sports Illustrated right out of the gate. As a college professor I try my best to remind them they will have to climb to those lofty heights. It is re-affirming to hear a professional sportscaster like Adam echo those sentiments.

"Know what you're getting into. Be willing to start at the smallest level possible, and be willing to work for free, especially during those college years. Don't expect anything in return, but find someone you respect and who knows the profession and hang out with them and learn from them. Just say, 'Hey, I'm here to learn from you' and let them know that you value anything that they can pour into you. I had that with a couple different people,

164

and they were gracious enough to give me the opportunity. I wouldn't be here today without what those guys gave me, guys like Gary Bateman and Brad Howard. The ability they poured into my life saying, 'Hey we believe in you and we trust you and here, go ahead and try this'.

"Again, though, really realizing what you're getting into. And then, you have to love it. If you don't love it, it's going to burn you out really, really quickly because it's a lot of late nights, it's a lot of long drives, especially in the high school ranks. You're going to places you don't even know existed before.

"Having a good attitude about it is key. You don't always want to go do every game; there's going to be some nice weather when you're thinking, 'Man, I wish I could stay at home and be with the family.' But when you're there, do the best you can with it and realize that you have a chance to do something that not very many people get to do. A lot of people would love to be

It is not for the awards that he does it, but that hasn't stopped Adam from picking up some hardware, including a runner-up finish in the sports feature category at the 2017 Missouri Broadcasters Association Award Banquet.

able to do what we do—getting to watch sports and get paid for it. To me, there aren't many better things in the world to do."

TIPS AND STRATEGIES
FROM THE PROS

As a college professor, I am always searching for advice from professionals in the field. What do my students need to know before they graduate? What skills do they need to develop? What can they expect when they enter the "real world"? This project gave me a great opportunity to pick the brains of some great sportscasters.

I wanted to know how they prepare to call a game, what some of the biggest challenges are that they've faced, what they enjoy most about the profession, and if they've tried anything in their preparation that didn't work.

As I advise students, I need to know what types of classes to drive them to (or if a degree in broadcasting or journalism is even necessary) and in what extracurricular activities they should partake. I also thought it would be interesting to learn how they see themselves.

Words like journalist, artist, and entertainer are used to describe the men and women on the call. So how do they see themselves? Finally, I asked the participants in the project who their favorite sportscasters are. But I also wanted to know what attributes make them stand out.

Some of the responses to these questions were expected, based upon what I've observed and read. Others, though, were completely unexpected, making this part of the interviews a real treat.

How do you prepare for a game?

(Brad Boyer): It's a full week deal. You start off with your two-deep, your starting line-up, so you've got a board to put together. I've got all my statistics on this board. You're creating new if you're the opposition. I'll have last year's stuff on there. I'll have their long runs and the long plays of the season. I'll have hometown, high school and the honors that they've received, as much as you can jam on the board. I have a full board of information, but I'll probably only use a third of it, if that, during the broadcast. It's good to have it all even though you may not use it all.

Bottom line is score—time—names. Those are the three things that you have to focus on in a game. You cannot distract the play-by-play, the storytelling, by too many statistics. They are there to enhance the broadcast. That's one thing I try to emphasize with my young broadcasters. If you didn't have any of these numbers, you could still call an effective game by what you see and just describing it. Time and score and names. It's the easiest thing to forget. While it may sound too repetitive to you, it's hugely important. You are the eyes for your audience.

(Nate Bukaty): When I talk to students, I tell them preparation is never ending. For me, there are three main components to preparing for a game. The first is your written research. You get all the particulars on each player—height, weight, where they're from, where they've played in their careers, how you pronounce their name. That's a definite challenge. I can give you a chapter on that. Anymore, when I go through the rosters I do a Google search on every player's name and find out what articles have been written about each player going back to the last time we played and find out all I can on those guys, things that are interesting. I do that for every single player on the roster.

167

I equate preparing for a sporting event like preparing for a semester final. You have covered all this material, now we're going to get eight questions or whatever. You have no idea which parts of the semester's worth of material you're going to get, but you have to know all the material. If you don't know it, that's the one thing that comes up.

> *"I equate preparing for a sporting event like preparing for a semester final. You have covered all this material, now we're going to get eight questions or whatever. You have no idea which parts of the semester's worth of material you're going to get."*
>
> ~ Nate Bukaty on game preparation

Next is watching games. You need to watch the team, especially in a sport like soccer where it's this guy has the ball and you have to notice who it is right now. Now this guy has it. You have to know who that guy is right now. You can memorize their jersey numbers and all that, but you can't always see their jersey numbers when you're sitting up in the press box, so you need to know what they look like and how they play. You'd learn that by watching the games.

You also need to watch the other team's games, and hopefully you get their broadcasters because they know everything about their team. So, in the middle of a game they'll bring up these stories and anecdotes that you maybe didn't see in your research or you never heard about and you can go look it up. So the more you watch their games, the more you understand their team.

And then the third part is talking to people. I make sure I go to training at least once every week and pull players aside and talk to them and ask questions. One thing that we have that the fans don't is access to the people. The fans can go look up all the stats and information that I have if they want to, they can watch the games if they want to, but one thing that they don't have is the ability to go sit down with (head coach) Peter Vermes and talk to him for a half an hour or go grab a player and talk to him for half an hour. Sometimes it's not just about the game itself. It's talking to Ilie Sanchez, who's from Barcelona, about the civil unrest that's going on in his home country, and I find out his mom flew to Kansas City to live with him this whole summer because he's living in a foreign country for the first time in his life. But she was so upset by all the civil unrest that was going on, and his brother was involved in it, so she flew home to be back in Barcelona. That's something you can use in a broadcast because I do feel like one of the big things about broadcasting a game is exposing the humans that are on the field.

(John Coffey): Generally, on Sunday or Monday after the game I put my depth charts together. Even though the SIDs may not have game notes ready, I'll go to their previous weeks and get the two-deeps and then if they change I can make a change later. I spend the first night putting in the two-deeps for the opposing team. Then the next night I'll go back in and put in the stats, and then the night after that note some things that I can gather by that point in the week. That way I have repetition of looking at them night after night to get acquainted with the other team.

Then late in the week, once I have my charts together, I'll take those and with the football team, I get their Hudl deal so I'll go on in and look at whoever we're playing, pull the video off of there and just put names and numbers together with who I see. A lot of times it'll be a player that maybe doesn't pop up on the two-deep who is getting some playing time, so I'll put them into my charts at that point.

For my charts it's on legal size sheets—our offense on one with their defense and so forth. I've got it on a legal binder and just kind of flip them back and forth, try to have all my stats and everything on that legal sheet so I don't have to be looking all over trying to pull up the stats; they're all on there next to the player.

(Art Hains): Football, I've got a chart. I've got my Bears football chart that I keep for the whole season and it gets pretty marked up before the end of the year. Players get hurt and there are lineup changes and I have to make adjustments to it, but I just update it from week to week.

The other team I have to generate it new. I like to try to start that on Monday. Usually the other team doesn't have their notes up yet on Monday, so I have to go off their notes from the week before. Then there might be some changes in the lineup that I have to adjust. But you know, by the middle of the week I've updated my chart and I've prepared my chart for the other team so I'm ready for football in that regard.

Basketball, I just keep a notebook, the Bears on top and the visitors on the bottom. Then I'll just make notes on there, and again with our team it's just a matter of updating. I do a page for every game, so I've got those going back years. Alongside the player, out to the side, I've got notes about him—height, year in school, hometown, scoring average, rebound average, all that. That way you have a sheet in front of you at the game. The discipline comes in writing all that down and then making the relevant notes out to the side, whether it's a team note or a note about the coach or about the series or about the history. I can just look down at my sheet and if something comes up in the game, if it's relevant to what's going on right now, then you try to grab that stat and emphasize your point with it.

Baseball, I really do very little prep and that's a bit of a weakness because you don't know the lineup until about 30 minutes before the game. In my scorebook I include the history between the teams and current trends and what's going on. But as far as defining it down to the individual players, I scribble in the lineup real fast and then if you're really a serious baseball broadcaster you've got an index card file on the players. I know usually pretty much what our lineup is going to be, at least one through five, but I'm not quite as strong on the preparation of that simply because of the last-minute nature of the lineup.

(Greg Hassler): First of all, you cannot have enough preparation. You have to know the guys. You have to know how to say their names. It just drives me nuts when people can't say their name right. You have to know the coach's name, you have to know what each guy has done over the year, you have to know maybe a superlative of some kind.

Once I get all the details and all the players, then I research the school. What's the school all about? It's fascinating what you learn—notable alumni when you go to the notable alumni section of the Wikipedia page of that school or maybe something about that town. I mean we would go up north and into South Dakota and all the flood damage and all the people that died in these floods back in 1800. It's unbelievable stuff that you read and you can have that for your broadcast. You may never use it, but you have it.

You go to a bio page, you click on each individual person and you learn about them. There may not be anything, but all of a sudden, man clicking on this girl's bio you find out her dad played five years in the NBA. That's something you should write down.

I always like to have that nugget, like Mankato, Minnesota. The postmaster spelled it wrong in the early 1800s, so the name was changed. Who knew? I didn't know that. So, I wrote it down and talked about it during the game. That makes it better for the listener and more stuff for me to talk about.

(John Kelly): Number one, I follow the game every single day and every single night. I think I watch as much hockey as anyone. When I'm not doing a game, I'm watching hockey at night. And in the afternoon, I'm watching NHL Network, and I'm watching their show where they interview players and go through highlights and things like that. Obviously with the internet now you're always up to date with the latest trades or injuries or trade rumors. You always read the columnists, the insiders. So that's part of my everyday routine is just following hockey and consuming as much as I can.

I look at it this way: If the Blues have three games in a week, I look at it as though I have three finals. So I'll prepare for final number one, a Tuesday night game against New Jersey, and for 24 or 48 hours that's all I'll think about. I'll write my notes and read stories about the opposition, obviously go to practice, the day of game I go to the morning skate and talk to the players, talk to the coaches. I get the storylines—who's injured, what are the line combinations, things like that. I have a book like most announcers and when I come home after practice I put that all in the book so it's condensed and I know where it all is. I have a scorebook as well.

So, it's two-fold. It's the game-day prep that takes a day or two, but it's also being around the game every day and following the game and the storylines and things like that.

(Kevin Kelly): For football, preparation starts right after I get home from doing a game on Friday night. I will get some information on the next opponent for each of the three teams that we cover for the Saturday Morning Coaches Show. I will look for more information over the weekend. Then on Tuesday evening, I will do some more research. Wednesday evening, I will do pre-game interviews with the area coaches. I try to have all the starting line-ups by Wednesday night as well. Thursday night, I will put my charts together for the game and then study them on Thursday night and again Friday in the press box before the game. I have a chart that's probably legal sized piece of paper, and I have boxes that'll be the offensive line, wide receivers, quarterback, running backs. It'll be lined like this and then the defense on the other side. So it'll be, let's say the Jefferson City Jays offense. Inside the box will be their number, their position, their name—last name first—then senior. And it's color-coordinated, too. The Jays would be a red number with black names and then who they're playing against would have their numbers in blue and their names in green. So then it would be placed on a piece of cardboard, and then you flip it and it has the starting offense for the other team, and the Jays defense on the opposite end.

In basketball, I will be looking for information on teams one or two weeks before an area team plays that school. When I get my information, I take a regular sheet of paper, I'll draw five circles and inside the circle will be their last name, their first name, their number, year, height. All of that information is inside each one of those circles. Then above the circle I keep fouls, below the circle I keep a running tab of their scoring so that every time they score I can just say "that's 16 tonight for him".

(Mike Kelly): Football, I generally start preparing on the Sunday before the game, so I will pull off stats and the two-deep that was released for the previous game of the opponent. I'll start working on Sunday on updating two-deeps, numbers, stats—things like that. I generally try to get the first template done on Sunday, and then I update that throughout the course of the week, depending on what is released by the individual teams during the week. Then I'll update if there are any injuries of note that happen during the week and things like that. I also have access to video from the Mizzou football program that allows me to watch video of the opponent through an app. I'll do that as well.

Basketball is a little easier because it's only a 15-man roster. I will sit down before the game and do my own notes on eight-and-a-half by 11 paper where I will put together the rosters. Then next to each player's name I do field goal percentage, three-point percentage, free-throw percentage, points, rebounds, assist-to-turnover ratio. Then for the team I have rebounds, points, and turnovers.

You'll have a program with the rosters, but I prefer having my own because it just helps me familiarize myself with the roster. And then I'll dive into the game notes to see if there are interesting stories and trends and things like that. You read a lot of newspapers each day. Obviously with Twitter you follow different stuff that happens so you try to do that and try to get a feel for what's out there.

(Mike McClure): For high school, we notify the coaches in advance to let them know which games I'm broadcasting. The first thing you need to do is get a numerical roster, and then email the coach and ask for the offensive and defensive starters and for a copy of updated stats. You used to be able to get a lot of stuff out of newspapers but because of the changes, not so much anymore. The internet is really helpful. Go on there, look and you can get some good information. The MSHSAA (Missouri State High School Activities Association) website has been a great resource. We can go back and look at their scores. There are ways to find information; you just have to put in the time and dig and find it.

Talk to the coach, and it takes a while to earn the coach's trust. I'm not going to go share information with the opponent. Monett's playing Aurora. I'm not going to go share Monett's information with Aurora, and I'm not going to share Aurora's information with Monett. What they tell me stays with me. That's the only way to build up confidence and respect and trust in my craft and what I do. I think that gets around, so coaches may share information about a key injury or things that are coming up.

College is easier because of the internet and the information that's available. You still put in the hours, still talk to people, but you can do a lot more on your own versus relying on coaches and sports information directors.

> *"It kind of stands to reason, but it's way better to be over-prepared than under-prepared."*
>
> ~ Art Haines on what works in game prep

(Dan McLaughlin): Wake up, probably scour the internet just to see if anything is happening on the national level with the game of baseball, then really dive into the pitching matchup of that night. I have a big score card I developed that I keep and I travel with that. I'll make notes on that scorecard for that night's game. I get to the ballpark really early. If I'm on the road, I get to the ballpark by 1:30, 2:00, if I'm at home I get there by 2:30, 3:00 (for a 7:00 game).

Once I'm there at the ballpark I'll go down to the clubhouse—probably both, but more so our clubhouse—just to talk to people, see what is going on, go on the field for batting practice, visit with people. Sometimes there are specific things I'm looking for from a player or a coach that I want to ask about and bring up on the broadcast. Then I'll head upstairs, look over the game notes, do the final research that I may have to do, and get ready for the game.

(Greg Schmidt): When I get my schedule every August I'll email all the administrators of all the home schools of all the places we're going to go, and say, "August 18th we'll be at your field to broadcast, is that okay?" Then I'll send out another email to the next guy, "August 25th we'll be at your school to broadcast, is that okay? This is what we'll need." I'll take care of the whole season at once. I'll get that out of the way before the season even starts.

The Monday before that particular week, I'll email the host administrator, remind them we're coming and ask them to please send me a roster. I'll email the visiting AD to tell them we're going to be there to broadcast, please send me a roster. Then I'll email both coaches saying I'm going to need 15 to 20 minutes of their time over the phone the middle of the week.

I talk with the coaches over the phone for 15-20 minutes, get a little bit on their starting lineup, get a little background on them that's pertinent on some of the kids they have who are injured and won't play, who's injured and only half speed, that type of stuff. I combine that information on the teams with what they did when they met last year.

> *"When you're home, you pour into the family. You can never balance it out for what they do for you and for your career, but you do every little thing possible while you're there to make memories."*
>
> ~ Adam Winkler on balancing the job with down time

I leave home to go to KMMO, pick up the equipment, tape my pregame show, probably leave KMMO at 4:15 to 4:30. I'll arrive at the field at 5:15 for a 7 o'clock kickoff, and set up my equipment. I usually have it arranged ahead of time with the coaches, so we do our pregame show. We tape the pregame show on the field during warm-ups with each head coach for about 3 minutes ahead of time, we get that ready, and then once that's done, about 6:15 or so, then it's on the air at 6:40.

When the game is over, I head back to the station and join the crew there helping provide scoreboard show coverage and post-game interviews with many of the coaches that phone us from throughout the area. The football scoreboard show usually lasts until about 12:30-12:45 a.m. making Fridays in the fall a pretty full day.

What has worked for you in your preparation and in calling a game? What hasn't?

(Art Hains): It kind of stands to reason, but it's way better to be over-prepared than under-prepared. You know if you've got some stuff that you haven't used at the end of the night then that's not the end of the world, but if you run out of ammo then it's tough. You can never be over-prepared.

(Greg Hassler): You always try to find shortcuts, to find different stuff. But you just have to sit down and do it, you know. By a couple of games, you'll know your team; it's the other team that you sometimes have a hard time figuring out. It took me a while to figure out what stats are important and what stats aren't, to know what matters and what doesn't. That just takes experience and time.

(Kevin Kelly): I would say that one of the frustrating things, and maybe something that doesn't work all the time, is getting information from the other school. Sometimes that just ends up being a situation where you just don't ever make the connection. They're not available when you're available, or you're not available when they're available. Then you have to find another way to get it. You sit down, you go through stuff, and you talk to the coach that you work with here. You ask, "What did you see?" and "What do you expect?" Those things that you would ask them in an interview. Are they going to play five wide receivers? Are they going to run an offset-I? But it's always nice to be able to contact the other coach and get that information.

(Mike Kelly): I think anytime that you get into a game when it's a blowout, you invariably think to yourself, "Do I have enough material?" and then at some point in time you also have to balance that with, particularly on radio, call the play. TV, a blowout is worse, I would assume, than for radio because they have to figure out a way to tell stories and justify and fill. For us, it's continuing to call the play and then go from there, but you know you also have to figure out "why". Why has this happened? So those are things that you're always looking for in terms of notes or stats during the game, things like that.

(Greg Schmidt): Until about four years ago we would do the pregame stuff to our football broadcasts live from the field itself. You find out that if you go on live there's a lot of commotion in the press box. Sometimes you have to stop for the national anthem or a pregame prayer or something like that. When you would do the bulk of the pregame stuff live in the press box itself things never went the way you wanted as far as a timeline is concerned, so we found three or four years ago the best thing to do is to tape at least half of the pregame show ahead of time in a studio and play that. It took me 40 years to figure this.

What is the most difficult aspect of the job of sportscaster?

(John Coffey): Probably the time that it takes to do it properly. You know, I think a lot of people think you just show up and turn on the mic and you go. To do it right it takes a lot of time in the game prep, and I mean it's like doing homework for classes. I kind of look at it as your exam is on Saturday, or for basketball you get a couple tests a week.

(Greg Hassler): You can't play every game at home. There is a lot of travel. You miss a lot of stuff. I have a daughter, and I've seen a lot of her stuff and I've missed a lot of her stuff. But on the other hand, you still have to feed her and put a roof over her head and all that. That's the way it goes; it's the life we lead. You still have to provide for them even though you can't be at everything.

(John Kelly): I think the most challenging part today is literally calling the game in the broadcast positions we're given that are so high in most arenas. It just is physically challenging to see the ice from the top of a 19,000-seat arena. In the old St. Louis Arena, in the old Chicago Stadium, the Montreal Forum, the Boston Garden—a lot of these old buildings would be 50-percent closer and it was so much easier to physically read the numbers. And sometimes you didn't even need to see the numbers; you could tell by how long a player's hair was or how he skated.

I remember my dad, when I was maybe in my teens, he was sort of complaining to me one day that all the players are wearing helmets now. He started when the players didn't wear helmets. When the Blues came around in '67, only a few players wore helmets. And I remember in the mid '70s my dad complaining when most of the players started wearing helmets that it's hard to tell the players apart now.

173

(Mike Kelly): I've been very blessed. I only know one time where a coach really had an issue with what I said. It was when Missouri played San Diego State a few years back. Prior to a TJ Moe touchdown, San Diego State gets possession of the football and they've got a running back by the name Ronnie Hillman who had rushed for almost 200 yards that night. If they give the ball to Ronnie Hillman three times and they get one first down, ball game's over, and I said that on the air. "It looks like San Diego State's going to win." Now, why, oh why, oh why they threw the ball on first and second down, and it created a three and out and Missouri got the football back, I have no idea. (Note: Moe scored on a 68-yard pass from Blaine Gabbert with 51 seconds left to give Mizzou the win in 2010.). But Gary Pinkel took exception to the fact that I thought the game was over, and you know, I pointed out to him the facts that led me to reach that conclusion. And he took exception that I said that this would have been their first win on the road against a top-25 team in like 20 years, and he didn't think that I should as a broadcaster use that. That's newspaper print material. I was like, no that's not print material; that's germane to the broadcast and, you know, we agreed to disagree, but that's the only time anybody has ever said anything, so I've been really lucky in that regard.

(Dan McLaughlin): I can answer this, but if people read it, they don't care. I don't think they should care whether or not we're tired or we got off on a road trip at 5 in the morning or that we've been on the road for two weeks. No fan cares about that, nor should they. They should just worry about how their team is doing and watching the game. I try never to bring that stuff up because I just don't think it's worth it. We're away from our families, we travel a lot and, it's the job we signed up for and if we want to do something else, we should do something else. If we complain, then shame on us.

(Adam Winkler): The hours by far, especially if you have a family. Trying to balance an 8 to 5 job and then another five hours a night doing a ball game. That can be taxing on your family. Your kids want to see you, especially when they're young. It's tough that you leave before they get up and you get home after they go to bed. You might not see them for a day or two, depending on what your schedule is like, so that's the biggest challenge. You have to have an understanding spouse who knows that's what you do and they just kind of accept the schedule as it is and move forward with it.

When you're home, you pour into the family. You can never balance it out for what they do for you and for your career, but you do every little thing possible while you're there to make memories. When the kids get a little bigger, I'm sure they'll be involved. We'll be bringing them to games, letting them sit in the broadcast booth and letting them enjoy those types of things. You have those chances to do that as a high school play-by-play guy, and that gives your kids the opportunity to be involved with you.

What is the best part about it?

(Greg Hassler): I like the coaches, especially at D-II. The coaches are more approachable because they aren't superstars. They're very talented guys with great backgrounds. I like the events. I like the home events, obviously, but I also like being on the road. I'm a single guy, and I just like getting out there, seeing different things. And we're fortunate because we have good teams. I may not be so optimistic if we were 2-17 in the league each year. That wouldn't be any fun. But I like getting out there on the road; it's almost a break from reality, actually. You know how people say when they buy a ticket and go to a sporting event, that is their break from work? You're getting away from everything negative. That is your escape for that three-hour period. Well, that is how it is for me, only a lot more often. I put on that headset and I have escaped from reality.

(Mitch Holthus): I love competition. It's the passion, and other than playing, coaching, or officiating, if you're going to do play-by-play of an event, it's the closest thing there is to that. You can prepare—and I do a prodigious amount of preparation—but you have no idea what's going to happen. It's not reading a teleprompter, and you have to be able to react. It's my pilot light that turns me on. I don't know what's going to happen, and I've got to be able to react. Can I say the right words in a split second? Because there is no rehearsal. I love that part of it.

What I've learned to love about it is that it is a conduit to making your life really count for others. That may sound like a trite or a self-serving answer, but it's really true. It's Cameron Black, who has never seen a game. Never seen anything in his life. It's the theatre of the mind created for him. All that Cameron has is the theatre of the mind. That's all he has. So, if what I do is performing and drawing a tapestry that creates the theatre of his mind, that's pretty awesome. There's not many things you can do in life that gets to do that. As years have gone on, there's more and more examples of something like that. But it gives you a chance to make your life count the way the Lord wants you to, to make it count in ways that you didn't think you could, to maximize it in the benefits you can have for others.

> "You know how people say when they buy a ticket and go to a sporting event, that is their break from work? Well, that is how it is for me, only a lot more often. I put on that headset and I have escaped from reality."
>
> ~ Greg Hassler on the best part of being a sportscaster

(John Kelly): The best thing is announcing the games. You get to the rink and you might have issues in your life, like everybody, but when you get behind the microphone and you sit down for three hours, you forget about everything else and you enjoy the game and you enjoy the broadcast and you are sort of in your own world. I do that 70, 75 times a year. The preparation is not hard, but it takes a lot of work. It takes effort. But the games themselves are the best part.

(Dan McLaughlin): I can't speak for everybody, but for me, it's doing my hometown team. This is the team I grew up cheering for, I learned a lot of history about them, it's the team I love, I want to see the franchise do well in all aspects—of business, of on-field play, of being good stewards of the city, and we're part of the fabric of the community, and being a part of that is probably the best part of it for me. Just realizing I'm tied into an iconic franchise, and I've been doing it for a long time.

(Erik Sean): There are a lot of people who would love to be doing my job broadcasting Division I athletics, and I never take it for granted. The way I look at it, I get to go to the game, I get in for free, they feed me when I'm there and give me everything I need to eat and drink, they give me the best seat in the house. Just a perfect seat. They let me broadcast the game and then I get a paycheck. I mean, I'm stealing money. I love what I do,

175

and if you love what you do and you really put your energy into it and you really prepare, your listeners can tell, and they'll appreciate it. Just think about how great of a job you've got. Never take it for granted because there are a lot of people that would switch places with you.

What kinds of classes would you recommend for someone wanting to be a sportscaster?

(Brad Boyer): You know the one that probably needs the most work for young broadcasters is writing. I know that doesn't have anything to do with the actual calling in a game, but in this world where you're putting stories up on the website writing is a big part of it.

(Nate Bukaty): One of the things that I really appreciate, and I don't know if colleges still do this, but when I was at KU, if you graduated from the journalism school I believe only a third of your courses were actually in journalism. The other two-thirds of your courses were in liberal arts or whatever else. You got to pick a concentration of different courses, and I picked English, history and psychology. If you want to be a good journalist, the more knowledge you have the better you'll be, the more well-rounded you'll be.

I would encourage anybody who's going to try to become a broadcaster to take as many different classes as possible and really take them seriously and learn. Just learn. My co-host on the morning show has an English degree. I would encourage going to journalism school. I would encourage taking broadcast classes. I would encourage taking classes, like I said, to be well-rounded in all mass media forms.

(John Coffey): Speech classes obviously for the sportscasting part. At Northwest there are also some classes the coaches teach, like there's a couple football coaching classes and I think basketball teaches something. Some of our students take those classes where the coaching staff lets them sit in and watch them break down game films and things like that. And then there's a couple officiating classes I think would be good for them to take.

Writing classes are good. Any type of reading classes; even though it might be outside the realm of sports, any knowledge you can bring into to the broadcast is good. You look at Vin Scully. How many different things he talks about during a game that's probably not even sports related but he's able to bring in at the right time to make it work. I think the more knowledge you have the better.

(Art Hains): Obviously electronic media where you get some practical experience, probably TV and radio. Running the equipment, working in front of the camera and behind the camera.

I can't emphasize enough the importance of writing. I know newspapers are going away and all that, but you still have to have a writing background. People might say, "Well, you're talking; you don't need to write well". I think it's important to be able to express your thoughts on paper in that way so I'd say writing is very important.

> *"Learn to write the King's English. The ability to communicate, written and verbally, is a commodity that you can't put a price on."*
>
> *~ Mitch Holthus on the classes aspiring sportscasters should take*

(Mitch Holthus): I have my own company, so I'm still involved in sales and marketing. So, get your sales background as well. I have a business degree and a journalism degree. Try to get a broad-based background.

Learn to write the King's English. The ability to communicate, written and verbally, is a commodity that you can't put a price on. And it's very important to have interpersonal skills. There's a struggle with having interpersonal skills. You need that.

Women and men who want to get into this field don't understand the psychology of sport. What do you ask Travis Kelce when you've lost six out of seven games? How do you deal with Coach Reid? How do you deal with players? Empathy. Having a heart for people. One thing I'm kind of proud of is when we go through times like this, people will come to me. "I just want to talk to you." Well, I'm not a counselor, but are they drawn to you or are they repelled by you? And so, I'm thinking, this is part of my mission. It's not just to say "Touchdown! Kansas City!" You have to learn empathy and understand how to communicate, how to listen. Have a heart. That comes from taking psychology classes, that comes from being involved in a leadership program where you lead and you also follow.

> *"I think you have to have a feel for the sport and the game. I remember my dad telling me that a game is a build-up and a crescendo."*
>
> ~ John Kelly on the attributes of a great sportscaster

(John Kelly): You have to have the degree, to me. You have to go to classes and you have to learn the writing and the rules and laws of broadcasting and all that, but as far as becoming an on-air professional, you have to do it. No offense to any professor or teacher; they can help you, they can instruct you. But you have to do it. It's trial and error, it's reps.

The other thing that's really important—and I got a minor in journalism—is that, no matter what position you have in broadcasting, you're going to have to write. I think that being a strong writer is never going to hurt you in broadcasting. If I were to advise a young broadcaster, I would say get as much hands-on experience as you can and be a strong writer.

(Kevin Kelly): I think that it helps to take a newspaper reporting class. I think it helps, obviously, to take broadcasting classes, but I think newspaper reporting and the writing type classes, even though you're doing voice play-by-play, I think those things help. I really do. To me, it helps me do play-by-play. I write every day, and I think to have that kind of background helps.

Any type of reporting classes are going to help you because play-by-play is not the only thing you do in connection with a play-by-play broadcast. You're doing interviews and that type of stuff, and we'll come back from a pregame interview and we're pulling off a tape cut and then we're writing a story. So I think those two things really work well.

(Ryan Lefebvre): What I tell high school kids and kids who are just getting into college is that English is your most important subject right now. How you speak, speaking grammatically correct, speaking with authority because you have a grasp of the language is so important. A lot of your communication now is not conducive to speaking grammatically correct and in full sentences. But that is what is going to separate you when you want to get into it. So, when you're texting, be texting like you are going to be sending it to a professor. My mom was an English major and corrected my English my whole life, even in front of girls, and it was embarrassing. But I was grateful for it.

(Erik Sean): One thing I will say if you're going to get into radio period, make sure that you take as many writing classes as you can—creative writing, whatever. I sit and type my sportscast and I write every single day of my professional life. Being able to word things, being able to write, and having a grasp of the English language, having a grasp on vocabulary is so important. If you're working at a radio station you're writing promos. Maybe you're in the creative services department where you're writing copy or you're writing commercials. You're writing news, whatever. One of the key things in radio is you're going to be doing a lot of writing, and so make sure to take your English courses and your writing classes seriously.

(Adam Winkler): I was only required to take like two years of radio or something like that, and it wasn't in depth because the degree wasn't for that. The degree was kind of more a self-taught thing on my end at Ottawa.

Obviously, speech would be something that you'd want to get involved in just because of the amount that you're doing to make sure you're saying the right thing at the right time. That just helps with your confidence because as a broadcaster you're going to be called to do public speaking. You're going to be up in front of crowds. Home is behind the radio mic. You can be talking to four million people, and it doesn't bother you at all. But you get up in front of 200 people speaking to a crowd, and you're scared to death.

Journalism would be another thing. I took newspaper and yearbook just to help out with those. It's not a passion of mine. I don't love to write, it's nothing I want to do, but those classes are needed to at least learn the basics.

What kinds of activities would you recommend?
(Brad Boyer): I've had people say, "How do you do play-by-play?" I don't know how to teach play-by-play. I can give you tips, but it's just something you have to do, and you have to find your style. It's not the easiest thing in the world. I have people say, "Well I think I could call a game," and I'm like, "Oh, yeah? You would? Just try to do it in front of a TV and see how it works." This was something I did, and the first time I did it I was awful. But you just sink or swim. Just get out there and do it.

(Nate Bukaty): You have to get internships. You have to make connections. Almost every job that I've gotten came because somebody knew who I was, remembered me from an internship I did or a job I did for them. You have to make the people realize how serious you are about the job, that you'll work weird hours, late hours, holidays, weekends nobody else wants to work. You have to make the time count, to make yourself stand out.

The best advice I got is go be bad somewhere for a while. Broadcast games where no one's watching you, no one's listening. Get some experience and grow as a broadcaster. That's important. You have to make contact. You can get all the experience you want, but if you don't have some people to help you get a job somewhere, it won't matter.

(John Coffey): I didn't do that growing up, and I probably should have. But any time you're in front of the public and speaking, that's good. Playing some of the sports will help, too. It gives you a little bit more understanding of what the athletes are going through. Depending on if you're going to a small school, you can compete in all those sports. I played a couple of years on the Northwest tennis team.

In college I worked on the campus station plus KXCV as an announcer and also worked part-time at a station in Bethany trying to get as much experience as I could. Anyone interested in doing play-by-play should practice as much as possible. When I was in college if I wasn't doing a game on the college station I would take my tape recorder and find a spot in the crowd and record the game and bring it to a couple of my instructors to critique each week.

Also, I stress to our kids even though their goal is to be a sportscaster it's important for them to develop strong writing skills and learn how to write a news story, cover city council meetings, do board shifts and go out and sell. Very rarely is someone going to get an all-sports position in their first job after graduation. The more skills they have the more employable they are.

> *"If you can do internships, remember you are beginning a career. My first job gave me $5 an hour and $50 a game, and I was having a blast. I loved it."*
>
> ~ Ryan LeFebvre on in which activities to participate

(Mike Kelly): I think you have to find a way to get hands-on experience. If you want to be a play-by-play person, you have to find opportunities to call games, whether that is sitting in the stands at a high school game with a microphone or sitting at Kauffman Stadium or Busch Stadium or inside Mizzou Arena or Allen Fieldhouse or someplace and having a microphone and doing play-by-play and developing your own style. Taping games, you know DVRing a game and sitting there in your apartment doing play-by-play into microphone. I think that's very, very important.

(Ryan Lefebvre): If you can do internships, remember you are beginning a career. You are starting a career right now. Try not to judge your first jobs on how much money you make or how big your market is. Judge your first job by how often you get to be on the air. The more you are on the air, the better you're getting, the better product you can have when you apply for your next job. I did three unpaid internships before I got my first job. My first job gave me $5 an hour and $50 a game, and I was having a blast. I loved it. I've been so blessed in so many ways to be doing Major League Baseball for 24 years. It's far beyond what I could have ever imagined. But I'm not having any more fun now than when I was doing it for $5 an hour and 50 bucks a game. I mean, I loved it. I loved the research, I loved setting up the equipment, I enjoyed doing the game, I enjoyed listening to the game afterwards and thinking "I'm going to do these three things better". I couldn't wait to do the next game because I was going to do those three things better, and then listening to the game and thinking, "That sounded better!" So, it's not any more fun for me right now. It's more rewarding and I get to provide for my family; there are a lot of nice things that come from broadcasting at this level for a long time. But the fun part of it hasn't changed.

(Mike McClure): Obviously playing sports and understanding the sport you're covering is very, very important. Honestly the most important thing is just get out there and do it.

Take your smartphone out to an American Legion baseball game in the summer, sit in the stands, fill out a score sheet, and start broadcasting. Or go to a high school football game and just practice. All I can tell you is work hard at it. The financial rewards are not there in the beginning; there's just not a lot of pay at the high school level. But if you stay with it and you do work hard at it, and if you are fortunate enough to have your own business and do this for a living, it's rewarding.

> *"There's a lot of trial and error, so I think if you really want to be on air, you just gotta get on air and you gotta practice and you have to find out what you like and what you don't."*
>
> ~ Dan McLaughlin on in which activities to participate

(Dan McLaughlin): I always say that, specifically if you are looking to be on air, you're not going to find it in a book. You either do it and go practice your craft and go work and work and work, or it's just not going to happen. There are things you can read about in a book that may help you with background, but if you're going to be on air, it's an applied skill. You have to work at it, you have to practice it.

When I speak to kids, I always tell them you have to get behind a microphone, whether you're practicing in your room calling a game or you go to a ballgame and you get in a booth and you send it to your recorder or you do what I did, which was call high school football games for $25 and high school basketball games, that's what you do. That's how you learn. The more you do it the more you'll learn.

There's a lot of trial and error, so I think if you really want to be on air, you just have to get on air and you gotta practice and you have to find out what you like and what you don't.

(Erik Sean): It doesn't matter if you graduated from Syracuse, which is one of the great broadcasting schools in the country. You could rock it and you could graduate from Syracuse with a degree. That doesn't mean that you can sit down and host a sports talk show for an hour or two hours or sit down and do a football game just because you've gone through all the classes and you've got the degree. It's about getting experience.

When I was first starting out, when I was stationed down in Florida I would get some people that would say to me, "Where are you from? Alabama?" I thought, What are you talking about? They heard a twang in my voice, a southern twang, and I thought, Man if I'm going to be a broadcaster I have to get rid of that. So those overnight shifts that I used to have at the radio station, I would go back to the Associated Press wire, and I would print a sports minute where you have four or five little sports stories. I would record myself doing a sportscast, and then I would listen to it and listen to my enunciation, and it was terrible. My inflection on the wrong word was obvious, and boy I could hear the twang in my voice—I'm talking too fast and not enunciating. Do it again and I would record again and I would do it again and do it again. I worked hard on trying to get my enunciation, my voice, my rhythm—all of those things. So, if you're going to be a successful broadcaster I suggest you start getting experience as quickly as you possibly can.

(Adam Winkler): You can't replace the hands-on, so my encouragement would be to find a university that has a radio station that you can get involved with. If their community has a radio station, that can be an advantage because you can say, "Hey I'm here to learn. Whatever you want me to do, I'm here to help out." To me that's the most invaluable. Experience. To have the hands-on experience and to do the play-by-play for four years and work with KOFO in Ottawa ... they gave me opportunities. And then doing internships like at 810 in Kansas City. That's the best thing that you can do.

What do you believe is your number one job? Journalist? Entertainer? Translator? Artist? Something else?

(Brad Boyer): Be a storyteller. The whole broadcast you're telling the story. The opening scene setter, right from the tip-off or the kickoff. Here's what's happening. The Bulldogs are receiving. They're going to be working left to right, or toward the east end zone of the Stoke Stadium field turf. Purple end zones, Bulldogs painted in white. Purple "T" at midfield. Stokes Stadium fans dressed in purple, full stands and fans are spilling out into the grass hill sitting, watching this game. Describe the uniforms.

Within all that, again, just the basics of what's taking place in front of you, the total story. I think you can ... I wouldn't say entertain ... but I would like people to say, at the end of the broadcast, it was enjoyable. But I think journalist is part of it. It all goes into the storytelling aspect. I'm presenting facts. That's journalism.

(Nate Bukaty): A lot of my friends and colleagues in the newspaper industry, they feel that being a journalist indicates an element of impartiality. I think a journalist is someone who catalogs something that happened. Isn't that basically the base definition? And if that's what a journalist is, then I think that is one of the first jobs of being a broadcaster. But not always are you impartial. If you're working for the network, then you're impartial. But if you're working for a team, you're working for the team.

I do think there's a huge element of being an entertainer because if I don't find the game interesting and compelling, why should you as a viewer? Most of us our goal is to capture those exciting moments and convey them to everybody. I don't think it's your job to be the entertainment; your job is to highlight the entertainment.

(John Coffey): The important thing is just to describe what you see. I don't think you want to become too much of a homer. To me it's obvious; we know who our audience is, but I think there's only been twice in the 32 years I've done the Bearcats I've used the word "we" and I got mad at myself each time. I have nothing to do with what's going on out on the field. Just describe what you see. That, to me, is the biggest job that you've got, and I try to do it in a way that is entertaining but accurate.

(Art Hains): A little bit of both journalist and entertainer. Journalist because even though I work for the university and I want the Bears to win, I am going to be as impartial as I can in describing what I see. I think the listeners, if they are listening to a team broadcast, they want you to be for the team. But I have shied away from really being a blatant homer.

I'll also acknowledge you are an entertainer to a degree, too. You're trying to not only inform but entertain and keep the listener engaged.

(Mitch Holthus): All of the above. It's blackening the oval of all of the above. Those are not mutually exclusive. Depending on the assignment, depending on the game, one of the categories can be emphasized at any given time, but they're all important. There is no one greater than the other, and no one less important than the other. It's all of that. It's one of the things I try to do with everything I do is to hit every one of those.

(Kevin Kelly): I don't look at it as entertainer, no. I would say that my job when I walk into a gym or to a football stadium is to be the eyes of the person that's listening and to the best that I can do paint them a picture to make them feel like they were there and they saw what happened.

(Mike Kelly): I think when you say you're a journalist sometimes you take yourself a little too seriously. Now, I do think that as you're using that palette to create the picture of what the listener is seeing as they drive, there's an element of journalism that comes into play and that is being accurate in what you describe. Don't fool the listener. If it's a bad pass, say it's a bad pass. If it's a ball that's dropped, it's a ball that's dropped. I think what happens is that sometimes maybe people try to soft sell what they're seeing.

You know, again, going back to the numbers. Therein lies the issue. So I think there are elements of journalism that come into play. Are we journalists? Yeah, we report facts. I will say this about journalism versus play-by-play. Go back to the earthquake in 1989 (during the World Series between the San Francisco Giants and the Oakland A's). Who had the best live coverage, the best live description of what was taking place? Jack Buck on radio and Al Michaels on TV because they were used to describing for their audience what they were seeing. Other newspaper or other television journalists didn't have that ability. These guys could capture the moment because they've done it.

(Ryan Lefebvre): I've come up with what I call a triangle. I'm a reporter because I'm trying to report on what's going on. Ernie Harwell told me one day that he thinks it's harder for us today than it was when he started because when he started you were just a reporter. Now fans want some opinion from you, they want you to analyze things more, which they didn't do back then. So, it's like I'm the reporter and, I'm not sure I want to use the word "columnist", but yeah, I'm a reporter and a columnist.

I don't think there's any shame in this at all: I'm an extension of the Royals public relations department. I will never lie to the audience, but I think despite what you may read on social media most fans want to hear the good in their team. I'm trying to get you to watch the team and hopefully come to see the game in person. So, there is a bias because I am an employee of the Royals too, and I'm not bashful about that at all. That is part of my job is to be part of the public relations team.

(Mike McClure): I hope you're a journalist. I don't want you to be the entertainer because that makes it about you and not about the game or the athletes involved in the game. Again, I think it's important to share informational nuggets that are pertaining to that night or that event, and don't just throw a nugget out there just because you have one, even though it's not applicable. Save it for your rain delay. At the same time, go back to the basics of tell the score, tell me who's leading, and tell me where we're at in the game.

(Dan McLaughlin): I think my number one job is to give people enjoyment, to make the games enjoyable, to make the games fun, to make the games exciting, to maybe laugh a little bit, to make the calls exciting, which I take a lot of pride in.

I take pride in always making sure that I come to the ballpark with energy. The minute that game starts there's a lot of energy coming out of me, and so my number one thing is to make the game entertaining for the fan and to make it enjoyable and then also to sell the game of baseball. I think that's another part of my job, too. You know, I'm trying to make people not only watch the games on TV but to come on down to the ballpark and experience what we have. Let us tell you why you should buy a ticket and let us tell you what the game experience is like when you're here and that they are really going to enjoy it, whether it's you're on a date or you're bringing your kids to the game or you're reconnecting with your grandfather or your grandmother, whatever. Those are the things I try to explain and hopefully do—sell the game, sell the Cardinals and make it enjoyable.

(Greg Schmidt): Journalist. I'm old school. I still believe that you're relaying information. I still believe that you're telling people what is happening. Now, you can mix a little entertainment in. There's other aspects along with that, but number one you're a journalist. You're supposed to be doing a game between two area teams.

(Erik Sean): I think you're a communicator, and when I say that you are a communicator you are communicating exactly what is going on, and the audience should be able to see it in their mind because you have communicated it to them in such a way that they can see it. That makes me feel the best when somebody comes up to me or will send an email or something like that and just say, "Man, I can totally see what's going on when I listen to you broadcast." Again, that is the ultimate compliment because you've got to be able to paint a picture, you've got to be an artist.

(Adam Winkler): My number one job is to describe exactly what's going on in front of me and be the eyes of those who are listening. That's what I'm supposed to do. That involves different voice inflection and different types of emotion. But my job is to describe what's going on in front of me to the best of my ability.

I always think about the story Danny Matthews told when he was being inducted into the Royals Hall of Fame. He was talking about a letter that a lady had sent him from western Kansas saying, "I'm blind, but I listen to you every single night and you're my eyes." I still think about that, so when I sit there and do a game, I picture that one person just sitting in a chair listening. If someone is not there at the game, that can be the person I'm broadcasting to tonight, and I try and describe it as detailed as I can.

> *"Be a storyteller. The whole broadcast you're telling the story. The opening scene setter, right from the tip-off or the kickoff."*
>
> ~ Brad Boyer on the role of the sportscaster

What are the four or five attributes you believe set the great sportscasters apart from the good ones?

(Nate Bukaty): Number one is definitely worth ethic. You have to approach the job with a sense of urgency. You can't feel like you've ever made it. To me, the guys who are great you can just tell how much preparation has gone in, how passionate they are about their job.

Some of the great ones are natural. They're naturally gifted speakers. They're not forced, they don't sound like they're trying to be a character or put on some sort of front or do an impression of a broadcaster. They are articulate. They know how to organize their thoughts into words that are easy to understand. They're able to paint a picture extemporaneously with their words.

Third is they have a feel for what moves, and that can be the big moment, it can be how to put the big moment in the context to kind of capture it. You have to have a feel for what gets people. You talk about Jack Buck. Some of those moments: "I don't believe what I just saw. I don't BELIEVE what I just saw". You know, that's not Charles Dickens. It's a simple sentence, but the way he said it and the way he said it both times captured the unbelievable emotion of the moment of Kirk Gibson's home run (in the 1988 World Series). I think the great ones have that. They have that knack and that feel for what moves people.

(Art Hains): They have a way of capturing the moment and painting the picture. The biggest compliment you can receive is when somebody says, "I felt like I was there." That's the idea. I worked with Brad Sham in Dallas. He was my boss at KRLD, and he's now, I think, the second-longest tenured NFL announcer.

Brad always talked about painting the picture, the word picture, and in a timely manner. A clear description of what's going on in the game but also what's going on otherwise—the color of the sky, the direction of the wind, the flags, the leaves blowing—anything you can do to bring the listener there in his or her mind.

(Greg Hassler): Obviously voice and delivery are very important. Knowledge of what you're doing, knowledge of the sport. And game prep. That's very important. I also think taking it seriously, taking what you're doing seriously, but not taking yourself seriously. Don't walk in there thinking you're big-time. You're not. You're rolling in there, calling the game, and then driving home six hours. There is nothing big-time about that. You have to enjoy it and take it seriously.

(John Kelly): I think you have to have a feel for the sport and the game. I hear too many announcers call a goal and quite honestly, I couldn't tell if the goal was scored in game three of the regular season in the second period to make the score 4-1 or if the goal was scored in game seven and overtime. The great announcers know the difference and know when to use emphasis and when to use drama in their voice. I remember my dad telling me that a game is a build-up and a crescendo and you shouldn't be quite as energetic and as enthusiastic in the first period as you are in the third period because the third period is more important in most games.

A great announcer like a Jack Buck with a call like "Go crazy, folks! Go crazy!" — why can he come up with that and why can't an ordinary or an average announcer come up with that? I don't have an answer for that, but that's one thing that separates a great announcer is he has the ability to separate the greatest moment with the best call. When a Jack Buck comes up with that or Al Michaels with his famous "Do you believe in miracles" call, they are obviously great announcers who had the ability to capture a great moment with an iconic call.

> *"I think there are elements of journalism that come into play. Are we journalists? Yeah, we report facts."*
>
> ~ Mike Kelly on the role of the sportscaster

(Kevin Kelly): I think the visual picture that they provide. The great ones, you close your eyes and they've got you right there. You can see everything even though you're not there. You can visualize everything that they're telling you and they're on top of it in terms of all of the players and the play and all that information that goes along with the broadcast that they relate to you.

(Ryan Lefebvre): Knowledge of the game. Knowledge of whatever game they're broadcasting. And you don't have to play it to have a knowledge of the game. I mean, people say that I played the game. I was a college player; I didn't play Major League Baseball, so I don't put myself in that I played the game. I probably learned more about the game as a broadcaster than as a player.

> *"Being accurate, being descriptive, paying attention to detail."*
>
> ~ Greg Schmidt on the attributes of a great sportscaster

Being yourself on the air and not trying to sound like another announcer. I think the really good ones sound the same off the air as they do on the air. Their personality is the same off the air as it is on the air.

Being humble. Look, I could go away tomorrow, and the Royals would still open and play 162 games. But the Royals go away and I go away. I think there comes a point we have to realize the broadcast is not about us; it's about the players and the fans, and we're in the middle, we're the conduit, that's all that we are.

And preparation. You have to be prepared. There are three things that I would require out of everyone on our crew—not that I hire people—but what I require myself: be prepared; treat everybody with respect, and that's everyone on the crew because we're all in this together, we all need each other; and don't make the broadcast about you. Pretty simple.

(Mike McClure): Knowledge of the game. The passion for what they do. Not resting on their laurels; always wanting to get better. Some just have "it", and when I say "it" I mean they have the voice made for radio or the voice made for TV. It sure doesn't hurt when you have the voice. People want to hear an Art Hains, a Vin Scully, a Jack Buck.

(Greg Schmidt): Being accurate, being descriptive, paying attention to detail and not only paying attention to detail but being able to relay that in a manner that's concise, using as few words as possible.

(Adam Winkler): I think number one you have to have a knowledge of the team that you're covering. People know if you have a knowledge of the team you're covering or not. Take a look at Mitch Holthus. Man, you know he knows every single thing about every single guy on that team and the opposing team. That comes from preparation and the amount he pours into that.

Number two, you have to be able to capture the moment. Some guys have that knack for just being able to capture the moment and say the right thing. I think that comes from preparation, too, and from the ability to recognize, "Alright, this might be coming up. This is what I'm going to go to."

Number three is kind of reining in your emotions because if you're in love with the team that you're covering, honestly your emotions can sway really high or sway really low with how the game is going. You have to realize that you have no bearing over what happens in the game, so jumping on an official or saying this is a stupid play call or something like that is not good.

I think number four, you have to really love what you're doing. If you don't love what you're doing, people are going to be able to pick it up. A play-by-play announcer can go through the motions of a game and just call a game and get by, but people can tell if you're just getting by. You have to love what you're doing, you have to enjoy the opportunity to be a play-by-play broadcaster because the jobs are few and far between. Trying to get into this profession is tough; once you're in, you want to stay in and not get out.

About the Author

This is Joe Moore's first book. He is an associate professor of communication at the University of Central Missouri, and has published several publications and made many presentations regarding sport communication. He started the sport communication minor at the university and took over the reigns as program coordinator for digital media production in 2012.

Prior to joining the ranks of academia, Moore served 15 years as a sports information professional. In that time he worked in support of hundreds of sports broadcasters. He also has served as a color commentator for a total of eight seasons.

Moore, his wife Heidi, and their three children—Gaby, Gavin, and Grant—live in Warrensburg.

Made in the USA
San Bernardino, CA
11 December 2018